TO LIVE IS CHRIST

The Life and Ministry of Paul

Beth Moore

LifeWay Press
Nashville, Tennessee

Third Reprint 1999

ISBN 0-7673-3412-4
Dewey Decimal Classification Number: 248.84
Subject Heading: CHRISTIAN LIFE \ PAUL, APOSTLE

This book is the text for course CG-0420 in the subject area Bible Study
in the Christian Growth Study Plan.

Unless otherwise noted, Scripture quotations are from the Holy Bible,
New International Version, copyright © 1973, 1978, 1984
by International Bible Society.

Scripture quotations marked NASB are from the
New American Standard Bible. © The Lockman Foundation, 1960, 1962,
1963, 1968, 1971, 1972, 1973, 1975, 1977. Used by permission.

Scripture quotations marked NKJV are from the *New King James Version.*
Copyright © 1979, 1980, 1982, Thomas Nelson, Inc., Publishers. Used by permission.

Scripture quotations marked KJV are from the *King James Version.*

Printed in the United States of America

Photographs by Ken Touchton and Bob Schatz
Map by Bob Stephenson

LifeWay Press
127 Ninth Avenue, North
Nashville, Tennessee 37234-0151

For more information on discipleship and family resources,
training, and events check Web site www.lifeway.com/discipleplus

To all those who have followed
in the footsteps of the apostle Paul
risking life and loneliness
to take Christ's gospel
to the uttermost parts of the world.

The Author

Beth Moore realized at the age of 18 that God was claiming her future for Christian ministry. While she was sponsoring a cabin of sixth graders at a missions camp, God unmistakably acknowledged that she would work for Him. There Beth conceded all rights to the Lord she had loved since childhood. However, she encountered a problem: although she knew she was "wonderfully made," she was "fearfully" without talent. She hid behind closed doors to discover whether a beautiful singing voice had miraculously developed, but the results were tragic. She returned to the piano from which years of fruitless practice had streamed but found the noise to be joyless. Finally accepting that the only remaining alternative was missions work in a foreign country, she struck a martyr's pose and waited. Yet nothing happened.

Still confident of God's calling, Beth finished her degree at Southwest Texas State University, where she fell in love with Keith. After they married in December 1978, God added to their household three priority blessings: Amanda, Melissa, and Michael.

As if putting together puzzle pieces one at a time, God filled Beth's path with supportive persons who saw something in her she could not. God used individuals like Marge Caldwell, John Bisagno, and Jeannette Cliff George to help Beth discover gifts of speaking, teaching, and writing. Twelve years after her first speaking engagement, those gifts have spread all over the nation. Her joy and excitement in Christ are contagious; her deep love for the Savior, obvious; her style of speaking, electric.

Beth's ministry is grounded in and fueled by her service at her home fellowship, First Baptist Church, Houston, Texas, where she serves on the pastor's council and teaches a Sunday School class attended by more than two hundred women. Beth believes that her calling is Bible literacy: guiding believers to love and live God's Word. *To Live Is Christ: The Life and Ministry of Paul* grew from her fervent desire that women know greater intimacy with God.

Beth loves the Lord, loves to laugh, and loves to be with His people. Her life is full of activity, but one commitment remains constant: counting all things but loss for the excellence of knowing Christ Jesus, the Lord (see Phil. 3:8).

Foreword

A few years ago a beautiful, vivacious young lady came to see me and shared what God had laid on her heart. As I sat there talking to her I never *dreamed* God had planned such an awesome future for her.

Beth Moore had always led the early morning slimnastics class for our Women's Retreats. She did it beautifully, so of course I asked her to do it again this particular year. She agreed to lead the class and then said: "Marge, I'd love to do a seminar on something else besides slimnastics."

I asked what she would speak on.

She replied: "Why, Jesus, of course!"

That sounded wonderful to me, so she did her seminar. It was so real and humorous and warm. She exuded vitality, energy. and zest for the Heavenly Father! I knew then that God would use her in a mighty way.

Beth's desire to help others know Jesus and His Word is contagious. She is the same wonderful person in her personal life as you will see on the video and get to know through the book. What a treat to journey with Beth in the footsteps of Paul the apostle.

Marge Caldwell
Author, Speaker, Marriage Counselor

Contents

Introduction

Welcome aboard! I'm so glad you're joining me on an expedition through Scripture with the apostle Paul! Our travels will take us by land and sea to places we never dreamed we'd go. Exciting adventures await us from the pages of reality, often far exceeding the pages of fiction. I hope you'll soon agree: the apostle Paul was a remarkable man! His persistence and undying passion will no doubt convince you he truly encountered the risen Christ. Decades after Jesus interrupted Paul's plans, the apostle's account of the event remained consistent. Something dramatically changed the life of a brilliantly devious persecutor. I pray that same Someone will also interrupt our lives with His glorious presence as we take this journey together.

I have been a fan of the apostle Paul for years. In my estimation, his writings embody a passion for Christ unparalleled in New Testament Scripture. I have accepted many of his words as a personal challenge. "I want to know Christ" has become my plea. "To live is Christ and to die is gain" has become my hope. And to borrow his words once more, "Not that I have already obtained all this,…but I press on" (Phil.3:12). I genuinely love Christ. And I am a fan of all those past and present who have loved Him with their whole lives.

Having admired the apostle for years, I was somewhat surprised by a few questions which came to me when several people learned I was writing a Bible study on his life. I received questions like, "What about all the controversy?" and "How can you, a woman, write a Bible study about a man who obviously had no tolerance for women in ministry?"

Sadly, the controversy surrounding small bits of the apostle's teaching have often kept students from delving into the heart and liberating theology of the whole man. You know what? I think you're really going to like him—once you get to know him. When we've turned the last page, even if you don't like him you'll have to agree he loved and served his Lord with every ounce of breath and every drop of blood he had. His passion for Christ was indomitable. Reason enough to study his life and be challenged by his Spirit-breathed words!

Perhaps you are familiar with *A Woman's Heart: God's Dwelling Place* and *A Heart Like His: Seeking the Heart of God Through a Study of David.* You will find *To Live Is Christ* to be similar in format but quite different in content to these previous studies.

All 3 Bible studies are 10-week interactive courses inviting your personal involvement. Each week contains 5 lessons which will each require 30-45 minutes for completion. If you spend this kind of time in the Word of God, I assure you, He will change your life. I urge you not to miss a single lesson. Get completely involved, picturing yourself as an eyewitness to the events you're studying. Ask God daily what He wants to say to you personally.

Ideally, these courses are targeted for group participation once a week. An 11-session video set will greatly enhance your experience. Participating groups will meet weekly to view the 50-minute video and join in discussion of the previous week's study. The listening guide for each video segment is located at the end of each week.

Each week's introduction includes 5 Principal Questions. Each Principal Question is derived from 1 of the 5 lessons for the week. Discussing the answers to these questions weekly in small group will help ensure each person's basic understanding of the material.

In addition to these 5 content-oriented questions, you will find Personal Discussion Questions in each lesson identified with a symbol like this 📖. These learning activities help group members personally apply the material by relating the events to their own lives. These are also formatted for discussion each week; therefore, the weekly small-group discussion will ordinarily consist of 5 Principal Questions and 5 Personal Discussion Questions designed to further enrich each person's experience.

No one will ever be expected to share personal experiences with the group. Sharing is strictly voluntary, and we hope no one will share anything causing herself or others discomfort. Please answer the questions in each lesson whether or not you choose to share them in small group. Any questions you skip will reduce the effectiveness of the study in your personal life. I want you to get the very most out of this journey! God will do amazing things among us if we grant Him full access to our minds, wills, and emotions!

Each daily lesson is introduced by a Scripture called Today's Treasure. Your daily treasure is the Scripture best representing the theme of the lesson.

Each lesson will invite your full participation through Bible reading and various kinds of questions and activities. You may find multiple choice exercises, yes/no activities, fill in the blank statements, creative thinking exercises, hypothetical situations in which I ask you to imagine yourself in a Bible character's position, or straightforward questions which you will answer in your own words. I will occasionally ask you to write a Scripture for special emphasis. These interactive exercises are designed for your sake. I don't want you to simply read my journey through Scripture. I want this book to become your journey. Your full participation will guarantee God's freedom to accomplish a fresh and wonderful work in your life.

I primarily use the *New International Version* of the Bible in *To Live Is Christ*. If you do not own one, you will still be able to answer virtually every question without significant confusion. If you're able to get your hands on an inexpensive paper back NIV, however, I think you would be blessed by an easy-to-read version which, in my opinion, does not compromise the text.

Now that we've discussed the similarities in format, how are the Bible studies different in content? The subject matter is different, of course. *A Woman's Heart*: is based on the Old Testament Tabernacle and was designed to enhance each student's grasp of God's majestic plan in the Old Testament fulfilled in the New Testament.

A Heart Like His, an in-depth study of King David, was designed to reveal the complexities of man: his potential and his relationship to God. We delve into the good, the bad, and the ugly!

Your present journey, *To Live Is Christ*, traces the life of the apostle Paul from his presumed childhood to his death, centering on one man's amazing ministry. If you respond to this study like I did, you'll be greatly refreshed by the obvious mercy of God to allow those who have really blown it to repent and serve Him wholeheartedly and effectively. You'll also be amazed by Paul's tenacity, and through his example I think you will find encouragement to persevere in trials. You will also become acquainted with Paul's humanity and perhaps realize he was not so unlike the rest of us—proof God can greatly use any of us if we are fully available and readily cooperative!

I was greatly affected by the study of Paul's life in many ways; but above all, I sense like never before a quickened awareness of the personal calling God has placed on my life. I feel a renewed sense of my purpose in God's plan. I am praying for you to have the same response. You are a Christian in this present generation for a very good reason. Your life has purpose. He planned your visitation on this planet and wants to fulfill 1 Corinthians 2:9 in your life. May these pages enhance your love and devotion for Christ so dramatically that He is freed in your life to do more than your eyes have seen, more than your ears have heard, and more than your mind has conceived!

Allow God to do a fresh work in your life for the next 10 weeks. Let every journey through His Word be a new experience, a new opportunity. Resist comparisons to other studies. Welcome changes. Invite Him to have His perfect way for the next 10 weeks so you can cry out with the apostle Paul, "For to me, to live is Christ!" Beloved, when you can say those words and mean them, you have discovered abundant life at its fullest. I'm so honored to have you along.

I conclude each lesson with a margin question asking you to consider how God wants you to respond to what He showed you today. I encourage you to expand your learning beyond the pages of *To Live Is Christ*. Keep your own personal journal. Record what God does and teaches you as you pursue this journey.

I have used several resources for study of Greek and Hebrew words. Definitions taken from the *The Complete Word Study Dictionary: New Testament*[1] are enclosed in quotation marks with no reference. I have also used Strong's *Concise Dictionary of the Words in the Greek Testament*.[2] Words taken from Strong's are enclosed in quotation marks with the word Strong's in parentheses.

In the first week's study I have extensively used words and explanations from the *Code of Jewish Law*.[3] These are indicated by (Code, volume #, page #). Sources used less frequently are footnoted.

[1]Spiros Zodhiates et al., eds., *The Complete Word Study Dictionary: New Testament* (Chattanooga, TN: AMG Publishers, 1992).
[2]James Strong, *A Concise Dictionary of the Words in the Greek Testament* (New York: The Methodist Book Concern, 1890).
[3]Rabbi Solomon Ganzfried, trans. Hyman E. Goldin, *Code of Jewish Law* (New York: Hebrew Publishing Company, 1993).

Goals for To Live Is Christ

Matthew 4:18; 5:1-2; Acts 1:1-2

Potential Learning Disabilities in the Christian Classroom

1. Spiritual _____ _____ Disorder: This term applies to the

person who has trouble paying attention for very long (Neh. 9:30-31; Isa. 42:20-22).

2. Spiritual _____: When we can't be still (Ps. 46:10-11). The Hebrew meaning of the

word *still* is _____.

3. Spiritual _____: This disorder is present when we have a tendency to keep getting

things _____ (Isa. 29:16-17; 64:8; Job 38:2-13, 16-21).

4. _____ Impairment: When we only see what's _____ to us

(Prov. 29:18; Matt. 28:18-20).

5. _____ Impairment: (Isa. 50:4-5).

Morning by morning He wakes us to _____ from Him.

When I have a word for you and you turn your back I call that _____.

The First Footprints

Day 1
Set Apart from Birth

Day 2
The Childhood of a Pharisee's Son

Day 3
At the Feet of Gamaliel

Day 4
Strangled by the Law

Day 5
Meanwhile in Jerusalem

When a little boy named Saul played make believe with his friends in a Jewish neighborhood in Tarsus, he could never have imagined the real life drama that awaited him. As God carefully watched the small child at play, at school, and at worship, I wonder if He thought, *Someday, My child, you will work for Me.* You and I have the opportunity to witness the unfolding of one of the most dramatic stories in Christendom. Our journey begins with some safe suppositions based on chronicles of ancient Hebrew life, but we will quickly move into well-documented scriptural accounts. This week we will imagine what Paul's childhood and upbringing might have been like, then we will set our sights on Jerusalem where strange twists of events will take place. We will seek to answer the following questions.

Principal Questions

Day 1: How would you describe the events surrounding the circumcision of an infant boy in an ancient Hebrew home?

Day 2: What are a few ways the ancient Hebrew home emphasized Scripture in the life of a young boy?

Day 3: How would you describe Gamaliel, Saul's primary teacher in Jerusalem?

Day 4: What would you imagine Paul's life was like as he attempted to live by the law faultlessly?

Day 5: What important event occurred in Jerusalem in the years following Saul's assumed departure?

I hope you'll jump into this journey with both feet. May the pages of Acts and Paul's Epistles have our footprints all over them by the time we complete our last mile. Let's get started. I'll meet you in Tarsus!

D A Y 1
Set Apart from Birth

Today's Treasure

"God, who set me apart from birth and called me by his grace, was pleased to reveal his Son in me so that I might preach him among the Gentiles"
(Gal. 1:15-16).

Through the next 10 weeks we will explore the life of the apostle Paul in a respectable degree of chronological order. To understand the man who was struck blind so he could see, we need to grasp the impact of what it meant to go from Saul the persecutor of Christians to Paul the first Christian missionary. Paul grew up in an orthodox Jewish home in a Gentile city. The Bible gives us only a few pieces of information about his upbringing; but based on those tidbits, we may draw a number of conclusions.

We know that Paul was reared as closely to the letter of the Jewish law as possible (see Phil. 3:5-6); therefore, based on Scripture and the traditional Jewish code of law, we can describe many details of his young life. We will begin our study of the apostle in the most appropriate place—his cradle.

Today I depart from my usual style of Bible study to paint a portrait of Paul's inauguration to Hebrew life. The following narrative describes the events which most likely began soon after his birth. The story line is fictional to help you picture the events, but the circumstances and the practices are drawn from Scripture and the Jewish code of law. At the conclusion of today's lesson, I will ask you to review a number of terms and find the biblical basis for several of the practices you read. Sit back and imagine the beginning of one of the most significant lives in all Christendom.

"I thank Thee, O living and eternal King, Who hast mercifully restored my soul within me; Thy faithfulness is great" (Code, I, p.1).

The words fell from his tongue while his eyes were still heavy from the night's rest. His morning prayers invited unexpected emotion this particular dawn as he soberly considered the honor that lay before him. Eight days had passed since the birth of his friend's son. Today would be the child's *Berit Milah*. He would stand beside the father at the infant's circumcision as the *sandek,* Jewish godfather, assuming solemn responsibility—second only to the parents, over the child's devout religious upbringing.

Adorned appropriately, the *sandek* and his wife made their way through the busy streets of Tarsus toward the home of the new parents. Tarsus was a beautiful city—a difficult admission for any man of the *diaspora*, separated from his Jewish homeland. Other than being Gentile, the city had everything a man could want. Scenic? Like few others. The refreshing Mediterranean breezes seemed to ricochet off the Cappadocia mountains, filling the air with a natural, sweet incense. No, this was not Mount Zion. But the mark of the Maker was most assuredly engraved on the countryside.

The moment was suddenly disturbed by the Greek merchants, obviously amused at the peculiar attire of the Jewish couple. The *sandek* thought to himself, *It would behoove us at times never to have learned their language.* Impossible, however. After all, Tarsus was their city. The Hebrew people within this Gentile city's walls were blessed to enjoy a relatively healthy community of God-fearing men. He would not complain ... although he might be tempted. Not today, anyway. He had far more important things on his mind.

"I think they are naming him Saul," said his wife.

"We shall not presume his name until we hear it from the lips of his father," he responded.

He had intended to arrive first so he could assist the father with preparations; but a few members of the *Minyan*, a quorum of 10 Jewish men, had already gathered at the door. Normally, the woman of a Jewish household would offer warm welcomes to visi-

diaspora—the settling of scattered colonies of Jews outside Palestine following the Babylonian Exile

tors at her door, but the newborn's mother was treated with utmost care during the days following her delivery. Friends and relatives assisted the father in any preparations that had to be made for *Berit Milah*, a tiny infant boy's first initiation into Judaism.

The small house was filled with people. The father, a Pharisee and Roman citizen, was an impressive man. He was one of a few men in the community who seemed to command a certain amount of respect from both Jew and Gentile. When all had finally gathered, the ceremony began. The *sandek* took his place in a chair next to the father who remained standing. The new father was not a particularly tall man, but the *sandek* couldn't help but notice that his stature seemed particularly stretched today. And why not? What could make a Jewish man stand taller than a newborn son?

The infant was placed on the *sandek*'s knees, and the father leaned over him with greatest care to oversee the circumcision of his beloved son. He then handed the knife to the *mohel*, the most upright and expert circumcisor available in Tarsus. The father watched anxiously for the interval between the cutting of the foreskin and its actual removal. He could not help but smile as he competed with his wailing son for the attention of the quorum as he spoke the benediction, "Who hath sanctified us by His commandments and hath commanded us to bring him into the covenant of our father Abraham" (Code, IV, p.43). With the exception of the *sandek*, all who gathered stood for the ceremony and responded to the benediction with the words, "Just as he has been initiated into the covenant, so may he be initiated into the study of the Torah, to his nuptial (marriage) canopy, and to the performance of good deeds" (Code, IV, p.44).

No one could deny the blessings of good health God had already bestowed on the infant boy. The *sandek* had to hold him securely between his calloused palms to keep the child from squirming completely off his lap. His tiny face was blood red, his volume at full scale. This may have been his first bout with anger, but it would not be his last. Had the ceremony not held such sober significance, the *sandek* might have snickered at the infant's zeal. He did not dare grin, but he might wonder if God would. Tears of joy stung his eyes. The child laying on his lap was yet another piece of tangible evidence that God was faithful to do as He promised. In a society where a child could be discarded as rubbish, nothing was more important to the Jew than offspring. Yes, God had been faithful to a thousand generations.

The circumcision was completed but not soon enough for the master of ceremonies. The *sandek* cradled the child with a moment's comfort, and then handed him to his father whose voice resonated throughout the candlelit home, "His name is Saul!"

As if only a few could hear, the guests rehearsed the words in one another's ears. "His name is Saul! His name is Saul!" A perfectly noble name for a Hebrew boy from the tribe of Benjamin, named for the first king of the chosen nation of Israel. A fine choice met with great approval. While a great feast ensued, the mother slipped the agitated infant from his father's arms and excused herself to nurse the child.

Custom demanded that the father host a feast to the limits of his wealth. A man who offered less than he could afford at his son's circumcision was entirely improper. If baby Saul's father was anything at all, he was painfully proper. Yes, this would indeed be a child well-reared. "I have much to learn from the father of Saul," the *sandek* surmised.

Darkness was quickly falling when the *sandek* and his wife finally reached their home. The day had been long but the fellowship sweet. Gathered with those who feared God and worshiped Him only, he had almost forgotten this city was not their own. Tarsus, the city of the Greeks, had given birth to another Hebrew. "Dear wife," the *sandek* thought out loud, "Our Saul seems special, does he not?"

"Dear man," she teased, "he looked like every other eight-day-old infant boy I've ever seen: mad as a wronged ruler!" They both laughed heartily. She prepared for bed as he reached for the Torah, trying to fight off the sleep quickly overtaking him. He repeated the words of the *Shema*; and then he walked over to the *Mesusah*, fastened to the door-post of the house, and placed his fingers on it. The *Mesusah* was a small, longitudinal-ly-folded parchment square, on which twenty-two lines some of the most vital Words of God were written. He responded to the touch with the familiar words of his own father every night of his life, "The Lord is my keeper" (Code, II, p. 62). He crawled into bed, remembered their words, and smiled once again. Then he whispered as his thoughts drifted into the night, "I still say he's special. Full of zeal, he is. Just something about him…."

*E*ach of the following are Hebrew terms shedding light on the life of Paul. To understand the ancient orthodox Jew is to understand much about the apostle Paul. Based on the information given through contextual clues in the narrative, match each of the following terms to their definitions.

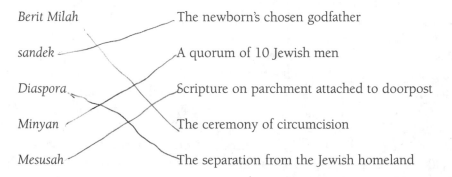

Berit Milah   The newborn's chosen godfather

sandek   A quorum of 10 Jewish men

Diaspora   Scripture on parchment attached to doorpost

Minyan   The ceremony of circumcision

Mesusah   The separation from the Jewish homeland

1. In Today's Treasure Paul spoke of being "set apart from birth." Read Genesis 17:1-11 and describe the significance of circumcision. How did circumcision set any Jewish male apart from others?

It was a token of the covenant between God and them.

2. Based on Psalm 127:3-5, briefly describe what a newborn son would represent to a Jewish father.

Children are an heritage of the Lord - His reward.

3. The *Shema*, the Hebrew word *hear*, remains one of the most important biblical phrases in Jewish life. The words of the *Shema* are found in Deuteronomy 6:4. Write them in the space below.

Hear O Isreal: The Lord our God is one Lord.

4. The home of any devout Jew in Paul's generation would have been marked by a *Mesusah*, which actually meant *doorpost*. The parchment inside the *Mesusah* contained the words of Deuteronomy 6:4-9 and

Deuteronomy 11:13-21. These Scriptures were the absolute watchwords of the Jewish faith. Read both passages carefully and explain why you think they were nailed to the doorposts.

To keep the word before their eyes + on their hearts, to remind them and to teach them to Love the Lord their God and serve Him. He in return will provide for them – sending forth rain for their crop He will provide food for their cattle that they may eat.

5. Search the narrative and find the factual response of the gatherers to the father's benediction during the circumcision ceremony. Based on their threefold blessing over the newborn, what were three obvious priorities of the devout Jew?

- ☑ marriage
- ☐ the homeland
- ☐ separation from Gentiles
- ☑ blessings
- ☑ good deeds
- ☑ studying the Torah

6. Based on God's command in Joshua 1:8, the devout Jew read Scripture just before he went to sleep. Do you ever read Scripture just before going to sleep at night? ☐ Yes ☐ No If so, what benefits have you discovered?

Sometimes – reassurance + rest also peace + comfort

Based on what you've read today, in what ways is an orthodox Jewish home of Paul's generation like a Christian home of our generation? How is it different?

_____

_____

I hope today's lesson spurred some distinct images of the ancient Jewish home and Paul's probable beginnings. We have so much to learn together. You're off to a great start! Let's conclude by considering how we've been personally affected by our glimpses into history. Answer the question that appears in the margin. Note that I will ask you to answer this question each day of our study.

DAY 2
The Childhood of a Pharisee's Son

Today we will draw more conclusions about Saul's childhood based on traditional Hebrew practices. The familiar utterances of Proverbs 22:6 were not mere words to the ancient Hebrew. The passage represented one of the sternest commands of God toward the Jew. "Train a child in the way he should go." To the strict Jew, only one way existed

How does God want you to respond to what He showed you today?

To love Him and obey His commandments. To keep His words before our eyes and that He is our provider and that He wants to bless us in this new covenant of Christ. He wants to have a covenant relationship with us as with Abraham.

Today's Treasure
"Train a child in the way he should go, and when he is old he will not turn from it" (Prov. 22:6).

for a child to go: the way of his father and his father's father. Theirs was the responsibility to direct the child in that familiar way. The words of Deuteronomy 4:7-9 had been rehearsed in the ear of every faithful Jew from the time of Moses.

*R*ead the verses. How did Moses distinguish between Israel and other nations?

_____

_____

Compare verse 8 with verse 9. What had their eyes seen that they were never to forget or let slip from their hearts?
- ☐ the miracles by which God delivered His people from Egypt
- ☒ the righteous decrees and laws of God
- ☐ the worship at the tabernacle

To whom were they to teach what they had seen? *To their Sons*

You can be sure the infant Saul was reared as closely to the letter of the law as possible. The apostle described his home life in very few words in Philippians 3:5. In what ways did he specifically describe his heritage?

Circumcised on the 8th day, of the stock of Israel, of the tribe of Benjamin, a Hebrew of the Hebrew and a Pharisee.

Paul told us he was "a Hebrew of Hebrews." A Jew would have known exactly what he meant. Virtually nothing but Jewish influence touched him in his early childhood.

Unlike the typical family today, the father assumed primary responsibility for training the child. The *Code of Jewish Law* states, "It is the duty of every father to train his children in the practice of all the precepts, whether Biblical or Rabbinical…It is also incumbent upon the father to guard his children against any forbidden act" (Code, IV, p.47). As a Pharisee, Saul's father would have assumed his responsibility with great sobriety. We may have to fight the temptation to automatically attach a negative connotation to the term *Pharisee*. F.B. Meyer's words may help us gain a proper perspective:

> The word *Pharisee* is a synonym for religious pride and hypocrisy; but we must never forget that in those old Jewish days the Pharisee represented some of the noblest traditions of the Hebrew people. Amid the prevailing indifference the Pharisees stood for a strict religious life….Amid the lax morals of the time, which infected Jerusalem almost as much as Rome, the Pharisee was austere in his ideals, and holy in life.[1]

Some gave the Pharisees a bad name, just as some Christians give Christianity a bad name. Saul's father was not likely one of them, although a number of scholars wonder if he might have been excessively strict, based on the apostle's words in Ephesians 6:4.

*I*n Ephesians 6:4 what did Paul warn fathers not to do?

The fathers were not to provoke their children.

Could this have been the voice of experience? Did God specifically inspire the apostle Paul to write these words because he had personally experienced the injury harshness could cause? We do not know, but the possibility certainly exists. No doubt, Paul's upbringing was strict but to what extent we do not know.

*T*raditional Jewish fathers, especially Pharisees, raised their children according to the principles taught in the following Scriptures. Read each one and record how you believe each might influence parenting.

Proverbs 1:7 *Teaching to reverently to fear the Lord and teaching the instruction or law*

Proverbs 30:17 *Being disrespectful & disobedient to parent can result in harm to that child.*

The *Code of Jewish Law* certainly condemned overt harshness in childrearing. Jewish parents considered children the utmost blessing from God and loved them dearly. The ancient historian Josephus said of the Jew, "We lay greater stress on the training of the children than on anything else, and regard observance of the Law and a corresponding godly life as the most important of all duties."[2] Although young Saul grew up in a very strict home, he enjoyed the utmost devotion of his father to his godly upbringing: something only the very fortunate among our children enjoy.

The rabbinic laws taught fathers to begin teaching their children the ways of God from their earliest understanding. Having been reared in a Baptist church famous for hearty amens, I had to smile as I read the words of the *Code of Jewish Law* stating, "It is well to train a child to respond *Amen* and other responses at the synagogue. From the time that an infant begins to respond *Amen*, he has a share in the world to come" (Code, IV, p.47). I can just imagine Saul as a three- or four-year-old responding, brow properly furrowed, with a serious "amen" at the appropriate times in a synagogue service.

As little more than a toddler, Saul learned to say the *Schmone-Ezre*—the primary prayers of the Jews—morning, noon, and night. He learned to pray before and after every meal. He actively participated in the traditional feasts as soon as he could talk. Even today in an orthodox Jewish Passover celebration, the youngest child in the family asks the traditional questions which provoke the father to retell the rich history of Israel's exodus from slavery.

*R*ecall a time in your childhood you learned about your Christian heritage. Brainstorm and list several ways children today can be involved in recalling their Christian heritage.

_____

_____

_____

A child of normal intelligence read Scriptures by five years of age. At six years old, Saul began his education at the school of a rabbi. These schools were ordinarily attached to the community synagogue. The Jewish population was large enough to have at least one active synagogue in Tarsus. Lessons were tedious and teachers were strict, but Jewish children were rarely caught roaming the streets!

Soon after his sixth birthday, Saul memorized Deuteronomy 6:4-9, the words on the tiny scroll inside the *Mesusah* on the doorway of his home. Far more impressively, he also memorized Psalms 113–118! We cannot begin to understand what the Hebrew held dear without at least a brief consideration of each of these Psalms.

*I*f Saul could memorize six chapters of Scripture as a young child, the least we can do is read them! Read each one. What might have been primary concepts important to a child's early education about God.

Psalm 113 *That God is worthy of our praise*

Psalm 114 *The earth trembled at the presence of the Lord.*

Psalm 115 *Our God is in the heaven and will bless those who trust in Him. Not to trust in man made idols*

Psalm 116 *The Lord hears our cries and responds with mercy and delivers us.*

Psalm 117 *Praise Him His mercy kindness endures forever His Truth endures forever.*

Psalm 118 _____

Reflect on your own childhood for a moment. Were any of the truths you recorded above taught to you as a young child? If so, which ones and who taught them to you?

_____

_____

A contemporary Jewish man wearing phylacteries and praying at the Western (Wailing) Wall in Jerusalem.

Imagine all six Psalms being seared into your soul in childhood! Being a Hebrew was not just a religion. Judaism wasn't even just a way of life. Being Hebrew defined who you were, how you thought, what you felt. By the time Saul was 10 years old, he knew the intricacies of the oral law. Young Saul's mind was thoroughly steeped and vastly stretched with constant memorization. He had little choice but to "meditate on the law both day and night" just to prepare for the following day's lessons.

The years between 10 and 13 are transforming years for any boy, but a particular metamorphosis took place in a Jewish boy's life. He matured more rapidly than our modern day Gentile boys do. By the age of 13, for all practical purposes, he was considered a man. At the age of 13, a boy in our society is considered to be an alien. Thirteen years old was something a Jewish boy lived for. It's something we often hope our boys live through!

By 13 years of age, Saul was considered a son of the law. He assumed all the religious responsibilities of the adult Jew. He started wearing *phylacteries*, called *tefillin*, during weekday morning prayers. *Phylacteries* were 2 black leather cubes with long leather straps. The cubes encased certain passages from the *Torah* written on strips of parchment. Saul wore one of the cubes on his left arm facing his heart. The other cube was placed in the center of his forehead. The leather straps on the left arm were wound precisely 7 times around his arm.

The *Code of Jewish Law* prescribed that a Jewish man 13 years or older was to put on the *tefillin* at the first moment in the morning when enough daylight existed to recognize a neighbor at a distance of 4 cubits (Code, I, p.27). These practices seem very strange to us perhaps, but we should appreciate their attempt to interpret Scripture as literally as they knew how.

*E*xodus 13:9 is one of the Scriptures from which *phylacteries* originated. Below describe how the *phylacteries* were a literal act of obedience.

It was a sign to the one who wore it et the Word of God was before His eyes — memorized

The left arm was chosen because it was ordinarily the weaker. They were to wear God's Word as a banner and shield over their weakness.

that God's law may be in his mouth for with a strong hand God brought them out of Egypt

We don't practice the outward expression of the Jew, but we are wise to share the inward principle. How has God's Word been a shield of protection in a time of weakness for you?

During a very trying situation I found that reading the Word has provided such peace & strength to endure especially not knowing the outcome until passing through it

Saul would have placed the *phylacteries* around his forehead and arm in total silence. If interrupted while putting on the *phylacteries* on any given morning, he would have started the procedure all over again, repeating the appropriate benedictions. You see, a 13-year-old Hebrew boy could not even get out of bed in the morning without remembering to whom he belonged. As he wound the straps of the *phylacteries* around his head and arm, he was reminded of his binding relationship to his Creator. Soberly he assumed the responsibility of one associated with God. The law of the Lord was his life.

*A*s you conclude today, reflect once again over the tedious practices of Saul's young childhood. Choose one of the following adjectives which you feel best describes a childhood like Saul's; then explain your choice in the space provided.

☒ devoted ☐ unreasonable ☐ exemplary ☐ fanatical ☐ blessed

Saul was reared in the traditions handed down from generation to generation in reverance fear and live for the God. He was also reminded that He belonged to God in a binding relationship

How does God want you to respond to what He showed you today?

That I have a trusting relationship with Him. That He will bless me when obedient to Him. To live a life fully devoted to Him. To walk in a reverant fear towards Him. To respond to His love.

D A Y   3

At the Feet of Gamaliel

Our previous lesson concluded with a picture of young Saul at 13, the age of passage for a Jewish boy. Although Saul's education in the home of a Pharisee was probably typical, his response was certainly atypical. Regarding his studies, we might say, "He took to it like a duck to water." Only, instead of feathers, he had *phylacteries*.

Saul was an exceptional student. Hebrew fathers were not notorious gushers, so his father probably refrained from extolling his son's brilliance. Yet, he no doubt considered the wisest approach for Saul's future. He was not unlike a modern father looking for the best university for his gifted son. He wanted the best for his son.

Today's Treasure
"'I am a Jew, born in Tarsus of Cilicia, but brought up in this city. Under Gamaliel I was thoroughly trained in the law of our fathers and was just as zealous for God as any of you are today'"
(Acts 22:3).

The search for the best continuing Jewish education was brief. He set his sights on Jerusalem, the homeland—the fountain of Jewish learning. We should take off our hats to the Pharisee from Tarsus as we consider his approval of Saul's trek to Jerusalem. Who would help him with the family trade? If Saul's dreams to become a rabbi persisted, who would inherit the family business? Scripture lends some evidence to believe Saul's father may have made these decisions entirely alone. The apostle made no mention of his mother in any of his writings; but in Romans 16:13, he spoke of the mother of Rufus filling a maternal role in his life. Some scholars suggest Saul lost his mother at an early age.

Mixed emotions filled the heart of the young man as he prepared for the journey to Jerusalem. Like most teenage boys, his emotions probably swung to the same extremes as his changing voice. Like any 13-year-old going so far from home, he was probably scared to death. Yet, as a Jewish 13-year-old, he was considered a man. He packed his bags with articles foreign to us, but common to the ancient Jew. He included prayer shawls, *phylacteries*, sacred writings, and customary clothing. He probably didn't gaze with affection over familiar contents in his room prior to leaving. The Jew was not given to domestic decor and did not believe in images on the walls.

All his life Saul heard about Jerusalem. His father made the journey often. Three annual feasts beckoned Jewish men from near and far to the city of Zion. A proper Pharisee traveled to Jerusalem for the annual Passover feast. Saul likely stayed home and watched over the family affairs while picturing the busy streets and solemn assemblies of the sacred city. Saul probably devoured every detail his father expressed about Jerusalem upon his arrival home. Now it was his turn.

*B*ased on Psalm 137:5-6, how would you describe the importance of Jerusalem to the devout Jew?

Very important

Most assuredly, Saul's father sought a Jewish traveling companion for his young son. Someone who could provide proper supervision for the young student would be traveling from Tarsus to Jerusalem. As Saul boarded the boat at the docks of Tarsus, he had no idea just how common the nauseating heaving of a sea vessel would ultimately become to him. The compass pointed due south as Saul gazed at the ancient coastal cities of Sidon and Tyre in the distance. After several rather unpleasant days on board, he probably arrived at the port of Caesarea with a chronic case of sea legs. There he exchanged rubbery limbs for the peculiar soreness of riding on the back of a beast over rough country. Thirty-five miles later, he caught the first glimpses of the city set on a hill—Jerusalem, the City of David.

Several wonderful Psalms help sketch vivid mental images of the ancient Jew's Jerusalem. Read Psalm 48:1-14 and Psalm 122:3-4 carefully. Use their descriptions to create a brief paragraph young Saul might have written to his best friend in Tarsus after seeing the city.

_____

_____

_____

_____

Do you have a special place that reminds you of the presence of God?
❑ Yes ❑ No

Young Saul's eyes beheld a far more cosmopolitan city than had his ancestors. Just a few decades prior to Saul's visit, Herod the Great sought the favor of the Jewish populous by rebuilding not just the temple but the entire city of Jerusalem. Built of pristine white stone, the desert sun danced on the city walls. Saul probably dismounted just before the city gate. The elders sitting at the gate looked up only long enough to notice the young traveler. His dress and manner assured them that he was a newcomer, but he was no stranger. No heathen was he. Noting his age, they probably nodded with approval over his father's obvious choice of further education—a budding rabbi, no less.

A model of the Roman theater in Jerusalem.

Just inside the gate, Saul cast his eyes on the impressive fruit of Herod's labors: a large theater, a palace, an amphitheater, a hippodrome for horse and chariot races, imposing fortified towers, and perfectly blended architecture. But all this paled in comparison to the structure on top of the hill which demanded his attention—Herod's temple. Herod rebuilt the temple bigger and better than its predecessor. Huge, richly ornamented white stones mounted on one another created a lavish feast for the eyes. Young Saul witnessed one of the most magnificent buildings in the entire world.

Saul probably ran up the main street of Jerusalem to the house of the Lord. He surely conjured up pictures of King David dancing down that very street. He hurried up the many stairs to greet magnificent porches surrounding the entire enclosure. Then he walked to a wall, one which held tremendous significance for the Jew; but one which would hold far more significance for a Jew who would ultimately become the world's most renowned missionary to the Gentiles.

A reconstruction of Herods Temple from the Model of Jerusalem located at the Holyland Hotel.

𝒮aul later wrote the words of Ephesians 2:14 in his letter to the Christians at Ephesus. Write his words in the space below.

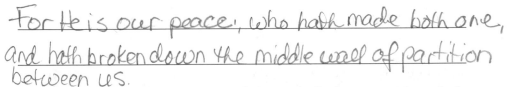

For He is our peace, who hath made both one, and hath broken down the middle wall of partition between us.

The apostle was not simply referring to a figurative wall of partition. He was referring to an imposing structure he faced on the temple grounds as an adolescent many years before. Being raised in a Gentile city, young Saul had no problem reading the notices inscribed in Greek and Latin. This literal middle wall of partition in the temple forbade access of the defiling heathen to the inner sanctuaries of the house of God. As a young man born into a position of religious privilege, he stood a little taller—chest a little broader—as he read those words. What a contrast of emotions he would feel many years later, as he came to despise the prejudice of those who would not recognize the walls crumbled by the cross. To them Saul would write: "For he is our peace, who hath made both [Jew and Gentile] one, and hath broken down the middle wall of partition *between us*" (KJV).

Within days, Saul took a seat in the most impressive classroom in the entire Jewish world. His esteemed teacher was the rabbi Gamaliel, grandson of the great Hillel—names of great importance in the history of Judaism.

Gamaliel continues to be so highly esteemed in Judaism that even the rabbi I interviewed for this writing spoke of him with genuine familiarity. So highly revered was Gamaliel, the Jews referred to him as "the beauty of the law."[3] About one thousand students populated the rabbinical college, also called the House of Interpretation during Saul's studies in Jerusalem.

*O*ne of the most wonderful concepts the Word of God teaches about the believer is God's prior plan for our lives. According to Galatians 1:15-16, when did God set the future apostle apart for His service? *From the womb*

What did He plan for Saul to do? *To reveal his Son in Paul to preach Christ among his brethren.*

NOTHING in Saul's life would be a waste unless he refused to let God use it. All Saul's religious training, his countless hours spent in Scripture and study, his brilliance in spiritual matters would all be parts of God's ornate plan. God would use what Saul learned at the feet of Gamaliel. "Gamaliel was clearly a remarkable man—the first to whom the title Rabban (Master) was given."[4] He was almost liberal in comparison to many of his contemporaries. Large-hearted, wise and open-minded, Gamaliel had been raised on the teachings of his grandfather, Hillel, whose words often had a remarkable similarity to the Greatest Rabboni who would ever live. A few lines from the teaching of Hillel are: "Judge not thy neighbour until thou art in his place; … my abasement is my exaltation; he who wishes to make a name for himself loses his name; … what is unpleasant to thyself that do not to thy neighbour; this is the whole Law, all else is but its exposition."[5] Do those words sound familiar?

Gamaliel's teachings strongly reflected those of his grandfather. God, in His wonderful wisdom, made sure that the law was taught to Saul with a touch of rare grace.

*G*od included a sample of Gamaliel's teachings in Acts 5:27-42. Read this portion of Scripture. Describe what you think Gamaliel must have been like based on this glimpse of his teaching.

Reasoned with Pharisees and to do anything to the disciples — reminded of several incidents of people following others which turned out poorly, also lest they would be fighting God.

Reread verse 42 carefully. According to Gamaliel's philosophy, would he now consider the purpose or activity of the apostles of human origin or of God? ❑ human origin ☑ God Explain your answer.

It seems that Gamaliel words of wisdom changed the priest — they enforced the apostles not to preach Jesus but they did

Yes, Saul was predestined to sit at the feet of one of Judaism's most grace-filled teachers; however, he soon developed his own ways of thinking. Saul's brilliance moved him to the front of every class. He was a born leader. You can be sure Saul rejoiced in taking a primary role in the endless debates on the interpretation of the law. "A large part of the students' time was spent in hair-splitting definitions, and arguments every whit as complex, and even bizarre, as those that centuries later were to trouble the scholars and divines."[6]

Saul spent five of the most critical years of his life in Jerusalem. He experienced the Holy City during some of its most prosperous and thriving years. Here his childhood dreams came true. He became a teacher, a rabbi. The son of a Pharisee became a Pharisee. Decades later, when he wrote his first letter to the Corinthians, he may have looked back over all the years of learning, the hundreds of debates, the trivial arguments, and stated a few words from the realm of personal experience.

*C*onclude today's lesson by reading 1 Corinthians 8:1-3. Fill in the following blanks according to verse 1, then write verses 2 and 3 in the space which follows.

*H*ow does God want you to respond to what He showed you today?

"Knowledge ~~puffeth ecp~~ , but love *edefies* ."

If any man think that he knoweth any thing, he knoweth nothing yet as he ought to know. But if any man love God, the same is known of Him.

The knowledge that puffed Saul's head was not wasted, but it wasn't until years later that he discovered love. As students of God's Word, let's commit to receiving the full benefit of studying Scripture. Don't study just to increase knowledge. Let every study of the Word of God increase your love for the divine Author!

D A Y   4

Strangled By the Law

"Arise, cry out in the night, as the watches of the night begin; pour out your heart like water in the presence of the Lord. Lift up your hands to him for the lives of your children" (Lam. 2:19). I always planned to have at least 10 children. Soon after we were married, my husband gave me the grave news: He only wanted a couple of children. I was devastated. I immediately retorted with the words, "But we agreed!" He smiled and responded, "No, Honey, you agreed." I have to snicker as I recall wondering if such a blatant omission from our premarital discourses was grounds for an annulment. (I am quite serious.) Little did my husband or I know that I was already expecting child number one.

Finally holding Amanda in our arms had a strange effect on each of us. Keith decided he might just change his mind and want three or four. I, on the other hand, decided maybe I would just have one. Nothing prepared me for the intense sense of vulnerability a seven-pound infant gave me. Someone suddenly had direct, unabashed access to my heart. I was terrified I would lose her. I prayed constantly for God to watch over her, then gripped the rail of her crib and stared at her while she slept just in case He was too busy. Most of the time, I simply held her through her nap time so I could be assured she was OK and in good hands. Reluctantly, I'm sure, God entrusted me with another child and I set out to drive her almost as crazy as I had my first.

No need for angels watching over my babies. They had me. Somewhere along the way, I decided they were not quite as fragile as I had assumed. They lived through my husband and me. They could probably live through anything.

Then they became teenagers. Although I'm far less obsessive, I find myself crying out in the night for them more than ever. I used to pray that God would surround them with people who were good influences. When my eyes began to open, I realized my prayers better adjust to greater reality. The truth is, godly influences are few. I pray for them to know what to do with bad influences and hope they become the good influences!

Today's Treasure
"If anyone else thinks he has reasons to put confidence in the flesh, I have more: circumcised on the eighth day, of the people of Israel, of the tribe of Benjamin, a Hebrew of Hebrews; in regard to the law, a Pharisee ... as for legalistic righteousness, faultless" (Phil. 3:4-6).

21

Young Saul left Tarsus with stars in his eyes. He headed for Jerusalem, the holy city of God. He did not leave home naive about the world. He grew up in a Greek city with every influence from the worship of idols to any conceivable sexual indulgence. But I don't believe he expected what he found in Jerusalem among those supposed to be the pious and the best. No, he was not naive about the heathen world. He was naive about the religious world. His father entrusted him to the finest rabbinic school, but he was not there alone. He was surrounded by good and bad influences. He saw people who were the real thing, and he saw people who were religious frauds.

We need look no further than the Word of God to see many of the influences Saul encountered among the Pharisees of Jerusalem. Saul was a contemporary of Jesus. Soon after Saul finished his education in Jerusalem and presumably headed back to Tarsus, John the Baptist began to "prepare the way for the Lord" (Matt. 3:3). In no time at all, Jesus was on the scene, teaching in the same synagogue where Saul recently stood. Saul found influences like the wise teacher, Gamaliel, but he also experienced influences like the ones Jesus so aptly described in the Gospels. In fact, many of the Pharisees and members of the Sanhedrin Christ encountered were Saul's instructors or classmates.

The term *Pharisee* was meant to represent genuine piety and deep devotion to God. Although righteous exceptions certainly existed among the Pharisees, in the days of Jesus and Saul the term became synonymous with hypocrisy and cynicism.

𝓜atthew 23 is an entire discourse addressed to the teachers of the law and Pharisees. Read the chapter carefully and compile a list, on a separate sheet of paper, of specific ways Jesus described the same people Saul encountered in Jerusalem. (For example, don't just note that they were hypocritical, but describe the ways they were hypocritical.) Be sure to note the reference. Follow the example below.

<u>Reference</u>	<u>Description</u>
v. 4	make demands they themselves do not keep

Take a thorough look at your list. Godly people are valiant people. They are people with the courage to ask God to spotlight areas of weakness, sin, and failure. Then God can strengthen, heal, and complete what is lacking.

As we look at the sins of the Pharisees, let's ask God to give each of us an honest, probing heart. Could any one of the phrases you've listed describe you? Allow the Holy Spirit time to speak to your heart. Would you be humble enough to put a check mark by those the Holy Spirit highlights as possibly applying to your life? Will you agree to allow God full access to those areas of your life? This exercise will not be shared in small group unless someone feels led by the Spirit of God to share by her own initiative.

𝓑efore we feel like crawling in a hole because we share some of the same hypocrisies as the Pharisees, let's reconsider Matthew 23:37. What did Christ long to do in spite of the Pharisees' wrong actions or motives?

To draw them as a hen gathered her Chickens under her wings

Oh, the mercy of our God! Glance back at the descriptions you've written. The people Jesus confronted were considered the cream of the crop! Yet, they were religious frauds and hypocrites; and Jesus loved them—even in the depth of their depravity "while we [they] were still sinners" (Rom. 5:8). Will we ever be able "to grasp how wide and long and high and deep is the love of Christ" (Eph. 3:18)?

*A*ccording to Matthew 23:37, why didn't Christ gather them together "as a hen gathers her chicks under her wings"?

They would not come to Him

What personal application could you draw from this point? Write a prayer expressing your thoughts to the Master.

Thank you Lord for calling me and allowing me to abide under the shadow of Your wings. You are my refuge.

Saul knew many of the people to whom Christ was speaking in Matthew 23. Saul himself was a Pharisee and probably returned to Tarsus to serve as a teacher of the law. Imagine how his thinking was influenced by his contemporaries. I believe Saul set sail to Jerusalem as a young adolescent with a pure heart; but somewhere along the way the negative influences outweighed the positive, and his purity began to erode. The law became his god. That's what happens when you take the love out of obedience. The result is the law. Without love for God and His Word, we're just trying to be good. Nothing will wear you out faster.

Have you been there? I have! Trying to obey God and serve Him before we've come to love Him can be exhausting. Has your attempt to serve God or be good for God's sake ever exceeded your love for God? ❏ Yes ❏ No If so, describe how you felt or what happened as a result.

Saul determined to be good and obey God. A graduate from the rabbinic school of Jerusalem, he packed his diploma and headed for a place to serve. Whether or not he divided his time between teaching and his father's business is unknown. One thing you can count on: he was absolutely miserable.

*H*ow do I know? Take a look at Philippians 3:6. What was his record regarding legalistic righteousness?

Teaching righteousness which is the law.

We cannot begin to comprehend what Saul's life was like as he sought to live by the letter of the law, because most of us are Gentile Christians. Daily rituals determined the first words out of Saul's mouth in the morning, the way he took off his night clothes and put on his day clothes, and how he sprinkled his hands before breakfast. He carefully avoided eating or drinking quickly and never ate while standing.

Saul pronounced numerous benedictions throughout the day. His entire day was filled with ritual, and at night he took off his shoes and garments in prescribed order. He avoided certain sleeping positions and chose others. For the sake of his heart and liver, he probably attempted to begin the night on his left side and end the night on his right. He purposely kept his turning to a minimum. Tossing and turning through the night is misery to us; but to Saul it could have been sin!

These daily rituals paled in comparison to all the laws regarding the Sabbath. Restrictions existed for the almost unimaginable. For instance, prior to the Sabbath a Pharisee cut his fingernails and toenails not in consecutive order but alternately. He then burned the nails. He avoided spitting in a place where the wind could scatter the saliva so he would not break laws concerning sowing on the Sabbath. Day in and day out, rules existed for everything.

Do you get the general idea of what Saul's life was like as he attempted to live by the law "faultlessly"? These examples are just a few of hundreds of man-made laws. I do not cite them in order to ridicule the Jewish people. I share a few of the written traditions with you to point out man's overwhelming tendency to tax God's instruction and put in His mouth words that do not belong there.

*C*an you think of any ways we have added unnecessary burdens to God's commands in our current "religious" practices?

_____

_____

The Sabbath could not have been further from God's intent by the time Christ was "made flesh to dwell among us." The day of rest was hardly recognizable to the One who ordained it.

*B*efore we conclude today's lesson, read Christ's encounter with the Pharisees on the Sabbath in Mark 2:23-27. Explain in your own words how rules for the Sabbath twisted the truth in verse 27.

_____

_____

*H*ow does God want you to respond to what He showed you today?

_____

_____

_____

_____

_____

_____

The devout Jew might cite Isaiah 56:2 as a motivation for keeping all the rules regarding the Sabbath: "Blessed is the man … who keeps the Sabbath without desecrating it." One translation for *blessed* is *happy*. Happy is the man who keeps God's Sabbath. I doubt much room existed for happiness in the life of one trying desperately to keep man's Sabbath. Saul was strangled by the letter of the law. He tried desperately to keep all the outward acts of obedience while his heart slowly eroded. Saul gradually became the model for Isaiah 29:13: "These people come near to me with their mouth and honor me with their lips, but their hearts are far from me. Their worship of me is … rules taught by men." Inevitably, Saul's far-away heart would turn to far-away actions.

*T*ake a moment to pray that God will help us today to avoid the pitfalls into which these committed Pharisees fell. I have written my prayer below.

Oh, God, forgive us when we act like modern day Pharisees. Convict us at the very moment of our departure from the law of love You have written on our hearts. Give us hearts of devotion not heads full of religion.

D A Y 5
Meanwhile in Jerusalem

"What has been will be again, what has been done will be done again; there is nothing new under the sun" (Eccl. 1:9). I am reliving my teenage years all over again through my two daughters. I'm even watching them dress in some of the same styles I wore in high school. They were ugly then. They're even uglier now. Solomon was right. *There is nothing new under the sun.*" One way we repeat the past is all students wish away their school years. No doubt Saul also longed for an end to the hours of grueling study.

For Saul the end finally came, and he said his good-byes and headed back to Tarsus. I wonder how many days passed until he found himself wishing he could wake up back in Jerusalem. Based on Ecclesiastes 1:9, it probably wasn't many. And, of all the luck— he left just when things were about to get exciting.

The years immediately following Saul's departure from the city of the Jews were the most significant years in all history. His fellow Pharisees came upon a situation that tied their tassels in knots. It all started when the guy with the weird diet and the camel hair started preaching. You can read it for yourself. It makes fascinating reading.

*T*ake a look at Matthew 3:1-10. What did John the Baptist call the **Pharisees and Sadducees?**
❑ a whitewashed wall ☑ a brood of vipers ❑ blind guides

Read verse 8 carefully. What do you think John meant?

Bring forth a suitable offering for repentance.

John didn't make many friends among the Pharisees. They didn't like him from the start; but they had no idea how much they would despise the One for whom John came to pave the way.

*R*ead Matthew 3:11-12. **Describe the ways John said Christ's ministry would exceed his own.**

John baptizes with water
Jesus will baptize with the Holy Ghost + fire.

Compare Luke 7:29-30. How frightening to think we could reject God's awesome purposes for our lives out of hard-heartedness and pride!

*W*hat are some ways you can avoid rejecting God's purposes for your life?

_____

_____

Christ loved the Pharisees. His bold approach was to tell them the truth so the truth could set them free, but they rejected it. In no time at all, this One became the thorn in their flesh. They would not rest until they became the thorn in His.

Today's Treasure
"The next day ... the chief priests and the Pharisees went to Pilate. 'Sir,' they said, 'we remember that while he was still alive that deceiver said, "After three days I will rise again." So give the order for the tomb to be made secure until the third day '" (Matt. 27:62-64).

Many of the Pharisees had ample reason to dislike Jesus. People who hide behind masks don't particularly like to be around those who peel them off. Jesus could look right through them. He exposed their self-righteous hearts by eating with sinners and healing on the Sabbath. Their attempts to corner Him in endless debates of Scripture left them looking foolish. Every confrontation seemed to fuel their hatred even more.

Not all the Pharisees agreed with the prevailing majority. Nicodemus was a Pharisee and a member of the Jewish ruling council. He came to Jesus obviously representing a number of Pharisees, because he used the words, "We know you are a teacher who has come from God" (John 3:2). He came in belief, yet he came in secret by night.

*R*ead John 12:42-43. How does verse 42 describe the number of leaders who believed in Jesus? *Many believed*

According to verse 43, why did they remain silent? *Because of the Pharisees — they would put them out of the Synagogue.*

Have you ever remained silent for the same reason? ❏ Yes ☑ No
If so, how did your silence make you feel?

_____

At one time or another all of us have remained silent regarding our belief in Christ because we wanted the approval of others. Can you imagine the turmoil in the hearts of these leaders as they sat mutely and watched the biggest miscarriage of justice ever known to man? The silent believers were driven by fear while the vocal opposition was driven by jealousy and pride. This Nazarene was an intolerable threat. They couldn't stop Him and, worse, they couldn't explain Him. Then one day, He finally went too far.

*R*ead John 11:38-53. Why do you think this particular miracle was the one that finally spurred the Sanhedrin to violent action?

✓ *All men will believe on Him.*

✓ *These also feared the Romans will take their place & nation.*

What prophecy did Caiaphas unknowingly speak? Choose one.
❏ Christ would come back from the dead.
☑ One man would die for all people.
❏ Darkness would fall on the entire earth.

"From that day on" what did the chief priests and Pharisees do?

They took counsel to put Jesus to death

Now I am going to ask you to read all of John chapter 18. Please do not skim the familiar passages. Pay particular attention to the input of the chief priests and Pharisees whom Saul would have known. We will be able to imagine Saul's likely response to Christ based on the responses of many of his fellow zealots.

*R*ead John 18 and answer the following questions.
Can you see a hint of irony in verse 28? If so, explain.

_____

_____

1. Keeping in mind the plans they had for Christ, according to verse 31 why did the Jews take Him to Pilate, the Roman governor? Choose one.
   ☑ They needed his approval to try Jesus.
   ❏ They knew Pilate would agree with them.
   ❏ They had no right to execute anyone.
   ❏ They had to obey the law.

2. What was Pilate's initial verdict in regard to Jesus? (v. 38)

   I find no fault in Him at all.

3. Now read John 19:1-16. On what basis did the Jews insist Jesus be put to death? (v. 7)

   We have a law, and by our law he ought to die; because He made himself the Son of God.

One of the most viable tools Satan ever uses to work against God's purposes is self-interest. His manipulation through self-interest is as old as the garden of Eden. Satan used self-interest in the hearts of the chief priests and Pharisees. Christ was their enemy because He threatened their positions and feelings of piety.

Describe a way the enemy has tried to tempt you with self-interest so you would reject the purposes of God in your life.

_____

_____

_____

For a while, the chief priests and Pharisees may have believed they had won. Pilate relented just as they hoped, and the Lamb of God was nailed to a cross. Just hours later, "When he had received the drink, Jesus said, 'It is finished'" (John 19:30).

*S*it back and really think about those three words for a little while. Actually, many things were finished at that incomparable moment. What things come to your mind as being finished as Jesus said these three words?

   He had finished the Father's work as the Sacrificial Lamb — to redeem mankind. Christ bridged the gap between God and man, enabling us to come before the Throne room of grace.

The Pharisees did everything they could do to make sure things stayed finished as far as they were concerned. According to Matthew 27:62-66, to what lengths did the Pharisees go to ensure no problems would follow?

Requested the sepluchre be sealed and secured because Christ said He would rise in 3 days.

Every loose end was tied. The tomb secured. The mouths stopped. Yes, it was finally over. Finally finished. Everything except their worst nightmare.

On the first day of the week, very early in the morning, the women took the spices they had prepared and went to the tomb. They found the stone rolled away from the tomb, but when they entered, they did not find the body of the Lord Jesus. While they were wondering about this, suddenly two men in clothes that gleamed like lightning stood beside them. In their fright the women bowed down with their faces to the ground, but the men said to them, "Why do you look for the living among the dead? He is not here; he has risen!" (Luke 24:1-6).

A few very important things were finished, all right. But the Lord Jesus was not one of them. It's strange, isn't it? The very thing He finished we can't seem to leave alone; and the very thing He hasn't finished, we try to halt. The work of Calvary is finished. No more payment for sin is necessary. He did it all by Himself on the Cross. We can't earn it. We can't add to it. It is finished. Yet we try to add our good works to his Salvation.

However, the work He is doing on everyone who has accepted Christ as Savior is not finished. Salvation is finished. Sanctification is not. Completion is not. Philippians 1:6 promises that "He who began a good work in you will carry it on to completion until the day of Christ Jesus." Yet we wish He'd stop picking on us the moment we're saved and let us be the boss. Like the Pharisees, we wish He'd stop interfering. Give this thought some consideration: sometimes more effort is required to keep rolling the stone back over the tomb than simply to cooperate with the work He seeks to finish in us.

As we conclude week one of our study, think about a difficult question: Do we just want the cross without the resurrection? Are we trying to stuff the living, working Christ back into the tomb so He'll just save us, and then let us alone? Or do we want to know "the power of His resurrection and the fellowship of sharing in His sufferings"?

In the next nine weeks we will get to see Saul make the journey from enemy of the cross to servant of the Lord. We'll see the power change a person from the inside out! The power to make someone entirely different—crucified with Christ and alive in the Spirit!

You can be sure the Jerusalem news finally hit the desk of a foreign Pharisee by the name of Saul. And we will find him more than willing to do his part for his fellow man.

How **does God want you to respond to what He showed you today?**

_____

_____

_____

_____

_____

_____

[1] F. B. Meyer, *Paul, A Servant of Jesus Christ* (Fort Washington, PA: Christian Literature Crusade, 1995), 17.
[2] E.KR. Johnsen, *Paul of Tarsus* (Minneapolis: Augsburg Publishing House, 1919), 20.
[3] F. B. Meyer, *Paul, A Servant of Jesus Christ* (Fort Washington, PA: Christian Literature Crusade, 1995), 26.
[4] Ernle Bradford, *Paul the Traveller* (New York: Barnes & Noble, 1993), 35.
[5] Ibid., 35.
[6] Ibid., 36.

The First Footprints

How can we make an invisible God visible to children?

1. By learning to _____ Him ourselves! (John 14:19-23; 5:17).

2. By exerting _____ _____ while you can (Prov. 4:1-4, 10, 20-21).

   Tender in Hebrew means "_____-_____, _____."

3. By personally _____ the relevance of God's Word (Prov. 3:5-6).

4. By seizing _____ to teach about God (Deut. 6:4-9).

5. By _____ with them! (1 Cor. 13:11).

6. By _____ them to God (Prov. 22:6).

   Train up in Hebrew means:
   1. "to disciple"
   2. "to dedicate"

WEEK 2

Finding the Way

Day 1
No Innocent Bystander

Day 2
A Sudden Change in Plans

Day 3
From Persecutor to Preacher

Day 4
A Pried-Open Mind

Day 5
New Church, New Name

God's Word doesn't just tell us what we want to hear. God tells us what we need to hear. We need to know that the heroes of our faith were flesh and blood just like us. Only Christ is divine and perfect. Every other hero struggled, sinned, and had moments of faithlessness. God intends for us to admire heroes of the faith, not worship them. He gave us glimpses into many of their frailties and blatant sins not only to balance us but to give us hope. God inspired Paul to tell us "we are more than conquerors through him who loved us" (Rom. 8:37). This week we'll discover just how much needed conquering in the life of a religious zealot. We will discover the answers to the following questions.

Principal Questions
Day 1: What was the connection and contrast between Saul and Stephen?
Day 2: What was most significant to you about Saul's conversion?
Day 3: When Saul set out to prove to the Jews that Jesus was the Christ, what was his method?
Day 4: How did God speak to Peter about prejudice?
Day 5: How did Barnabas and Saul begin their ministry together?

Only Jesus could turn such a self-proclaimed enemy of the gospel into one of the greatest lovers of the gospel who ever lived. If He could change Saul and mark eternity with his life, God can change us. Let's continue to offer Him a teachable heart this week and let the transformation begin!

D A Y 1

No Innocent Bystander

Imagine the unfolding events in Jerusalem. No messenger could run quickly enough to satisfy Saul's curiosity. I suspect that he kept abreast of the growing menace facing his fellow Pharisees. Finally, the sightings ceased. Jesus' followers circulated a preposterous account of His ascending into the heavens. The Pharisees really didn't care how He left. They were just glad He was gone. *If only we'd come up with that body,* they must have fretted. You can be sure students and teachers debated every conceivable theory.

A few no doubt wondered, *What if he really did come back from the dead?* After all, they remembered that unfortunate Lazarus incident. No one dared speak up. How convenient for the Pharisees if the stir had simply died down after Jesus was gone. Instead, as the months passed, the number of Jesus' followers grew as did their boldness. Saul was probably disgusted over the way the Pharisees mishandled the problem. If he wanted it done right, he'd obviously have to do it himself. So Saul packed up his things and headed for Jerusalem, salivating for the chance to be the hero. In his estimation, someone needed to deal with those fanatics. He was more than happy to be the one.

Saul arrived in Jerusalem just in time to hear an infuriating speech from an unforgivable infidel. The heretic addressed the Sanhedrin with unacceptable audacity.

His name was Stephen. No doubt, Saul did some quick research on the renegade while standing conspicuously in the crowd. Let's do a little research of our own.

Today's Treasure
"While they were stoning him, Stephen prayed, 'Lord Jesus, receive my spirit.' Then he fell on his knees and cried out, 'Lord, do not hold this sin against them.' When he had said this, he fell asleep. And Saul was there, giving approval to his death" (Acts 7:59–8:1).

Read Acts 6:1-15. Complete the following.

1. Sometimes God allows conflict in our churches to create awareness of need. How do these Scriptures offer evidence to support this statement?

Widows were neglected The apostles called a meeting and 7 men appointed over this business Which was done The people were happy

2. What evidence can you find to suggest God honored the addition of these seven men? Check all that apply.

☑ Many priests became obedient to the faith.
☐ The Grecian widows stopped complaining.
☑ The Word of God spread.

3. According to verse 7: "A large number of ___*priests*___ became obedient to the faith." What impact do you imagine this result had on the hard-hearted Pharisees and Sadducees?

Very upset & bothered

4. Verses 5-15 offer wonderful descriptions of the man called Stephen. Categorize each of the descriptions under the appropriate headings.

**Internal Manifestations
of the Holy Spirit**

Full of faith

Wisdom

**External Manifestations
of the Holy Spirit**

Wonders

Miracles

31

In our neighborhoods and work places we are surrounded by people with empty lives. Many of us remember our own agony of emptiness. And right here on earth's miserable sod, Stephen was full—not just because he accepted Jesus as Savior, but because he surrendered his whole life to Christ's will and purpose. The more Stephen poured out his life for Christ, the more Christ poured His life into Stephen.

I could never tell anyone that becoming a Christian makes life easier. But with a heart full of emotion, I will tell anyone that a life surrendered to Christ is a life that is full. My life has not been easy. I've made many mistakes, and I've been the victim of others' mistakes. Yet I would not trade lives with anyone. Why? Because my life is full. I believe emptiness causes more people to despair of life than does pain.

As evidence of Internal Manifestations of the Holy Spirit, you probably noted that Stephen was full of faith, full of God's grace and power. Only a person who is full of the Holy Spirit can possess the kind of power Stephen displayed and yet remain full of God's grace. Only in Christ can a man or woman become an instrument of impressive, unquestionable might—yet remain a vessel of humility, an object of grace. You see, a person full of the Holy Spirit cannot be full of self. Pride never accompanies power in the fully yielded life.

Among the External Manifestations of the Holy Spirit, you may have noted the description in Acts 6:15: "his face was like the face of an angel."

*H*ow might either of the following passages provide possible explanations for Stephen's face looking like that of an angel?

Exodus 34:29 _____

Ecclesiastes 8:1 _____

Now let's join Saul in the crowd and listen to Stephen's speech before the Sanhedrin.

*R*ead Acts 7:1-53. Reread the charges Stephen made against the Jewish leaders in verses 51-53. What do you think he meant by the following terms?
Stiff-necked _____

Uncircumcised hearts *Closed hearts*

Uncircumcised ears *Closed ears*

Read Acts 7:54-8:1. Complete the following.
1. Read 1 Peter 4:12-14 with Stephen's experience in mind. How did these verses spring to life as Stephen looked up to heaven?

_____

_____

2. The Bible mentions Saul for the first time in Acts 7:58. How is he first introduced to us in Scripture? Choose one.
❏ He cast the first stone. ❏ He incited the riot.
❏ He supervised the stoning. ☑ He had the witnesses' clothes at his feet.

3. Why do you think Stephen did not want the sins of his executioners held against them? There is no right or wrong answer. Just offer your thoughts.

He was so full of the Holy Ghost and love

4. What are several important advantages to forgiving your persecutors?

We will be forgiven of our sins
We will have peace of mind

Briefly describe an experience when you found forgiving difficult.

There were several incidents which caused a great deal of pain and hardship but the best thing is to forgive and forget.

5. How does Acts 8:1 prove Saul was no innocent bystander?

Saul was consenting to Stephen death.

Stephen. The first Christian martyr. What a shame, we may muse. Such a powerful life cut so short. What plans God must have had for him! What impact he would have had on the kingdom. Where were the angels of God? Where was his Shield? Where was the Protector? We are only privy to the chronicles of one day in the life of Stephen. Yet, what a day it was. I believe it was the day He was born to live.

Stephen's name in the Greek is *Stephanos*. The meaning of his name is <u>crown</u>. He received his calling from the same God who called Jeremiah, to whom He said, "'Before I formed you in the womb I knew you, before you were born I set you apart'" (Jer. 1:5). I believe that every day of *Stephanos'* life God looked on him with great affection, dreading the sight of his agonizing death. God was looking toward the moment when Stephen's name would become synonymous with his reward. While others saw a man, God saw a crown. To the believers who would soon face the same persecution and same earthly end, Christ urged, "'Be faithful, even to the point of death, and I will give you the crown [the *stephanos*] of life'" (Rev. 2:10).

We tend to equate victory with survival, don't we? To overcome peril is synonymous with living through it, in our estimation. How temporal our calculations! From glory's gaze, Stephen received the most awesome calling of all: he was counted worthy to die for the sake of Christ. Many of us may struggle recounting the names of all twelve disciples, but most of us can name the first Christian martyr without hesitation.

Worthy, indeed, was his calling. It brought the Son of God to His feet. He stood in Stephen's honor and watched from Heaven while the frenzied crowds of His chosen people dragged Stephen from the city. They cast the first stone. Then came the second. Then hits came so quickly that one could not be separated from another. Don't underestimate Stephen by imagining his senses were dulled. I believe he felt each jagged blow. While Christ stood in Stephen's behalf, Stephen stood in His. As the fatal blows buckled his body, he sank to his death interceding for those who stoned him, "'Lord, do not hold this sin against them'" (Acts 7:60). As his body lay in a heap, Stephen stood covered in blood—Jesus' blood.

Saul was there, giving approval to Stephen's death. The original Greek word for *approval* is *suneudokeo*. Are you ready for this? It means "to take pleasure with others." *Suneudokeo* is a word sometimes used of both parties in a marriage who are mutually pleased with something (see 1 Cor. 7:12-13). Applying the original meaning to Saul's actions, the scene becomes clearer. He was pleased with their actions, and they were pleased with his approval. A mutual admiration society. To provide further startling clarity, consider that the word describing Saul's action expresses continuous or repeated action. In other words, Saul was virtually cheering throughout the entire exhibit. He didn't just give his approval when Stephen breathed his last. He cheered on every blow, like points on a scoreboard.

As Jesus watched, He didn't miss a single nod of Saul's phylacteried head. Remember, Christ was up on His feet at the time. Can you imagine the alloy of emotions He must have experienced as He looked on the two key players in the Kingdom that day? One for Him. One against Him. One covered in blood. The other covered by prayer shawls. One who could not save himself from men. The other who could not save himself from sin. One dead in body but alive in spirit. The other alive in body but dead in spirit. One loved by God. And the other loved by God. Grace, grace, God's grace.

Just a day in the life of a man named Stephen. A shooting star. He had one brief performance. One chance on stage. But it was absolutely unforgettable. As the curtain fell on his life, He received a standing ovation from the only One who really mattered. I have a feeling that seconds later the two of them hadn't changed positions much. Christ was still on His feet. Stephen was still crumbled to his knees. How sweet to imagine the first heavenly words he heard that day: "Welcome, *Stephanos*, My joy and My crown."

D A Y 2

A Sudden Change in Plans

As I approach today's lesson, I am overwhelmed with emotion. I will never be able to translate on paper the emotions bursting the old wineskin of my heart with the new wine of fresh love. I wish I could somehow describe how I feel about my God this moment. How I long for new words. New shades of paint. New notes on a scale. I cannot enunciate the overflow of my heart to you. But I can share with you the source of the fresh wave of love: an ever-present Christ, ever-watchful, ever-interceding, ever-interrupting, ever-merciful.

If you asked me today what I question most at this point in my journey with Christ, my answer would not be, *Why do bad things happen to good people?* Nor would it be, *Why have You allowed me this suffering?* It would most definitely be, *Why did You call me? With all my failures and frailties, why do I have the privilege of loving You, of knowing You the little that I do?*

Today as the blinding light falls suddenly on a murderous persecutor, we still may be left in the dark to understand why we've each been called; but our eyes will be unveiled to the One who called. And we will sigh and confess, *How very like Him.*

Dr. Luke's account of Saul's conversion is recorded in Acts 9:1-9, 17-19. Paul's account of his own conversion is recorded in Acts 26:9-18. We should not be surprised that Paul's own descriptions are far more detailed. One of our friends could tell the story of our salvation but not with the passion and attention to detail we could tell it ourselves!

How does God want you to respond to what He showed you today?

_____

_____

_____

_____

_____

_____

Today's Treasure
"As he neared Damascus on his journey, suddenly a light from heaven flashed around him. He fell to the ground and heard a voice say to him, 'Saul, Saul, why do you persecute me?'"
(Acts 9:3-4).

*R*ead both accounts, then complete the following exercise to help you compile the events into one record for more thorough comprehension. Try to be as specific as possible.

1. Compare Acts 9:1 to Acts 26:9. How could these verses support the statement: "A person can be sincere in his beliefs yet be sincerely wrong."

_____

_____

2. Check any of the following which accurately describe Saul's actions against the followers of Christ.

- ☑ He threatened them.
- ☑ He arrested them.
- ☐ He ridiculed them.
- ☐ He tried to get them to commit blasphemy.
- ☐ He assaulted them.
- ☑ He voted for their deaths.
- ☐ He had them punished.
- ☑ He traveled to other cities to persecute them.

3. Why was Saul going to Damascus that eventful day? Choose one.
- ☐ to take men or women of the Way as prisoners to Jerusalem
- ☐ to have men or women of the Way cast from the synagogues
- ☐ to talk to the chief priests about the men and women of the Way
- ☐ other: _To bring men and women bound back to Jerusalem._

4. How did Saul describe the light from heaven? _Light from heaven_

_____

5. What conclusions can you draw from Christ's words "persecute me"?

Persecuting the Church which is His body therefore Saul was persecuting Christ

6. Why did Christ appear to Saul? List every reason given.

I believe He wanted Saul to know who he was persecuting and to save him

7. What might be several reasons why Christ struck Saul blind? Think in terms of physical reasons, spiritual reasons, and even emotional impact.

To stop him - give Saul time to think and reflect. To save him and prepare him for the plan He (Jesus) had for his life + ministry.

I can remember some of the first experiences in my life when this formerly dogmatic, closed-minded woman unwillingly discovered the shade of gray. I tended to see everything in black and white. I've concluded that for those who only see gray, God often emphatically and lovingly paints portraits of black and white so they are forced to acknowledge the new colors. For those who only see black and white, He introduces constant situations when answers aren't so easy, lists "A to Z" cannot be found, and points one, two, and three don't work. GRAY.

At a very difficult time in our lives when we were constantly called for school conferences concerning our son Michael, Keith and I were amused after meeting one of his new counselors. He couldn't have been a day over 25. He had a brand new psychology degree and our precious boy figured out. Everything he mentioned, we had tried at least 5 years before—and at least 500 times. We didn't say anything, in order to spare his dignity; but when we got in the car we said, "Wasn't God merciful to give him Michael early in his practice?"

I was tempted to say to him, "Mr. Black and White, meet young Mr. Gray. He's going to add a brand new color to your palette, and one day you'll be glad. Just like I was."

Life is full of grays, but today you and I get to enjoy a little black and white—the evil of a sinner's heart, the purity of a Savior's mercy.

The evil of a sinner's heart. After such noble beginnings, such strict reinforcement of God's laws, incomparable attainment of the knowledge of Scripture, and every external mark of righteousness—what happened? How did a brilliant young rabbi become a relentless persecutor of men and women casting his vote for the death of many? He certainly did not develop into a murderous zealot under the instruction of Gamaliel, his highly esteemed teacher.

*R*eview the counsel of Gamaliel in Acts 5:33-39. What advice would he have given Saul about the people of the Way?

_____

_____

Saul was not unlike Michael's bright young counselor. He thought he had all the answers. The obvious difference is that Saul's answers were lethal. Saul thought he was smarter than his teacher. No sense in waiting to see if the people of the Way would finally dissipate. He took matters into his own hands and tried to give them a much needed shove. Acts 26:11 describes Saul's mental state perfectly: he had become obsessed.

I'm certainly no counselor, but I suspect that most obsessions rise from a futile attempt to fill a gaping hole somewhere deep in a life. Saul's external righteousness and achieved goals left behind an itch he could not scratch. Can you imagine how miserable he must have been? Religiously righteous to the bone, inside he had nothing but innately wicked marrow. All that work, and it hadn't worked. All his righteous passion turned into unrighteous zeal, and he became dangerous.

The Greek word for *obsessed* is *emmainomai.* The root word is *mainomai* which means "to act like a maniac." Our best attempts at homegrown righteousness are still but a moment from the unspeakable. Passions can turn a new direction with frightening speed. May none of us forget it. The prophet Isaiah said, "All our righteous acts are like filthy rags" (Isa. 64:6). If all the righteousness we have is our own, it's just an act. And acts don't last very long.

The purity of a Savior's mercy. Saul, himself, would later say, "God demonstrates his own love for us in this: While we were still sinners, Christ died for us" (Rom. 5:8). Christ met Saul on the path to his darkest, most devious sin. For that very moment, for the depths of Saul's depravity, Christ had already died. Christ literally caught him in the act.

*F*ill in the following blank according to Philippians 3:12. Keep in mind that these are the same man's words: "Not that I have already obtained all this, or have already been made perfect, but I press on to take hold of that

for which Christ Jesus ___took held___ of me."

The *NIV* uses the words *took hold*. The original Greek word *katalambano* means "to lay hold of, seize, with eagerness, suddenness … the idea of eager and strenuous exertion, to grasp." Christ literally snatched Saul by the neck. Later, the persecutor turned apostle would write unforgettable words to Timothy, his son in the faith.

*W*rite 1 Timothy 1:15 in the space below.

This is a FAITHFUL saying: and worth of all acceptance that Christ Jesus came into this world to save sinners of whom I am Chief.

Read the next verse. Why was the persecutor shown such mercy?

For a pattern to them which should hereafter to believe on Him to life everlasting.

Paraphrase the apostle's declaration of praise from 1 Timothy 1:17.

To the King Eternal, immortal, invisible the Only wise God be all honor, glory forever and ever.

Glance back over Acts 26:16-18 and review the marvelous, eternal works Saul was called to do. Jesus sent Saul to open the eyes of many and turn them from darkness to light so they could receive forgiveness of sins. No greater calling exists, as well as no room for pride. God's chosen servant was never more than a flashback from humility. Perhaps this is the very reason God forgets, but we don't. Let's face it. No one can teach forgiveness like the forgiven. Perhaps, like me, your life has required a healthy measure of God's forgiveness.

Can you think of a person whose public testimony of God's forgiveness helped you to finally accept it yourself? Explain briefly.

_____

_____

Have you had a chance to share the joy of forgiveness with another person struggling with being forgiven? ❑ Yes ❑ No If so, explain briefly. Please protect the other person's privacy if he or she has never shared publicly.

One time my sister & I had a fight several days later we forgave each other & laughed at the things that transpired — but we did forgive each other.

Thank goodness, Saul ultimately became a zealous proponent of forgiveness of sin. As our lesson draws to a conclusion, let's end with some important thoughts about zeal.

- We can wholeheartedly believe in something and be wholeheartedly wrong.
- Sincerity means nothing if it is misdirected.

Saul believed in his cause with all his heart, and it literally led him down the path to destruction.

Anyone who knows me very well knows I am an avid, maybe rabid, basketball fan. The star player on our local professional team is one of the most devout believers I have ever seen. He observes every holiday. He devotes hours to prayer. He prioritizes his faith high above his profession to the point of observing a month-long daily fast which invariably falls during playoffs. He lives a strict and holy life. He testifies at every opportunity on national television—a devout believer. Sadly, he believes in a lie. All that devotion, all those righteous acts, and inside resides a dangerously unredeemed heart. Saul was sincere. As he stated in Acts 26:9, "'I too was convinced that I ought to do all that was possible to oppose the name of Jesus of Nazareth.'" The more I learn about God's Word, the less I think of opinions. Chiefly, my own.

*C*an you think of a personal opinion or a devout belief you used to have that you ultimately, based on God's Word, realized was incomplete or misguided? ❏ Yes ❏ No If so, identify the idea below.

_____

_____

*H*ow does God want you to respond to what He showed you today?

_____

_____

_____

_____

_____

Christ not only snatched Saul from Satan that pivotal day. He snatched Saul from himself—from his own misguided zeal, from his own obsessions. He can snatch you from yours, too. I'm living proof. I couldn't count the times any given month I thank God for saving me not only from Satan but from myself.

Having searched the life of Saul, how can we ever doubt that Christ can save? Is any too wicked? Any too murderous? Grace never draws a line with a willing soul. His arm is never too short to save (see Isa. 59:1). He can reach into the deepest pit or down the dustiest road to Damascus. Yes, some things are gray such as, why did He choose us? But some things are still black and white—I once was lost, but now I'm found, was blind but now I see.

D A Y   3

From Persecutor to Preacher

Today's Treasure
"*Saul grew more and more powerful and baffled the Jews living in Damascus by proving that Jesus is the Christ*" (Acts 9:22).

Few things are more precious than the expressions on a newborn's face as he or she is suddenly cast from the darkness of the womb into the bright lights of the delivery room. I vividly remember both laughing and crying at my daughters' faces screwing up indignantly as if to say, "Would the same wise guy who turned on that light mind turning it off?" Many years ago when a grown man was born again on a dusty road to Damascus, a light came on that no one was able to turn off. We will soon discover many who tried. Today we will consider Saul's eye-opening initiation into true discipleship.

*R*ead Acts 9:10-31. Our emphasis today will be on the events following Saul's encounter with Ananias. Complete each of the following.

1. The Lord told Ananias he would find Saul at a certain house praying. Use your imagination for a moment. In your opinion, what are a few things he may have been praying about?

Forgiveness for being directly involved in the martyr of many Christians

2. If you could describe Ananias' initial response to God's instruction in one word, what would it be? _____

3. What was Saul's first action after he regained his sight? Choose one.
   ❏ He began preaching. ❏ He wept.
   ❏ He went to Jerusalem. ❏ He was baptized.

4. Saul began preaching in Damascus. What was his message?

_____

5. Think of three adjectives you believe would best describe Barnabas based on today's reading.

_____ _____ _____

6. Why did Saul's fellow believers insist he be sent to Tarsus? Choose one.
   ❏ He was about to be imprisoned. ❏ He was causing a riot.
   ❏ The Grecian Jews tried to kill him. ❏ He made too many enemies.

In our previous lesson, we discovered Paul's testimony of his conversion to be more specific than Luke's version of the events. By comparing both, we were able to arrive at a clearer picture of God's glorious interruption on Paul's journey to Damascus. Once again, we will find Paul's account of his infancy as a Christian to be far more specific than Luke's.

*C*ompare Luke's version in Acts 9:19-30 with Paul's own version in Galatians 1:14-18. For the sake of clarity, number the following events in chronological order.

____ Grecian Jews in Jerusalem tried to kill Saul.
____ Saul began preaching in the Damascus synagogues.
____ Saul went to Arabia and later returned to Damascus.
____ The brothers sent him off to Tarsus.
____ The brothers got him out of Damascus in a basket.
____ Barnabas brought Saul to the frightened apostles.
____ Saul traveled to Jerusalem but was rejected by the disciples there.

Paul was careful to tell the reader that he did not consult any man but went immediately into Arabia following his conversion. Apparently Paul thought he'd better get to know the One who obviously knew him so well. Unlike us, Saul's primary need was not discipleship. He knew more about Scripture in his young years than most learn in a lifetime! He needed to come to grips with the Author.

When his quiet exile with the Savior was over, he once again approached the ancient city of Damascus. What strange thoughts must have clouded his mind. He first came to Damascus to profane the name of Christ. Now he came to preach the name of Christ. He first came to Damascus to take followers of the Way prisoner. Now they would make room for him in their homes. He had to know he would be the talk of the town, yet the inevitable mockery did not slow him down.

We are told "Saul grew more and more powerful and baffled the Jews living in Damascus by proving that Jesus is the Christ" (Acts 9:22). The verse tells us two wonderful things about Saul:

1. He grew more powerful. The Greek word is *endunamoo,* also used in Hebrews 11:34 as a description of Samson. The supernatural power Samson possessed physically, God gave to Saul spiritually! Saul was probably a man of small physical stature. A writer in the second century described him as: "A man rather small in size, bald-headed, bow-legged, with meeting eyebrows, a large, red and somewhat hooked nose."[1] Little about his physical appearance was intimidating, but when the Spirit of God fell on him, he became the spiritual heavyweight champion of the world!

2. He proved to the Jews that Jesus is the Christ. The word *proved* means "to cause to come together, to bring together,…to join or knit together."

Let's insert one of these phrases in the Scripture so we can see the picture God is drawing for us. "Saul … [knit together to] the Jews … that Jesus is the Christ" (Acts 9:22). What did he knit together? The old with the new! He knit the teachings of the Old Testament Law and Prophets with their fulfillment in Jesus Christ. As the *King James Version* says, "Saul … confounded the Jews … proving that this is very Christ." His speech to them was probably much like Christ's speech to the two travelers on the road to Emmaus.

*R*ead Luke 24:27. What was Christ's text? _____

What was Christ's subject matter? _____

Both Christ and Saul proved He was the promised Messiah by knitting the promises of the Old Testament to their fulfillment in Jesus. The proof was there. All they needed to do was believe. Unlike the Gentiles, the Jews knew Scripture. They just hadn't recognized the One about whom the Scriptures were written!

Saul was hardly the kind of man to be ignored. Saul with the gospel was like my daughters with the radio. He kept turning up the volume. Inevitably the Jews conspired to kill him, so Saul took the first basket out of town. According to his testimony in Galatians 1:18, Saul wanted to get acquainted with Peter anyway. From the look of things, this was a perfect time for a visit to Jerusalem.

Can you imagine how differently Saul must have approached the city this time? Every step he took had new significance. Damascus was northeast of Jerusalem, so Saul walked past the Mount of Olives and the garden of Gethsemane. He walked through the Kidron Valley, dodging the hardened ground over ancient graves. He walked through the city gates where his face was recognized instantly. The chief priests waited for his return with prisoners. Instead, only one prisoner returned: a prisoner of Jesus Christ.

Talk about feeling alone! Perhaps one of the most pronounced characteristics of the Jewish people was a very strong sense of community. Being surrounded by Gentiles as Saul and his family had been in Tarsus probably only tightened the bonds of togetherness. He had always known the security of belonging. His conversion not only freed him from the bonds of sin; it also suddenly freed him from the bonds of human security.

God had issued Saul an undeniable apostolic calling. He probably assumed his place of belonging was with the other apostles. "When he came to Jerusalem, he tried to join the disciples, but they were all afraid of him, not believing that he really was a disciple" (Acts 9:26). As despicable as he had been, our hearts sting for him a little, don't they? Perhaps each of us can relate to the unique stab of loneliness.

Two wonderful words begin the next verse: "But Barnabas." We will meet many historical figures through our study. Some will be honorable. Others will not. A few will be heroes. Without a doubt, Barnabas was one of those. Acts 9:27 tells us "Barnabas took him [Saul] and brought him to the apostles." The original Greek word for *took* is *epilambano* which means "generally to take hold of, e.g., to take the hand or take by the hand." Few things touch my heart more than Christian men who risk vulnerability in obedience to Christ. Barnabas reached out a helping hand to a discouraged man. Saul took that hand. Two lives bonded in that moment.

Barnabas offers us an example we don't want to miss. Although we will have a number of opportunities to get to know him through our series, let's take a brief look at the man God used to reach out a warm, tangible hand of acceptance to Saul.

*R*ead the first mention Scripture ever makes of Barnabas in Acts 4:36-37. What was his original name?_____

Who renamed him and why this particular new name?

_____

Encouragement. The root of the word is *courage.* What do you think *courage* has to do with *encouragement?*

_____

_____

God used Barnabas over and over to give others the courage to be the people He called them to be. When Barnabas brought Saul before the other apostles, they may have remembered how each of them had been the focus of his encouragement at one time or another. Now he encouraged them to accept a new brother.

We have each experienced a critical need for encouragement at some time in our lives. When we're surrounded by other believers and the music is playing and emotions soaring, the call of God on our lives can be easy to hear and accept. Then we have to go back home, back to work, and back to the trenches to live our faith. Difficulties and losses arise. Life changes. Things don't work out the way we expected. We need encouragement: a courage transplant from another believer so we can continue to pursue the abundant life of the Lord Jesus even in the midst of our discouraging circumstances.

Reflect for a moment on the seasons of your Christian life. Who has been a Barnabas to you and how did he or she encourage you?

_____

_____

Many probably criticized Barnabas for being gullible concerning Saul. Barnabas was willing to give people a chance even when others didn't. How many people have returned to former lifestyles because no one believed and accepted them when they attempted to change? If we end up being duped, better to have erred on the side of belief!

Few things bear the immediate fruit of encouragement. Look ahead in Scripture for just a moment and inspect some of the fruit of Barnabas' ministry for yourself.

*R*ead Acts 11:22-24. What evidence do you see in verse 23 of Barnabas' living up to the name the apostles gave him?

_____

What results did his ministry have according to verse 24?

_____

_H_ow does God want you to respond to what He showed you today?

_____

_____

_____

_____

_____

_____

Because Barnabas—a good man full of the Holy Spirit—believed in people, many people ended up believing in Christ. Now, that's results.

Barnabas persuaded the apostles to accept the new convert, and the most powerful preacher in all Christendom was set loose in Jerusalem. Consequently, Saul did such a fine job of debating the Grecian Jews, he nearly got himself killed. We see an end to this chapter of Saul's experience in Acts 9:30. The brothers pushed Saul on a boat to Tarsus to keep him from losing his head. I can't help but snicker at the words which follow Saul's departure: "Then the church throughout Judea, Galilee and Samaria enjoyed a time of peace" (Acts 9:31). Saul had a way of stirring things up. No doubt, Tarsus had enjoyed her last breath of peace for a while. Saul was on his way.

Meanwhile, "The church throughout Judea, Galilee and Samaria … was strengthened; and encouraged by the Holy Spirit, it grew in numbers" (Acts 9:31). Sounds like Barnabas still hung around awhile, doesn't it? Let's look for ways to be a Barnabas in another's life this week. Take every opportunity to encourage fellow believers.

The answers to the activity on page 39 were 6, 2, 1, 7, 3, 5, and 4.

D A Y   4

A Pried-Open Mind

Today's Treasure
"For God, who was at work in the ministry of Peter as an apostle to the Jews, was also at work in my ministry as an apostle to the Gentiles" (Gal. 2:8).

In lesson 3, you compared the events of Saul's post-conversion life based on Acts 9 and Galatians 1. Today we'll explore a very important historical marker in those events.

*L*ook back at Galatians 1:18. With whom did Saul stay for 15 days after

he arrived in Jerusalem? _____

Fifteen days is a long time to have company—if not for Peter, for his wife! (Yes, Peter was married! See Matt. 8:14-15.) At that point, she was still keeping a strictly kosher kitchen. She had no idea how differently she and her husband would soon be looking at the food on their table—a fact which will have more significance later in our lesson today. Imagine the discussions between Peter and Paul—two giants of our faith.

*T*hink back on the things you know about both Peter and Paul. Whether you have limited or extensive knowledge of their backgrounds, heritage, encounters with Christ, and ministries, you can probably think of several similarities and differences that made their union very interesting. Note as many as you can in the columns below.

Similarities	Differences
_____	_____
_____	_____
_____	_____
_____	_____

You can be sure most of the items you've noted were topics of discussion between the two at some point. Scripture tells us Saul went to Jerusalem to get acquainted with Peter. The Greek term suggests far more than simple acquaintance. The term *historeo* means "to ascertain by inquiry and personal examination; to know or to visit, so as to consider and observe attentively and gain knowledge." *Historeo* is the word from which we derive the English word *history*. Remember, Saul was a student at heart! Surely all great teachers are! Saul didn't go to Jerusalem just to make a new friend. He went straight to Christianity's foremost professor for a history lesson! The tables turned as an uneducated fisherman became the scholar, and a highly educated rabbi became the student. Saul had so much to learn and, perhaps, unlearn. Peter also had volumes to learn from Saul whether he realized it or not. At least one lesson he would learn soon.

Not long after Saul's informative visit with Peter, Saul's new brothers in Christ urged him to go back to Tarsus (Acts 9:30). Saul is not mentioned again in the Book of Acts until late in the eleventh chapter. However, something happens in Peter's life in the interim which I believe flowed from his encounter with Saul. After Saul departed for Tarsus, Peter traveled to various places and was a vessel of God's powerful Spirit. No doubt he kept thinking about Saul. True to human nature, their differences probably clouded his mind more than their similarities.

*I*n the columns I asked you to fill in earlier, you may have listed one of their foremost differences in ministry. Galatians 2:7 perfectly describes a marked contrast in their callings. Choose one.
- ❏ Peter was to proclaim the law. Saul was to proclaim God's grace.
- ❏ Peter was to stay in the realm of Judea. Saul was to travel abroad.
- ❏ Peter was a proponent of marriage. Saul was a proponent of singleness.
- ❏ Peter was entrusted with the Jews. Saul was entrusted with the Gentiles.

Before we assume the two men simply shook hands and went their separate ways, let's try to crawl into the mind of the apostle Peter. Scripture pictures Peter as unduly interested in what Christ called others to do. Having just received his personal commission from Christ, John 21:21 tells us Peter looked at John and asked, "'Lord, what about him?'" The scene makes me laugh every time. Peter seemed to always say what others just thought. As I often say about one of my beloved children with the same habit, his brain stem was his tongue. He never seemed to have a thought that didn't come out of his mouth! Christ's answer? "'What is that to you?'" (John 21:22).

Follow my line of thinking. I suspect that in the months following Saul's visit, Peter often thought of Saul's calling and was relieved it wasn't his! Can you imagine how many times he must have thought about Saul being called to minister to the Gentiles and thought, "Better him than me!" From a deeply rooted Jewish point of view, the difference in their ministries was mammoth! Saul may as well have been called to lepers or animals! Peter may have even wondered if Saul's punishment for persecuting the church was to get the leftovers. In no time at all, God taught Peter a very important lesson through a vision. The reading I am about to ask you to do is somewhat lengthy, but I hope you will find the account interesting.

*R*ead all of Acts 10 and in the space below write the Scripture which you believe best summarizes the chapter.

_____

_____

I see at least four applications emerge in this unique chapter of Scripture:

1. God often uses repetition as an effective tool. Have you ever noticed how God uses reiteration in our lives to make sure we get the point? People frequently have come to me after a message I've delivered and said, "OK, you're the third person this week God has used to speak to me about that issue. I give up!" I've also been on the other end of the experience. The first time or two God tries to get through to me I might be able to resist the point. The more the hammer hits the nail, however, the more I'm forced to chalk it up as more than coincidence.

*D*escribe the last time God used repetition to get through to you.

_____

_____

God sometimes uses repetition like a crowbar to pry open our minds. He used Saul to first force Peter to look at the Gentiles as beloved of God. Then God persisted by giving him a very unappetizing vision. Next, He used Cornelius as human affirmation of divine revelation. Finally, He displayed His absence of partiality as "The circumcised believers who had come with Peter were astonished that the gift of the Holy Spirit had been poured out even on the Gentiles" (Acts 10:45).

2. God often places similar visions on the hearts of separate people. We don't often hear of Christians today having visions like those in Acts 10. But when God is preparing to do a new thing, He definitely places visions on the hearts of various people. Sometimes they may be miles apart in proximity or ministry, yet God will tender both hearts toward a similar work. At times God has overwhelmed me with a burden that ultimately became a vision. At those times He has raised up someone else with the same vision.

This Bible study and the two preceding it are examples of God giving a similar vision to separate people. God placed a burden on my heart for women's in-depth Bible study. The burden turned into a vision as God confirmed His intentions. Still, I had no idea I would be a part of the vision! I just thought my job was to needle my denomination until in-depth Bible study became available! Soon, I was invited to be part of a think tank focused on the needs of Christian women. The participants flew in from all over the United States. Without exception, we all shared the same vision!

I've experienced the same phenomenon at church. I've seen a lay leader share a vision for our church which he strongly believed the Lord had given him. Then tears gathered in the eyes of several others who each sincerely testified, "God shared the same thing with me!"

*H*ave you ever witnessed or been part of a similar vision God gave to separate people? ❏ Yes ❏ No If so, explain briefly.

_____

_____

3. God shares vision most often with those who are prepared to receive it. Take a look at verses 9 and 10 once more. God gave the vision to Peter for several reasons.

- He had a personal need for the vision. God desired to provoke a change in Peter.
- He had an active prayer life. Verse 9 tells us "Peter went up on the roof to pray." Many Christians desire to hear from God and see Him revealed in their lives, but fewer have the active prayer life He uses as an avenue to reveal Himself. Prayer is essential because prayer places us in a posture to hear from God.
- He had an appetite for what God had to reveal. Notice verse 10 says Peter became hungry. Not coincidentally, God issued him a vision illustrated through food. God often uses spiritual appetites the way He used Peter's physical appetite.

God often shares a glimpse of something He desires to do with those who have a corresponding hunger for Him. For instance, my assistant has hungered for world missions most of her life. Although I also had a heart for international missions, her burden exceeded mine. Consequently, God first shared with her His desire for our ministry to be very involved in missions overseas. He then fueled my hunger and placed the same vision on my heart.

4. God always dishonors prejudice. Peter probably not only saw himself as different from the Gentiles, but better. His attitude is nothing new. Like most of us, his prejudices were handed down through the generations. Many prefer to think of generational prejudice as "the way I was raised" rather than a chain of sin they need to break.

Many otherwise strong, God-serving, Bible-believing Christians are steeped in prejudice. Peter was one of those. Yet his willingness to have his closed mind pried open was testimony to his godly sincerity. Peter soon discovered that his new attitudes were very confrontational. Acts 11 unfolds with the reaction of the other apostles who heard about Peter's encounter with Cornelius. We read that "The circumcised believers criticized him and said, 'You went into the house of uncircumcised men and ate with them'" (vv. 2-3). They were appalled! Yet Peter's lesson became one from which they all learned.

My hero on the subject of prejudice is my daughter Melissa. She was born color-blind. If she has any prejudice at all, it's toward prejudiced people. In the eighth grade, she fell in *like* with a hispanic boy at her school. She asked me if having a boyfriend outside her race was against Scripture. I explained that the words "unequally yoked" spoke of Christian beliefs rather than race.

This young man was the son of a very fine preacher. The boy was a committed Christian involved in his youth group. He was also a fine athlete, which gave the two of them many things in common. I listened carefully, drew a deep breath and said, "Melissa, I'm afraid you are just about to discover how cruel the world is. You are not doing anything wrong, but many people will probably talk about you as if you are. I will stand with you if you are determined to make a stand."

I was right. Rumors were all over our neighborhood by the time she walked down the hall with him the first time. Interestingly, the other teenagers didn't seem to notice. The parents were the ones who uproared! Most of my friends disapproved. Most of his parents' friends disapproved. The prejudice poured both ways. I was asked several times how I could let Melissa have a boyfriend outside her race. My answer was always the same. "Melissa is watching me carefully for biblical integrity. I must stand on the Word to raise my children. I must have no other standard." We took a fair amount of criticism, but our precious Melissa stood tall and ultimately emerged with more integrity than her accusers. Melissa and I formed a very strong bond through her encounter with prejudice. I ended up with her respect. She ended up as one of my heroes.

Have you ever taken an unpopular stand against prejudice?
❑ Yes ❑ No If so, explain briefly.

_____

_____

How does God want you to respond to what He showed you today?

_____

_____

_____

_____

_____

Having our minds pried open is rarely easy, but vision is rarely given to those who refuse. We are challenged to overcome prejudice on many levels, certainly not just race. Economics divide. Denominations divide. Ministries divide. Differences will always exist, but division doesn't always have to result. Although God chose Peter and Saul to minister to different groups of people, He intended for each of them to see the importance of the other in the overall vision. Saul later wrote, "For God, who was at work in the ministry of Peter as an apostle to the Jews, was also at work in my ministry as an apostle to the Gentiles" (Gal. 2:8). God had driven the point home to Peter through a series of visions in which He commanded, "'Do not call anything impure that God has made clean'" (Acts 10:15). Praise God, all who are in Christ have been made clean.

We must be careful to avoid spiritual elitism. Everything we are and anything we possess as believers in Christ is a gift of grace. Pure hearts before God must be cleansed from any hint of spiritual pride. We must aggressively fight the enemy when he seeks to nullify our growth and good works by making them invitations for pride and prejudice.

DAY 5
New Church, New Name

Today's Treasure
"For a whole year Barnabas and Saul met with the church and taught great numbers of people. The disciples were called Christians first at Antioch" *(Acts 11:26).*

Our Scripture reading today reintroduces Saul to the Acts account. We will witness the great turning point in his ministry. Saul boarded a boat for Tarsus, his homeland, after the Grecian Jews tried to kill him in Jerusalem (see Acts 9:29-30). Through Paul's own testimony in Galatians 1:21 we know that he went to Syria and Cilicia. Five years passed between his departure to Tarsus and the Scriptures we study today. Many scholars refer to these as the missing years. Although we have no details of Saul's life during this time, we can be sure the inhabitants of the cities he visited didn't describe him as missing! You can imagine he had an overwhelming presence everywhere he went! Probably the only reason the events of those five years are missing in the Book of Acts is because Luke, the writer, was not an eyewitness.

Consider a few things that might have happened during the interim years. In Acts 9:16, the Lord told Ananias He would show Saul how much he must suffer for His name. I believe God began fulfilling this prophecy almost immediately. Figuratively speaking, he was thrown into many fires during his ministry, yet few would have been any hotter than those in Tarsus. He was the local hero among the Jewish community in his hometown. Most people probably knew that his departure years before was for the express purpose of dealing with those menacing followers of the Way. Now he returned as one of them. I doubt anyone threw him a homecoming party. We have no reason to assume his father had died, yet we see no reference to his reaction to Saul's conversion. His father may have acted as if his son had never been born.

Even today when a Jew from an orthodox family turns from Judaism, parents sometimes consider the defector to be dead. Some observe something like a funeral. Others prefer to blot them from their lives and consider them never born. Many families do not react so harshly and permanently, yet remember—Saul's father was a Pharisee! His son's defection was a fate worse than death.

We have no idea how long Saul stayed in Tarsus. I certainly could not blame him for later traveling to other parts of Syria and Cilicia!

Scripture suggests a concrete reason to believe these interim years were **quite difficult. Read the apostle's testimony of his sufferings in 2 Corinthians 11:22-27. Which of his experiences were new to you?**

_____

_____

God wasn't kidding when He said Saul would suffer for His name, was He? Yet, many of the perils mentioned are not recorded in Acts. The most likely time these sufferings took place was during the interim period not detailed in the Book of Acts. As Saul reenters the picture today, let's assume his life has been anything but uneventful!

Our reading in Acts will pick up immediately following Peter's explanation to those who criticized him in Jerusalem for going "into the house of uncircumcised men" (Acts 11:3) and eating with them.

Please read Acts 11:19-30. What caused the gospel to reach as far as **Phoenicia, Cyprus, and Antioch? Choose one.**
- ❑ persecution   ❑ invitation
- ❑ imprisonment   ❑ famine

God purposely employed a wonderful word when He described the immediate effect of persecution—believers were scattered. The original Greek word _diaspeiro_ means "to sow here and there or to scatter as seed." You can be sure Satan was working feverishly by fueling persecution and division against the growing numbers of believers. As a result of persecution, many believers fled hundreds of miles from Jerusalem, yet Satan still did not get the ultimate victory! God used the persecution in Judea to scatter His seeds all over the civilized world. Why? To grow a great harvest!

Please celebrate with me that Satan cannot do anything to us God cannot use through us! No matter what gains the enemy has had in your life, if you will cooperate with God and allow Him to direct your life henceforth, God will turn defeat into victory! Satan does not have to have the last word in the circumstance he authored in your life.

*H*as Satan been the instigator of something in your life that has brought hardship or disappointment? ❑ Yes ❑ No If so, take time to ask God to help you remain faithful and rejoice in the good He will bring from it.

I hope you didn't miss a marvelous event in verse 20! A couple of gutsy believers who had been scattered to Antioch broke the mold. They "began to speak to Greeks also, telling them the good news about the Lord Jesus."

When God desires to do "a new thing" (Isa. 43:19), He purposely seeks out a few righteous renegades who don't have a problem breaking the mold! Mold breakers are usually people who don't care much about popularity or tradition.

I have a good friend at church who is a mold breaker. He has been used of God to help make our church a viable presence in the new millennium. I don't mind telling you, he has had as many enemies as friends. These men from Cyprus and Cyrene were mold breakers. The soil across the street from the synagogue looked awfully fertile to them—so they scattered and spoke!

*H*ow did the Greeks respond to the good news? Choose any which apply.
❑ **Many believed.**   ❑ **Many were grieved.**
❑ **Numbers were baptized.**   ❑ **Many turned to the Lord.**

The two responses you chose above are crucial to the understanding of true conversion. The people did not simply believe. James 2:19 tells us even the demons believe. We can believe Christ is the Son of God, be convinced He died and rose again for the sins of mankind, and still be lost. That's head knowledge. When I personalize Christ's gift of grace on the cross, I am saved. That's heart knowledge. Look back at Acts 11:21. One difference between the head and the heart lies in the word *turned*. Head knowledge doesn't always change a thing. Heart knowledge does. Life turns at that moment. We can't just go back to living as if nothing ever happened. The externals may evolve more slowly as we break habits and alter lifestyles, but the internals change instantaneously. Life takes an inevitable turn.

Can you think of a way your belief was characterized by a *turn*?

_____

_____

I have to snicker as I read the words in verse 22, "News of this reached the ears of the church at Jerusalem." Antioch was about 300 miles north of Jerusalem, but juicy news travels faster than a speeding bullet! Barnabas was dispensed to Antioch immediately. After so many rumors, don't you know he was refreshed to see the reality! When Barnabas arrived in Antioch, he "saw the evidence of the grace of God" (Acts 11:23). Reality superseded rumor, and he was glad!

Philippians 2:13 reminds us "it is God who works in you to will and to act according to his good purpose." The Jerusalem church leaders probably conferred over the best ambassador for Antioch and ultimately chose Barnabas. I believe that their choice was foreordained by God. He willed for Barnabas to go to Antioch for "his good purpose."

*R*emember what the name Barnabas means? Son of _____

Why do you think Barnabas would have been the perfect choice to send to a group of people who had recently believed and turned to the Lord?

_____

According to verse 23, what did Barnabas encourage the new believers to do?

_____

Barnabas encouraged them to plan in advance to remain faithful to the Lord! I cannot overemphasize the importance of this exhortation. This principle is one I've diligently sought to teach my children. I've tried to make them understand that the point of temptation or the pinnacle of pain is not the ideal time to decide whether or not to stick with Christ. The most effective time to resolve to remain with Christ is in advance of difficulty. Planning to stay faithful can greatly enhance victory.

I wish I could say I always resolved in advance to "remain true to the Lord." Certainly, there were times I didn't. But I finally learned the wisdom of Barnabas' good advice and have been so thankful for the fruit of safety it bears. Barnabas had seen the cost of believing in Christ first hand. He was teaching these new believers the kind of resolve that would hold up even against the threat of death. Under his faithful tutelage, a great number of people were brought to the Lord.

_R_ecall a time of temptation or trial when, because of your commitment to Christ, you made the right decision. Thank God for His Holy Spirit.

What decisions are ahead of you that you have not committed to Christ?

Although Barnabas was overjoyed at the great harvest the scattered seeds had ultimately produced, these missionaries were obviously in a situation over their heads. They needed a specialist, an expert discipler. They needed Saul. And right about then, he probably needed them. Barnabas headed for Tarsus, looking for Saul. So for a whole year Barnabas and Saul met with the church and taught great numbers of people. What a team they must have made—Saul the teacher, Barnabas the encourager. One taught the principles of a godly life. The other assured them they could do it with God's help.

The next phrase in Acts 11:26 conjures up many emotions in me. The disciples were called _Christians_ first in Antioch.

Christian:
an emotional word causing one man joy and another man fury–
one man peace and another man turmoil.
a dividing word unceasingly drawing a line. Either a man
is or he is not, either for or against.
a uniting word. Unlikely pairs drawn together in
work places and neighborhoods over one single bond.
a defining word for which countless people have lived and
countless people have died.

The Greek word the believers were called was _Christianos_. The name given was first adopted at Antioch. You may be interested to know that it "does not occur in the New Testament as a name commonly used by Christians themselves." _Christian_ was a label coined by unbelievers as a form of "ridicule."

*W*ere you aware the name was first used by opposers to make fun of believers? ❑ Yes ❑ No

Once again, how beautifully God stole the victory from Satan. The very word used as a mockery became the greatest privilege a man could boast.

*H*ow did Peter, Saul's contemporary, address this insult and encourage believers in 1 Peter 4:16?

_____

_____

Many responded just as Peter exhorted. In the infant days of the New Testament church, Polycarp received Christ as Savior and served Him faithfully as the bishop of Smyrna. The cruel Marcus Aurelius, governor of Rome, sent soldiers to apprehend the servant of God in Smyrna. *Foxe's Book of Martyrs* describes the events which followed:

> Hearing that they were come, he came down and spoke to them with a cheerful and pleasant countenance: so that they were wonder-struck, who, having never known the man before, now beheld his venerable age and the gravity and composure of his manner, and wondered why they should be so earnest for the apprehension of so old a man. [They asked] "What harm is it to say 'Lord Caesar,' and to sacrifice, and save yourself?" At first he was silent: but being pressed to speak, he said, "I will not do as you advise me." When they saw that he was not to be persuaded, they gave him rough language, and pushed him hastily down, so that in descending from the chariot he grazed his shin. But he, unmoved as if he had suffered nothing, went on cheerfully, under the conduct of his guards, to the Stadium. The proconsul then urged him, saying, "Swear and I will release thee;—reproach Christ." Polycarp answered, "Eighty and six years have I served him, and he never once wronged me; how then shall I blaspheme my King, Who hath saved me?" The proconsul again urged him. Polycarp replied, "Since you still vainly strive to make me swear by the fortune of Caesar…affecting ignorance of my real character, hear me frankly declaring what I am—I am a Christian!"[2]

*H*ow does God want you to respond to what He showed you today?

_____

_____

_____

_____

_____

_____

The crowd was enraged. A fire set. The flames refused to engulf him until finally Polycarp died by the sword of perplexed and frightened men.

Christians have been beaten, whipped, starved, humiliated, mutilated, tortured, hung, burned at the stake, crucified, and fed to lions, yet scarcely 2000 years after a man called Jesus of Nazareth walked the streets of Jerusalem, 1,734 million people alive on this earth today call themselves by the ever dividing, ever uniting word: Christian. God is still scattering the seeds a few righteous renegades planted in a city called Antioch. Had they only known what they were starting.

---

[1]Joan Comay, *Who's Who in the Old Testament* (New York: Crown Publishers, 1980), 322.
[2]John Foxe, *Foxe's Book of Martyrs* (New Kensington, PA: Whitaker House, 1981), 20-23. Used by permission of the publisher–Whitaker House, 30 Hunt Valley Circle, New Kensington, PA 15068.

Finding the Way

Acts 9:1-19

1. An initiation into _____ (v. 8). The road to service begins with _____.

2. The enforcement of _____ (v. 9).

3. An important "point" behind _____ (v. 17).

   The meaning of the word *sent* or *apostle* is "_____."

   Psalm 45:2; 1 Corinthians 15:9-10

4. A new kind of _____ (v. 11).

5. An open _____ (vv. 13-16).

   Ways to Confirm God's Will

   a. Is this command congruent with God's character?

   b. Have you received reconfirmation?

   c. Have you received sound counsel?

6. An overriding _____ (v. 14; Matt. 28:18).

7. A graceful _____ (v. 17; John 20:17).

   The word _____ means "learner, student."

WEEK 3

Miles and Missions

Day 1
One Blind Sorcerer

Day 2
A Light for the Gentiles

Day 3
A Prudent Pair

Day 4
Hardships on the Kingdom Road

Day 5
Harder Than It Has To Be

This week we pack our bags and join Paul on his first missionary journey! You'll soon see that the apostle's life was anything but boring. His many experiences will prove that living and moving in the center of God's will does not mean we avoid opposition. To the contrary, we often meet challenges because of our choice to follow God! Being a sold-out servant of Jesus Christ requires courage; but, praise His Name, He who requires it also supplies it. Throughout our study, we have the privilege to learn from the example of a man who knew opposition intimately. His key to victory was knowing the One in charge far more intimately. This week, let's discover the answers to the following questions.

Principal Questions
Day 1: Who was Bar-Jesus?
Day 2: What does being "appointed for eternal life" mean?
Day 3: Why was Paul stoned?
Day 4: How were the Gentiles who were turning to Christ being wrongly burdened?
Day 5: How does Acts 14:21-22 refute many popular prosperity gospels?

God will use the apostle Paul to help us clear up a few popular misconceptions in many Christian circles today. All the enemy has to do to spread a lie is twist the truth. Stay alert and open-minded. His Word is alive! (see Heb. 4:12).

D A Y 1
One Blind Sorcerer

Welcome to week 3 of our journey! Acts 11 concluded with the church in Antioch giving generously to the believers in Judea as they faced impending famine. Barnabas and Saul packed their bags and headed for Jerusalem as ambassadors of famine relief.

*O*ur study today will center on Acts 13, but I want you to be aware of several important events that took place between the time Saul and Barnabas left Antioch and their return. Please read all of Acts 12 and list at least three historical events recorded in the chapter.

_____

_____

_____

Today's Treasure
"While they were worshiping the Lord and fasting, the Holy Spirit said, 'Set apart for me Barnabas and Saul for the work to which I have called them'" *(Acts 13:2).*

Allow me to sum up the events of this chapter and build a bridge to the events to follow. A family of kings, all named Herod, ruled Palestine. The Herod at this particular time was Agrippa I, grandson of Herod the Great. Part Jewish himself, he enjoyed great popularity with the Jewish leaders of Judea—courting their favor at any cost. This favor cost him dearly. He tried to cut the apostolic head off the church by having James beheaded. He then imprisoned Peter with hopes for a similar end.

James was the first apostle martyred though tradition suggests that all but one eventually died for Christ. Herod's efforts to stamp out Christianity by killing the apostles was doomed to failure, because the true Head of the church could not be cut off!

Herod probably realized he was out of his league when Peter disappeared from prison. Left with no explanation, Herod had the guards executed and took a quick trip to Caesarea. There he did the inexcusable. He allowed himself to be worshiped as God. The tender side of me would prefer to think he died, and then was eaten by worms; however, Scripture reverses the order. Glad I wasn't in on that scene! Acts 12:24 gives quick relief! "The word of God continued to increase and spread."

*H*aving finished their mission, Barnabas and Saul returned to Antioch bringing a special attendant with them. What was his name?

_____

We will get to know him a little better as we reflect on our next reading. Read Acts 13:1-12 and complete the following.
1. According to verse 4, who sent Saul and Barnabas on their way?
   ❑ Simeon, Lucius, and Manaen   ❑ the disciples
   ❑ John Mark   ❑ the Holy Spirit

2. What role did Simeon, Lucius, and Manaen play in sending Saul and

Barnabas? _____

3. Why do you think Saul called the Jewish sorcerer a child of the devil?

_____

4. How did the proconsul ultimately respond to the teaching about the Lord? Choose any which apply. He...
❏ believed. ❏ was afraid. ❏ was amazed. ❏ was almost persuaded.

The first church in Antioch remains such an example to us. We've already seen willing evangelists, willing recipients, and effective discipleship revealed in the willingness of the infant church to give. Acts 13 unfolds with another mark of an effective church body—strong leadership. These five prophets and teachers didn't just hold important positions; they each had a personal passion for God. They worshiped and fasted, both Greek verbs indicate a practice rather than a one-time experience.

I am deeply burdened for Christian leadership. Many leaders are so busy and so stressed with the demands of "ministry" that they leave little time for the things that fueled their original passion. I believe that intimacy with God is the missing link in most stale ministries. No ministry is beyond becoming lifeless and flat. Freshness accompanies an active and current relationship with Christ.

The leaders of the church in Antioch were constantly ready to hear from God; therefore, when He spoke, they were listening! He said to them, "'Set apart for me Barnabas and Saul for the work to which I have called them'" (Acts 13:2). Again and again in Scripture we see God's perfect timing. In Galatians 1:15, the apostle explains he was set apart from birth (about A.D. 10). He did not receive salvation until around A.D. 36. He was not set apart for his signature ministry until around A.D. 46. Not one minute was wasted. God was training Saul during those formative years. Meanwhile, Barnabas the Encourager was proving his effectiveness among both Jews and Gentiles. When God's time came, both men were ready for the Holy Spirit to send them out (see Acts 13:3).

I grew up in a denomination that prioritized missions and spurred a love and appreciation in my heart for missionaries. This moment is precious to me. Meet the first international missionaries: Saul and Barnabas! Set apart to be sent off—just like so many other faithful ones who have followed in their footsteps, forsaking the securities of home and family to follow Christ anywhere. As of this writing, nearly 80,000 evangelical missionaries presently serve overseas.[1] I have no greater admiration for any group of people.

*D*o you know someone who has followed in the footsteps of the first missionaries? ❏ Yes ❏ No   If so, how has their example affected you?

_____

_____

The Holy Spirit not only sends, He also equips. God gave more than wisdom and experience to aid Barnabas and Saul in their journeys. He also gave them a helper. We will call him John Mark to minimize any confusion with other characters named John. Saul's helper would later write the second Gospel, the Book of Mark.

Any study of the apostle Paul would be lacking in clarity without a map to trace his travels. You will find a map on the inside back cover. You will be tracing Paul's three missionary journeys as well as his final trip to Rome. You need pens of four different colors to distinguish the journeys. I will tell you when to change to a different color.

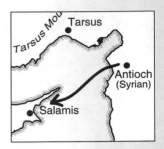

*Y*our starting point today is Antioch in Syria. Draw a line from Antioch to Cyprus where you will connect Salamis and Paphos.

Tracing Paul's travels will help us keep information organized and increase our understanding and appreciation of his ministry. When the Bible mentions a village or region in one of his journeys, draw the appropriate line. You might also draw arrows pointing the appropriate direction at each stop to help you keep his departures and arrivals clear.

Saul met some interesting characters in his travels! He got no farther than his second stop when he met a man I'm sure he never forgot. His name was Bar-Jesus (or Elymas). He was the attendant to Sergius Paulus, the proconsul or governor of Cyprus.

Bar-Jesus committed a serious offense against his supervisor and the kingdom of God. "The proconsul … sent for Barnabas and Saul because he wanted to hear the word of God" (Acts 13:7). Bar-Jesus did everything he could to oppose them and keep the proconsul from believing. The apostle rebuked the sorcerer. Reread verses 9 and 10.

Finally, we read that Saul was also called Paul! What a relief! I have tried to refer to him by the name consistent with the Scriptures we were studying. But, we all know him least by his Hebrew name, Saul, and best by his Roman name, Paul. Henceforth, we will call him by the latter.

Paul called Bar-Jesus "a child of the devil" (Acts 13:10). He was actually using a play on words because the name *Bar-Jesus* in Aramaic means Son of Jesus.[2] In effect, Paul was saying, "You're no son of Jesus. You're a son of the devil!" He not only meant the term to be taken figuratively, he meant it literally as I hope you will now see. The three descriptions given in Scripture support Paul's accusation against him. Consider how the following phrases apply to Elymas as well as to Satan:

- Full of deceit: The original Greek word *dolos* means "bait, metaphorically and generally fraud, guile, deceit." Remember, Bar-Jesus or Elymas was a sorcerer, which meant he was a magus, or presumed wise man, who "specialized in the study of astrology and enchantment."
- Full of trickery: The original Greek word *rhadiourgia* is often used for theft through "wicked schemes or plots."
- Perverted the right ways of the Lord: The original Greek word *diastrepho* means "to turn or twist throughout; to distort, pervert, seduce, mislead; to turn away."

So, Paul's accusation that Bar-Jesus was "a child of the devil" was quite appropriate.

Look back at the three phrases that describe Satan and his servants. Have you seen a recent example of the devil's deceit, trickery, or perversion of God's ways?   ❑ Yes ❑ No If so, describe briefly.

_____

_____

You can imagine Paul came up against the schemes of the evil one many times as he sought to do the will of God. As we study his life, we can learn to identify the works of darkness and be equipped to stand against them.

*A*cts 13:11 records the first miracle we see God perform through the apostle Paul. Use your imagination. Why do you think Paul might have struck Bar-Jesus blind rather than causing him not to speak, walk, or hear?

_____

_____

Satan is powerful, but he is no match for the Son of God. The proconsul "believed, for he was amazed at the teaching about the Lord" (Acts 13:12). This Greek definition is my favorite today. The word *amazed* is the original word *ekplesso* which is "found only in the sense of knocking one out of his senses." I can't count the times God has knocked me out of my senses through something He has taught me about Himself.

God wants to amaze us with the wisdom of His Word. He wants to blow our minds and widen our vision! He wants to show us how relevant He is. How can we do our part so He can do His? Serguis Paulus, the proconsul, revealed to us a marvelous link. Ultimately, he was "amazed at the teaching about the Lord" (v. 12), "because he wanted to hear the word of God" (v. 7). He was ready to receive, and God honored the desire of his heart! Let's learn to pray like the psalmist who said, "Open my eyes that I may see wonderful things in your law" (Ps. 119:18). He may just blow our minds.

Think of times you picked up your Bible and were interrupted, distracted. How often when you attend a worship service are you distracted while preparing to go, on the way, or at the service? Does your annoyance become anger directed at a child, spouse, or friend? Our anger needs to be directed at the source. Be aware that when you desire to study God's Word, Satan will do everything to distract.

*S*pend some time in prayer. Ask the Holy Spirit to empower you this week to recognize the source of your distractions and to channel your anger where it belongs—toward the evil one.

*H*ow does God want you to respond to what He showed you today?

_____

_____

_____

_____

_____

DAY 2
A Light for the Gentiles

Today's Treasure
"'Therefore, my brothers, I want you to know that through Jesus the forgiveness of sins is proclaimed to you. Through him everyone who believes is justified from everything you could not be justified from by the law of Moses'"
(Acts 13:38-39).

Today we join Paul and Barnabas as they continue their first missionary journey, departing Cyprus and entering the large Roman province of Galatia. As you trace Paul's travels on your map, you will see the distances they were willing to travel to preach the gospel. We don't do missionaries justice when we romanticize their ministries. Missionary work is extremely difficult. The travels are taxing and often frightening, as Paul and Barnabas discovered. Not everyone can take it as today's reading proves!

*R*ead Acts 13:13-43. You might find reading aloud to be helpful. I don't want you falling asleep during Paul's sermon! Complete the following.
1. Reread Acts 13:41. What is something God has done in your days (or your life) that you never would have believed even if someone told you?

_____

2. How would you arrange into good news and bad news Paul's sermon to the Jews in Pisidian Antioch (not the Antioch where believers were first called Christians)?

Good news: _____

Bad news: _____

3. How would you characterize the response to Paul's sermon? Choose one.
❑ unanimous acceptance   ❑ a poor acceptance
❑ a generally favorable acceptance

We will save our discussions of John Mark's departure for a future lesson in which the subject is raised again with greater detail in the Book of Acts.

Sometimes we yearn for God to crack open a receptive door to share our faith with a friend, neighbor, or coworker. We scramble to grab an opportunity that never seems to come. Other times, God swings open a door so quickly, we're too stunned to walk through it! In today's reading God swung the door open so quickly He almost blew the beard off the rabbi! Practically by the time Paul and Barnabas found a chair, they were asked to share a message of encouragement.

Paul was not about to miss a golden opportunity. Like any good orator, he chose his style and material to fit his audience. As he stood in the synagogue, he addressed Jews and those who believed in the God of Israel. I am convinced he had a very specific purpose as he introduced Christ to them through their own history.

Remember when Paul went to Arabia after his conversion and spent some solitary time trying to sort things out? You may recall he then returned to Damascus and "baffled the Jews ... proving that Jesus is the Christ" (Acts 9:22). On week 2, day 3 we discovered that the word *proving* means knitting together. In Arabia Paul had been knitting together the old and the new and found the two strands of yarn to be a perfect match. Paul's intention was to give the Jews in Pisidian Antioch a knitting lesson! He urged them to see how perfectly Christ knit the past with the present. They did not have to forsake all the chapters of their history. They just needed to accept the rest of the story!

Paul was such a prodigy of grace, he could not preach a sermon without it. He charged the Jews with having executed their own Messiah with "no proper ground" (v. 28), yet he extended the invitation to any "brothers" (v. 38) or fellow Jews, to receive forgiveness through Christ. What glorious news! If a person who had shared the responsibility for Christ's death could be forgiven, can any person be beyond forgiveness?

Look again at verse 43 before we proceed to our next reading. Paul and Barnabas' first experience in Galatia was obviously positive. "Many of the Jews and devout converts to Judaism" met with them after the message and received their encouragement.

𝒩ote the exhortation in verse 43. What did they urge the believers to do?

_____

Let these words be pressed into the soft concrete of your mind so they will be set in your memory when on day 5 we consider the letter he will write to them.

ℛead the rest of Acts 13. Complete the following based on verses 44-52:
1. What motivated a number of Jews to oppose Paul and Barnabas?
❑ fear   ❑ intimidation   ❑ jealousy   ❑ pride   ❑ guilt

2. Read verse 48 carefully. In what three ways did the Gentiles respond when Paul and Barnabas turned to them?

_____

_____

_____

3. What evidence can you find in these verses to support the belief that Satan, the one ultimately behind every opposition to the gospel, wants people of greatest influence on his side?

_____

_____

We will conclude today's lesson with some words of clarification and warning. First, we've come across a passage which may trouble you. Let's see if we can clarify what Scripture is saying. Acts 13:48 tells us "All who were appointed for eternal life believed." Does God only appoint certain people to receive eternal life, and deem all others doomed to eternal condemnation? I can't think of many issues more important than this.

*S*cripture clarifies Scripture. What do the following Scriptures tell you about God's desires for salvation?

2 Peter 3:9 _____

John 1:12-13 _____

Now look again at Acts 13:39 and fill in the blank.

"Through him _____ who believes is justified."

John 3:16 says "God so loved the world that he gave his one and only Son, that whoever believes in him shall not perish but have eternal life." Therefore, whoever in the entire world believes has eternal life. That's a universal invitation if I've ever seen one! First John 2:2 states that "He is the atoning sacrifice for our sins, and not only for ours but also for the sins of the whole world." John left no room for the idea that Christ died only for certain people. When Acts 13:48 tells us "all who were appointed for eternal life believed," Luke was employing a Greek military term somewhat foreign to us. *Tatto,* the original word for *appointed,* is used figuratively in the New Testament and means "to set in a certain order." The word was used originally to describe the order in which soldiers were arranged.

*R*ead Paul's own words in Romans 1:16. This verse describes the order or arrangement perfectly. Notice, salvation is for everyone who believes, but the order or arrangement is

"First for the _____, then for the _____."

Perhaps a paraphrase of Acts 13:48 based on the original definition of the word *appointed* would help: "When the Gentiles heard this, they were glad and honored the word of the Lord; and all who were appointed (next in order) for eternal life believed." In other words, the Jews in Pisidian Antioch had been given their opportunity; and now it was the Gentile's turn.

Receive a word of warning from Paul's encounter with persecution in Galatia. We read in verse 50 that "the Jews incited the God-fearing women of high standing and the leading men of the city" against Paul and Barnabas. Ultimately, in verse 50 the enemy of Salvation used the Jews just as they used the leading women and men of the city. Both were puppets on his strings. Little has changed. Satan still takes advantage of women and men, seizing their powers of influence for his own purposes.

I am asking the Holy Spirit to help us with a final assignment today: Meditate on the last seven days for several moments. Picture yourself in your usual roles as well as specific encounters. List ways in which you exerted the power of influence whether rightly or wrongly. I will get you started with a few questions I am asking myself: Did you influence your spouse in a decision at work? Did you influence a friend who was upset with someone? Did you influence a class or a group of people in a meeting? Did you influence your boss or employees? Did you influence your children in situations they were in? List every point of influence you can remember, and then add to the list as the Holy Spirit reminds you of others.

_____

_____

_____

_____

You're probably more influential than you thought. If you had lunch with friends this week, you probably influenced someone in some way. If a friend shared a problem with you, you influenced her somehow with your response. If you gave your opinion on a matter recently, you very likely affected someone else's. We are constantly exerting influence. Influence is a gift, a trust. We must be careful how we use it. Take heed. Satan can affect masses of followers through a few leaders.

Acts 13 concludes with Paul and Barnabas thrown from the city, but not before "The word of the Lord spread through the whole region" (v. 49). They had done what God sent them to do in Pisidian Antioch. The Truth had been told. Seeds had been planted. The results were up to Him. They shook the dust from their feet, laced their sandals, and headed for Iconium.

Perhaps you know how it feels to be obedient to God yet not see the results you wanted or expected. You may have met rejection, yet you're still fighting for the results you hoped for—trying to force a good ending. Is God pulling you forward while you dig your toes into the dirt, refusing to give up? Paul and Barnabas may have departed the city believing they had started well but finished poorly. They may have felt their efforts were in vain. Meanwhile, God looked from Heaven and saw His Word spread like a blanket over the region. Don't try to judge your own effectiveness. Another opportunity for ministry awaits you. Shake the dust off those feet and move on. Joy lies ahead.

A Prudent Pair

After leaving Pisidian Antioch in a cloud of dust, Paul and Barnabas traveled south in the province of Galatia to the city of Iconium. As you see on your map, they traveled quite a distance to their next destination. Few flat lands greeted them. The road literally rose up to meet them as numerous hills and mountains interrupted the landscape.

Paul was approaching 40 years of age by this time. No sooner than his head hit his mat, his calves surely cramped and seared from the journey. The brilliant stars finally soothed him to sleep. He and Barnabas probably settled into the kind of relationship necessary for people paired for days on end. Rich talks fit between long intervals of silence. Small talk momentarily eased their awesome responsibility. Between Paul's tenacity and Barnabas' encouragement, neither lacked motivation. By the time they could see Iconium in the distance, they were spilling over with the kind of joyful anticipation that can only come from the filling of the Holy Spirit (see Acts 13:52). A new challenge awaited them. Perhaps more of a challenge than they expected!

*T*oday's reading will be twofold. I want to pinpoint two major characteristics Paul and Barnabas shared. Read Acts 14:1-7 and complete the following.
1. How did some of the Jews and Gentiles temporarily overcome their aversion to one another for a common cause?

_____

2. How did God confirm the message of His grace?

_____

3. How did Paul and Barnabas respond when they found out about the plans to mistreat and stone them? Choose one.
   ❑ They faced their persecutors.   ❑ They ran for their lives.

4. After their experiences in Iconium, what did Paul and Barnabas do when they reached Lystra and Derbe?

_____

You may have been surprised to see them flee when they learned of the plans set against them. Shouldn't they have stayed and trusted God to guard them from attack since they were doing His will and preaching His message? Couldn't the same power used to perform signs and miracles be used to stifle their enemies? In seeking a few answers, I believe their actions offer us the first of two fitting descriptions of the dynamic duo: They were smart! I don't believe they were reacting out of pure fear. They were responding out of pure wisdom, and quickly!

*L*et the Book of Wisdom speak to their circumstances. What advice does Proverbs 22:3 offer?

_____

Identify a time when you or someone you knew faced danger and ran.

_____

In retrospect, do you think you should have stayed and faced the danger?
❑ Yes ❑ No

Most likely, your answer was no! You probably responded with prudence, not cowardice! Take a look at a few times in Christ's life when He knew danger awaited Him. Read each Scripture then describe how He responded.

John 7:1 _____

John 8:59 _____

Read Matthew 26:1-2. Why do you think Christ did not slip out of their hands this time?

_____

Check your response by reading John 7:30. Now you know for certain why Christ did not resist His accusers when they came to arrest Him. The time had come for Him to give His life as a sacrifice for sin. As you can see, Paul and Barnabas responded to impending danger the way Christ did on several occasions. They all had access to the supernatural power which could have changed things! Christ could have opened the earth and commanded it to swallow His pursuers in Palestine or the pursuers of His beloved ambassadors in Iconium. Yet, He chose to use another method. Christ did deliver Paul and Barnabas from an evil attack. He used their heads and feet to do it! I see two general principles at work regarding miraculous intervention in the New Testament:
- Miracles were used more often for authenticity than intervention.
- Miracles were used most often when natural means were either not available or not conceivable.

Jesus ordinarily used natural means of provision. When He and His disciples were hungry, they usually found something to eat. When they were thirsty, they went to a well and drew water to drink. He could have supplied anything they wanted supernaturally, but He chose natural means when available. He responded the same way to impending danger. He used His feet or maybe a boat, and He departed.

Whether God uses natural means or supernatural means to deliver us from danger, both are divine provisions. God supplied the healthy legs Paul and Barnabas used to flee. God provides the car we drive to the nearest public place when we're being followed. The person who walks on the scene out of nowhere and frightens off an attacker is an ambassador of God! This part of our lesson may be very difficult for some of you because you have been attacked or injured and wonder why you weren't delivered. I hope you will find comfort in our next reading because Paul has been in your shoes.

_R_ead Acts 14:8-20. Complete the following:
1. Why were bulls and wreaths brought to the city gates in Lystra?
    ❑ to offer sacrifices to the God of Israel
    ❑ to celebrate the healing of the cripple
    ❑ to offer sacrifices to Barnabas and Paul

2. Tearing the clothes was a Jewish expression of grief and anguish (see 2 Sam. 3:31). Why did Paul and Barnabas tear their clothes in verse 14?

_____

3. Earlier in our lesson we talked about God often choosing natural means over supernatural means in His provisions. How does verse 17 support this?

_____

_____

4. Imagine that you are Barnabas, watching Paul being stoned. What kinds of things might be going on in your mind?

_____

_____

We have seen a vital fact about Paul and Barnabas: they were smart! Now, we witness a second description of both men at critical moments: they were sincere.

Because of an old Greek myth, the people of Lystra were afraid not to honor Paul and Barnabas. They might have been two gods come down in human form! For generations a story about two Greek gods who visited earth circulated among the people of Lystra. They were met with scorn except for one poverty-stricken couple who showed them hospitality. According to the myth, the gods cursed the people but gave the couple an opulent palace. The people of Lystra were taking no chances in case these gods had returned.

The sincerity of Paul and Barnabas is refreshingly obvious. They not only tore their clothes in grief because the people had made such a preposterous assumption, they wasted no time in setting the record straight. They did not capitalize on a moment's glory. They did not use their attentions to get a good home-cooked meal. They rushed out to the crowd, shouting, "'Men, why are you doing this? We too are only men, human like you'" (v. 15). To me, Paul chose the best words of all in 1 Corinthians 1:29 when he said; "No flesh should glory in his (God's) presence" (KJV).

*D*escribe a situation when you have been tempted to take God's glory for yourself.

_____

_____

Think about this carefully: Barnabas and Paul could have used the crowd's wrong impression that they were gods, but they maintained their identity. A flashy miracle at just the right time and not one stone would have been thrown. The crowd would have bowed at their feet. Paul and Barnabas could have slipped out of town without a scratch; instead, Paul was stoned so severely they dragged him outside the city thinking he was dead. Can you imagine the pictures flashing in Paul's mind with every blow of a stone? I'm sure his memory replayed Stephen's radiant face. Paul probably could not bear to think of himself worthy to die for the name of Christ in the same way. He probably fell unconscious thinking he was about to breathe his last, but this was not Paul's time.

With joyful anticipation, Paul and Barnabas had arrived in Iconium only to have to quickly depart under threat of stoning. They had escaped one of the most painful forms of punishment ever devised. They wiped their brows, gave a sigh of relief, and headed into Lystra. Before they knew what had happened, the stones were flying; they had no place to run, nowhere to hide.

*A*s we close today, I want you to see something precious in God's Word. Many years later, Paul still remembered the events in Iconium and Lystra and shared a peculiar testimony. Read 2 Timothy 3:10-11. What does Paul say the Lord did during the events we've studied today?

_____

Any person in her right mind would prefer to be rescued before the first stone's thrown, not after the last! Yet, Paul described both his experience in Iconium (where he departed prior to suffering) and his experience in Lystra (where he departed after suffering) as the Lord's divine rescue. Perhaps his inspired choice of words will intensify your appreciation of his exquisite testimony. The original word for *rescue* in 2 Timothy 3:11 is *rhuomai* which is derived from a word meaning "to drag along the ground." *Rhuomai* means "to draw or snatch from danger, rescue, deliver." Please read the remainder of the definition with great care and meditation: "This is more with the meaning of drawing to oneself than merely rescuing from someone or something."

You see, God wasn't only interested in drawing Paul out of difficulty or danger. He wanted to draw Paul closer to Himself. Every time God delivers us, the point is ultimately to draw us closer to Himself. Whether we get to avoid pain and suffering or we must persevere in the midst of it, our deliverance comes when we're dragged from the enemy of our souls to the heart of God. We escape from the clutches of evil every time we draw near to the embrace of God. Delivered from evil. Drawn to God. The rescue has not reaped its ultimate work until we're under His wing (see Ps. 91:4).

*W*rite Jeremiah 31:3 in the space below.

_____

_____

Please conclude your lesson by writing a brief testimony of a time God used a difficult situation to draw you with lovingkindness to Himself.

*H*ow does God want you to respond to what He showed you today?

_____   _____

_____   _____

_____   _____

_____   _____

_____   _____

DAY 4

Hardships on the Kingdom Road

Paul and Barnabas departed from Lystra after target practice by a number of stone throwers. Acts 14:19 tells us Paul was stoned so severely his body was dragged from the city as dead. The next verse adds, "But after the disciples had gathered around him, he got up and went back into the city." We are safe to assume the disciples did not just gather around him and gawk. They surely prayed for him. Whether Paul was only delivered from impending death or completely restored physically, he was certainly rescued by his faithful God. While his persecutors dragged the apostle outside the city, His Savior dragged him further into His heart.

Today's reading unfolds in Derbe, the next city you will want to connect on your map. In just a few verses in Acts 14, you will see Paul and Barnabas backtrack through a number of cities on their way to the original Antioch where they were commissioned. Keep in mind the difference between the two cities called Antioch. The one mentioned first in today's reading is the city of Antioch in Pisidia or the one we've referred to as Pisidian Antioch. The latter mention of Antioch is the city in Syria where Paul and Barnabas founded the Gentile Christian church and were sent forth as missionaries.

*P*lease read Acts 14:21-28 and complete the following.
1. Why do you think Paul and Barnabas returned to Lystra, Iconium, and Pisidian Antioch on their way back to Syrian Antioch ?

_____

2. Write the exact words Paul and Barnabas said to the disciples in these cities according to verse 22.

_____

_____

3. Paul and Barnabas appointed elders in each church before they departed for Pamphylia. What evidences can you find to support the seriousness of these appointments? Check any which apply.
- ❑ fasting
- ❑ prayer
- ❑ worshiping together
- ❑ committing them to the Lord

4. Paul and Barnabas had suffered and survived many things. They had also performed miracles. How did they resist any self-praise in their testimony to the church in verse 27?

_____

Before we penetrate the heart of our lesson today, note the obedience of Paul and Barnabas to the great commission (see Matt. 28:19-20). Acts 14:21 tells us they ministered to the people in Derbe in two vital ways. They preached, which means "to evangelize" (Strong's) and they taught or *matheteuo,* which means "to instruct with the purpose of making a disciple." Paul and Barnabas were careful not to neglect evangelism or discipleship. Both are vital, life-giving elements in any New Testament church.

After Paul and Barnabas preached and taught in Derbe, "They returned to Lystra, Iconium and [Pisidian] Antioch." Remember, their final destination on this first missionary journey is Syrian Antioch. Locate Derbe on your map. You can see they chose the long route. Why didn't they simply head to (Syrian) Antioch, their mission home base, straight from Derbe? Why in the world would they backtrack through Lystra (where Paul was stoned and left for dead), Iconium (where they narrowly escaped being stoned), and Antioch (where they were persecuted and expelled)?

Acts 14:22 tells us exactly why they walked back into potential peril. They went to strengthen the disciples and encourage them to remain true to the faith. They faced risk to tell them, "'We must go through many hardships to enter the kingdom of God.'"

Paul and Barnabas didn't mean a person must go through trials to become a Christian. Remember, they were speaking to disciples in the faith. Their hearers' salvation was already secured. The key to their exhortation is found in the meaning of the word *must.* The original Greek word *dei* means "is inevitable in the nature of things."

*W*hy is hardship inevitable in the nature of things? Identify the two reasons for hardship in the life of the believer based on the following verses.

1. 2 Corinthians 4:17 _____

_____

When we're going through difficulties, they never seem light or momentary, but remember Paul is comparing them to "an eternal glory that far outweighs them all."

2. Ephesians 6:12 _____

When we receive Christ as our Savior, we ignite the ire of His enemy Satan; however, 1 John 4:4 reminds us "You, dear children, are from God and have overcome them, because the one who is in you is greater than the one who is in the world." Praise God!

As you see, hardships are inevitable for us because:

- God wants to give us eternal victory by working His glory in and through them.
- Satan wants to bring us defeat by causing us to struggle and fall.

Hardships are inevitable because of the glorious nature of God and the heinous nature of Satan.

Paul and Barnabas considered this message of inevitable hardships such a priority that they risked everything to go back to those three cities and tell it. Their message had two purposes which may seem to be a paradox to us. They told them hardships would be inevitable to bring them strength and encouragement. At first consideration, we may not find a message about unavoidable troubles very strengthening! Certainly, we don't find it encouraging! But let's dig a little deeper and see if we can discover some strength or encouragement from their message.

1. How could strength result from a message about inevitable hardships? Recognizing the inevitable nature of hardships can motivate us to redirect our energies. Fear of trials sometimes depletes more energy than facing trials! Help comes to us in times of trouble not before, when we're letting fear and dread overcome us. Once we accept the inevitability of hardship, we can redirect our focus from fear of trials to faithfulness. In the face of tribulations, we often sense a heavenly strength filling our souls right on time.

I know what it's like to let fear deplete your energy. As I mentioned in week 1, I was so afraid I would lose my first child to crib death that I could hardly rest. Every few hours I jumped out of bed to see if she was breathing. Losing a child wasn't my only fear. From the time my mother officially became a senior adult, I often cried on the way home from her house because I feared something might happen to her before I saw her next.

Had either tragedy happened, all my sleepless nights or buckets of tears would have helped me not a bit. God finally taught me to redirect my energies toward getting to know Him and love Him through His Word, so I can be equipped for anything.

The last year has been one of the most difficult seasons of my entire life. One crisis seemed to roll in behind another. I faced losses I thought I could not stand. My heart is very sore, but it's still beating. I am not glad my hurts happened. I'm not rejoicing over the loss. But I am alive, and life is still strangely abundant. Had God not taught me His Word and made Himself the uncontested love of my life, I think I might have wanted to quit. If you are like me and you tend to fear having your heart broken, ask Him to help you redirect your energies toward faithfulness instead.

2. *How could encouragement result from a message about inevitable hardship?* Realizing the inevitability of hardship encourages us in the faith rather than discourages us. After this past year, I would be pretty discouraged if I thought hardships in the lives of surrendered Christians were unusual and signs of carnality and disobedience.

A dangerous prosperity gospel fills our Christian airwaves today. Many believe that if you have enough faith, you'll be both healthy and wealthy! Many preachers and teachers are telling anyone who will listen that hardship is never the will of God. They proclaim that every difficulty is from the kingdom of hell; and if we stand in unwavering faith, we will be happy and physically prosperous.

My relatives had a name for that kind of teaching—hogwash. We will never become so spiritual that we will cease experiencing hardship.

*F*irst Peter 1:7 tells us one reason why difficulties will come throughout our lives. Fill in the blanks according to the *New International Version:*

"These have come so that your _____—of greater worth than _____,

which perishes even though refined by fire—may be proved _____

and may result in _____when Jesus Christ is revealed."

Hardship sometimes comes as a direct result of sin and disobedience. We usually are aware when consequences of sin have caused us deep suffering, but many other times trials have nothing to do with disobedience. Believing a heretical prosperity gospel can leave us terribly discouraged wondering what we've done wrong. We wonder why we can't seem to muster enough faith to be healthy, problem free, and prosperous.

Recently I grieved while I watched a friend claim and reclaim his wife's healing while she was dying of cancer. He was a member of a church that teaches you can "name it and claim it." He sent out letters asking many of us to pray certain healing Scriptures in her behalf and not waver in belief. My heart was so broken for him. I prayed every one of those Scriptures for her and claimed them on her behalf. Several days later, I learned God had taken her home before I had even received the letter. I was unknowingly praying for someone who was completed and perfected before the very Throne of Grace. She wouldn't have come back if she could have. She had been healed, but not the way we had prayed. I continue to pray for the family she left behind, because their grief may be intensified by disappointment in God and in their own faith.

*H*ave you ever gone through a time when difficulties seemed to roll in like the tide? Have you wondered if people thought something must be wrong with your spiritual life to have such trials? ❏ Yes ❏ No
Could you be honest enough to say you've wondered about someone else who seemed to have many difficulties? ❏ Yes ❏ No

Please be encouraged to know that difficulty is not a sign of immaturity or faithlessness. The Holy Spirit will do His job and let you know if you are suffering because of sin. Otherwise, remember—we must go through many hardships to enter the kingdom of God. Incidentally, unbelievers also suffer many hardships. The difference is this: ours are never in vain.

I hope we have shared some of the strength and encouragement Paul and Barnabas gave to the believers in Lystra, Iconium, and Pisidian Antioch. Those new converts saw living examples of perseverance through suffering. Paul and Barnabas departed from each city under difficult circumstances. They went out of their way to return so they could say, "We're OK! We've survived! And we're still believing and serving"! In seeing the joy and commitment of God's suffering servants, they knew they could survive, too.

*T*he time came for Paul and Barnabas to leave, but they did something to ensure an ongoing strengthening and encouraging of their new disciples.

Acts 14:23 tells us they appointed _____.

The original Greek word is *presbuteros* which means "older, a senior." A closely related Greek word *presbutes* literally means "an old man"! (Strong's) *The Holman Bible Dictionary* tells us the "elders in the Pauline churches were probably spiritual leaders and ministers, not simply a governing council."[3] Not coincidentally, Paul and Barnabas wanted to leave the new believers with ongoing strength and encouragement, so they carefully appointed elders who were not only spiritually mature but, if I may say so gently, OLD! However, the older men were not the only ones charged with responsibility.

*W*ho did Paul appoint in Titus 2:3-5 to "train the younger women to love their husbands and children, to be self-controlled and pure"?

_____

Why would elderly men and women be able to provide unique strength and encouragement to their congregations?

_____

_____

*H*ow does God want you to respond to what He showed you today?

_____

_____

_____

_____

_____

Life is difficult. The converts in Lystra, Iconium, and Pisidian Antioch were surely strengthened and encouraged as they saw living examples of people who were surviving hardships with victory and joy. Listening to Paul and Barnabas testify must have greatly impacted their ability to endure. We don't have Paul and Barnabas, but we have hosts of elderly people more than happy to tell us about the faithfulness of God—if we'll just stop, ask them, and listen.

Harder Than It Has to Be

I love to travel. I especially love meeting brothers and sisters in Christ. As much as I relish the new faces and places, there's no place like home. I heave a sigh of relief when I set my bags down inside my door and put my arms around my husband. I feel at home with my family. I experience the same feeling when I kneel to pray with my Sunday School class. I feel at home with my flock. They know me better than any group on earth. They have seen my ups and downs, yet I am bathed with love and acceptance every time I walk in the door.

Paul and Barnabas felt the same way about the church in Antioch. This was the first church they "birthed" together. Antioch was home base. The believers there welcomed them like family and savored their testimonies. The last verse of Acts 14 wraps the tumultuous chapter like an old terry-cloth robe wraps a tired body after a terrible day: "They stayed there a long time with the disciples." A welcomed respite.

Have you ever noticed that just when things seem to calm down a bit, something or someone comes along to throw a kink in it? Paul and Barnabas had worked hard in Antioch. The people were responsive and anxious to learn. A strong, viable Gentile church had emerged, but the church was young and very impressionable. Our reading today will center on a poor impression a few outsiders made on the church at Antioch. You will read about Paul and Barnabas returning to Jerusalem to settle a doctrinal question. This trek does not constitute a missionary journey nor the final road to Rome, so you will not need to trace it on your map.

*R*ead Acts 15:1-35 and complete the following.

1. **What issue was debated between believers in this chapter? Choose one.**
   ❏ **Jews and Gentiles eating together**
   ❏ **Gentile Christians in leadership**
   ❏ **circumcision as a requirement for salvation**
   ❏ **false teachers**

2. **Identify the background of the believers who were insistent on Gentile circumcision in verse 5. Choose one.**
   ❏ **Sadducees**   ❏ **Pharisees**   ❏ **rabbis**   ❏ **heathen**

3. **Each of the following people participated in the Jerusalem Council. Please note each of their contributions (or arguments) in the debate.**

Peter: _____

_____

Barnabas and Paul: _____

_____

James, Jesus' brother: _____

_____

4. The Jerusalem Council drafted a letter to the church in Antioch and appointed two leaders, Judas and Silas, to accompany Paul and Barnabas in their return. What four things did the council ask believers to avoid?

❑ sexual immorality   ❑ bickering   ❑ meat of strangled animals

❑ blood   ❑ divorce   ❑ speaking in tongues

❑ food sacrificed to idols

5. Acts 15:31 tells us the believers in Antioch were glad to receive the encouraging message. What other emotions do you imagine they probably experienced when they heard the news?

_____

Legalism—that one little word is probably responsible for causing more churches to die, more servants to quit, and more denominations to split than any other. Like a leech, legalism saps the lifeblood out of its victim. It enters the door in the name of righteousness to vacuum out all the dirt and ends up vacuuming out all the spirit. Don't confuse legalism with recognition and pursuit of godly standards.

_P_eter gave a great description of legalism in Acts 15:10. Based on his words, how would you define legalism?

_____

_____

Two sets of legalists emerge in our reading today:
- the Judean visitors to Antioch who told Gentile Christians they must be circumcised to be saved
- the believers in Jerusalem from the party of the Pharisees who told them they must also obey the law of Moses

Let's offer the legalists more grace than they offered Gentile believers. I'll assume they made a mistake rather than acted out of pure meanness. In giving them the benefit of the doubt, I see at least three mistakes they made in behalf of the new Gentile converts.

1. They drew a universal standard from their personal experience. Since they had been circumcised prior to salvation, they decided everyone else should as well. Through the ages, people have struggled with the same wrong assumptions based on their own personal experience. If God worked one way in their lives, any other way must be invalid. Let me illustrate with the story of two men.

The first man lives a godless, depraved life. The Spirit of God convicts him. He falls on his face, surrenders to Christ as Lord of his life. He serves faithfully and never falls back into the old patterns of sin. He becomes a preacher and boldly proclaims the message that people are not saved unless they instantly surrender their entire lives to the lordship of Christ. If they have ever fallen back, they were never saved at all.

The second man received Christ at a very early age, and then fell away in rebellion for years. He returns to Christ as the penitent prodigal, slips into his old ways several times, and finally reaches freedom in Christ. In his opinion, a person's state of salvation cannot in any way be judged by his actions. He believes a man can live like the devil for a season of his life and still be saved.

Both men are born again, but both men are mistakenly applying their experience to every other believer. Each of these men could find some degree of scriptural support, so who is right? God is. He is right and justified in saving whomever He pleases. There is only one way to be saved: by grace through faith in the Lord Jesus Christ (see Eph. 2:8-9). God uses many methods to draw people to Himself. He is far more creative than we want to think. Only He can judge the heart.

Let's pause a moment and let God expose any areas where we have tried to make our personal experience a standard for another believer. Try to think in fairly broad terms such as the areas of salvation, spiritual gifts, prayers, miracles, or healings. Any reflections?

_____

_____

2. They tried to make salvation harder than it is. James delivered a strong exhortation to the Jerusalem Council in Acts 15:19: "'We should not make it difficult for the Gentiles who are turning to God.'" What a frightening thought! We must ask ourselves a very serious question: Do we make it difficult for people around us to turn to God? Do we have a list of rules and requirements that turns people away?

Part of the exquisite beauty of salvation is its simplicity. Any man, woman, or child can come to Christ with absolutely nothing to offer Him but simple faith—just as they are. Salvation requires nothing more than childlike faith—believing that Jesus Christ died for my sins and accepting His gift of salvation. The heart and the life sometimes turn instantaneously like the first example. Other times the heart turns instantaneously but the life adjusts a little more slowly like the second example. Let's not make salvation more difficult than it has to be.

3. They expected of others what they could not deliver themselves. In Acts 15:10, Peter said, "Now then, why do you try to test God by putting on the necks of the disciples a yoke that neither we nor our fathers have been able to bear?" In essence Peter was asking, *Why are you expecting of someone else what you can't deliver yourself?* The question is one every believer should occasionally ask herself. Do we have almost impossible expectations of other people? Do we expect things of our mates we wouldn't want to have to deliver? Do we expect perfection in our children and tireless commitment from our coworkers? Are we yoke brokers just looking for an unsuspecting neck? Yoke brokers are miserable people because they are never satisfied with less than perfection. Their obsession with everyone else's lack of perfection helps them keep their minds off their own. Yoke brokers are selling a yoke no one wants to buy—their own.

*H*as anyone ever expected of you something you knew she couldn't do herself? ❑ Yes ❑ No If so, how did you feel?

_____

_____

Let's return to the simplicity of salvation. Not adding to. Not taking away. When we paint the picture of our salvation for others to see, we may use different colors, textures, and shapes on the edges of the parchment. But in the center can only be a cross. Anything else cheapens grace and cheats the believer. Paul wasn't about to let that happen to his beloved flock. God proclaimed His plan for Gentile believers centuries before Paul and Barnabas ever broke the mold of Judaism (see Isa. 42:6-9).

James reminded the Jewish believers in Acts 15:18 that salvation coming to the Gentiles had been known for ages. They were seeing the fruition of an old plan in which God would do a new thing. He gave His Son on the cross to set the captives free, not to imprison them under the impossible laws of men.

*F*ill in the blank according to Ezekiel 34:27, NIV.
"They will know that I am the Lord, when I _____
and rescue them from the hands of those who enslaved them."

God can break any yoke, even those we don't realize we're wearing. We can feel burdened and trapped yet not realize why. In session 3 we will learn to recognize some areas of slavery and how they can be broken.

Thank goodness, the message of freedom prevailed at the Jerusalem Council. Paul and Barnabas departed with a letter personalized for the Gentile believers in Antioch. Two men accompanied them from Jerusalem. The letter they were carrying was of utmost importance. At first glance it seems somewhat contradictory. Gentile believers didn't have to be circumcised to be saved, but they were urged to abstain from several practices forbidden under Jewish law. Were they free from the law or not? Yes and no. They were free from the law of Moses but not free from the life-giving laws of God.

The freedom God gives is to come out and be separate from the practices of the former worldly life. The letter to the believers in Antioch was a declaration of liberty; the four areas of abstinence would help them remain free.

We will study Paul's principles for sexual purity later, but let's pinpoint another area that offers us an important learning opportunity. They were told to abstain from food sacrificed to idols. Gentile believers might have reasoned that although they would not dream of sacrificing to idols anymore, what harm could be done by simply buying the leftover food at a good price after it was offered?

Satan sometimes tempts us the same way. We don't desire to go back to our old lifestyles, but certain parts of it seem so harmless—some of the old friends, old hang outs, and old refreshments. The elders warned that nothing is harmless about the practices of the old life. Eating foods sacrificed to idols could weaken them to former practices or cause someone else to stumble.

*R*ead Paul's exhortation in 1 Corinthians 10:19-21. How would you summarize Paul's point in your own words?

*H*ow does God want you to respond to what He showed you today?

_____
_____

The Gentile believers would not forfeit their gift of grace by eating foods sacrificed to idols, but they would risk their freedom and compromise their separateness. They were wise to avoid anything which would place them close enough to the vacuum to be sucked back in. Safety and freedom are found in staying so far away you can't even hear the vacuum cleaner running.

Paul and Barnabas were back home. Back with their beloved flock. They returned to tell them they were free and to tell them a few ways to stay free.

[1]Patrick Johnstone, *Operation World* (Grand Rapids, MI: Zondervan Publishing House, 1993), 643.
[2]John F. Walvoord et al., eds., *The Bible Knowledge Commentary New Testament* (Wheaton, IL: Victor Books, 1983), 388.
[3]Trent C. Butler et al., eds., *Holman Bible Dictionary* (Nashville: Holman Bible Publishers, 1991), 406.

Miles and Missions

Galatians 5:16-26

The Fruit of the Spirit

1. God's provision for believers to share the _____ of Christ (Gal. 2:20).

   • Love: We have a supernatural ability to _____ God's love (Rom. 5:8)

   • Joy: We have the supernatural ability to _____ joy even in _____ (Matt. 13:44).

   • Peace: We have a supernatural ability to have peace when our _____ are _____ (Ps. 46:1-4; Heb. 12:26-29; Col. 3:15).

Definitions of patience

   1. _____: The ability to bear up under difficult circumstances.

   2. _____: The ability to bear up with difficult people.

   • Patience: We have the supernatural ability to bear up with _____ _____.

   • Kindness: We have the supernatural ability to remain warm and _____-_____

   in an _____ world.

   • Goodness: We have the supernatural ability to be genuinely _____ to this world.

   • Faithfulness: We have the supernatural ability to _____ God and to _____ on our belief.

   • Gentleness: We have the supernatural ability to _____ and _____ to God's will.

   • Self-Control: We have the supernatural ability to exercise _____. (2 Tim. 1:7).

2. A _____-_____ completely contrary to our human natures (Gal. 5:17).

3. The supernatural outcome of _____ in the Spirit (Gal. 5:16).
   Live in the Spirit by walking with God through:

   • Daily _____ to His authority.

   • Daily _____ from sin.

   • Daily _____ the filling of the Spirit (Luke 11:13; Gal. 2:20).

Unexpected Sojourners and Wider Paths

Day 1
Divide and Multiply

Day 2
The Birth of a Spiritual Son

Day 3
The Leadership of Christ's Spirit

Day 4
The Midnight Song

Day 5
The Noble Example of the Berean Believers

This week we embark on our second missionary journey with the apostle Paul. The more we continue our journey, the more we will discover the importance of coworkers in the gospel. Paul rarely worked alone. Studying his life affords us the marvelous privilege of peeking into many other lives as well. Inevitably, however, where you find people, you find problems! This week we may see Paul at his worst and at his best. The same man who had the propensity to be irritable and unreasonable could be spiritual and tender moments later. Sound familiar? We have a lot to learn this week as we seek to answer the following questions.

Principal Questions
Day 1: Why did Paul and Barnabas go their separate ways?
Day 2: How would you describe Timothy?
Day 3: How can we be best equipped to discern God's redirection in our lives?
Day 4: How did God use the imprisonment of Silas and Paul for His glory?
Day 5: Why were the Bereans of more noble character than the Thessalonians?

This week may tug a little tighter on your heart strings. Don't pull back from God. Get emotionally as well as spiritually involved in your journey. Imagine how you would feel in Paul's sandals. Think about ways you might have reacted differently. Let God penetrate your heart and mind with His Word. Don't push Him to the comfortable perimeters. He wants to do something wonderful in your life!

DAY 1
Divide and Multiply

Today's Treasure
"They had such a sharp disagreement that they parted company. Barnabas took Mark and sailed for Cyprus, but Paul chose Silas and left, commended by the brothers to the grace of the Lord" (Acts 15:39-40).

Sailors speak of the call of the sea, but something stronger than the sea called Paul. He relished his days in Antioch. How beautifully the garden had grown from a few scattered seeds six years earlier! He enjoyed the privilege of returning to the same quarters every night and laughing over a meal with good friends. He busied himself with the work of a pastor. He loved these people and his partner, Barnabas. But filled with the Spirit of God, Paul felt compelled to go where the Spirit led.

We may plan to stay forever and commit with noble intentions to do one thing for the rest of our lives. But when the Spirit of God moves within us, we must move with Him or be miserable. Paul knew God had called him to Antioch only to send him out again. He had learned to obey both the abiding and the moving of the Holy Spirit. He had been allowed by God to abide in the comforts of Antioch for a season. Now the Spirit of God compelled him to move again.

I love being drawn into the story line and relationships of Scripture, but involvement also increases the disappointment when our heroes show their humanity. We are about to see how God uses flawed people like you and me.

*P*lease read Acts 15:36-41 and complete the following.

1. Acts 15:36 tells us Paul wanted to return to the towns where he and Barnabas had preached, to see the new believers. What do you think Paul might have wanted to know about the new converts?

_____

2. You've probably begun to develop accurate impressions of Paul and Barnabas. Based on your impressions, why do you think Barnabas might have insisted on taking John Mark on the journey?

_____

_____

3. Barnabas very likely possessed each of the character traits you've listed above. In Colossians 4:10 Scripture also notes another reason for his relentless support of John Mark. What was their relationship? Check one.
   ❏ brothers   ❏ cousins   ❏ childhood friends

4. In your opinion, was Paul being too hard on John Mark and why?

_____

_____

5. What negative repercussion resulted from the disagreement?

_____

6. Do you see any evidence of a potential positive repercussion resulting from the disagreement?

_____

_____

We need to draw personal parallels and application from our study of Scripture. We relate to the characters based on our personal experience. I can relate to one aspect of Paul's experiences. For many years, I traveled by myself, speaking and teaching. But somewhere along the way, I began to encounter loneliness. I sometimes took a friend with me, but as the scope of the ministry widened an occasional luxury turned into a practical need. God met the need by equipping me with a full-time assistant to whom I often refer. She does not work for me. She works with me. She shares my vision for people to know God through His Word. She completes what I lack. Her partnership also takes a load off my husband. I can return home to a man who delights in the highlights of my journeys but cherishes the transition of my attentions back to him and our children. My partner in ministry has increased tenfold my joy in serving abroad.

Paul and Barnabas had experienced far more together than my partner and I. Barnabas was the first to accept Paul and welcome him among the brothers in Jerusalem. Together they faced the kind of peril and persecution that bonds two people for a lifetime! They were a team. When the Holy Spirit compelled Paul to return to the towns where they had preached, he wanted his dear friend and partner to go with him. Imagine how difficult this severance must have been for them.

Dr. Luke shows the magnitude of difficulty in the description in Acts 15:39: "They had such a sharp disagreement that they parted company." Sharp disagreements spin from strong emotions. They each had strong emotions about John Mark and toward each other. Obviously, both Paul and Barnabas were upset by their differing opinions.

Somehow, disagreements between people have a strange way of inviting observers to pick sides. I've already caught myself trying to decide who was right and who was wrong. I feel a strange need to make up my mind and get in one camp or the other.

*H*ow about you? Are you the same way when two people you know have an argument? Which of the following best describes you when two people you know (especially in ministry!) have a sharp disagreement? Be honest!
❑ I try not to think about it.
❑ I can hardly think of anything else.
❑ I do not feel privately compelled to take sides.
❑ I usually find myself privately taking sides.
❑ I often verbally take sides by sharing my opinion with others.

Human nature often leads us to wrestle until we've hashed out who is right, who is wrong, and chosen a side. What does Romans 14:1 tell us about "disputable matters"?

_____

Let's start becoming aware of our tendency to get involved, at least emotionally, as judge and jury when people disagree. Next time we're in a similar situation, perhaps we should ask ourselves, *Does someone always have to be right and another wrong?*

Paul and Barnabas were Spirit-filled servants of God, yet they differed vehemently on whether John Mark should join them. We might assume either Paul or Barnabas was not under the leadership of the Holy Spirit; because the Spirit could not possess two opinions. Or could He? I believe both men could have been under the direct influence of the Holy Spirit and yet, still have differed. How? The Holy Spirit might have been saying yes to Barnabas and no to Paul. He might have wanted Barnabas, but not Paul, to take John Mark. Why? So God could divide and multiply. Paul had matured so effectively under Barnabas' help and encouragement, they had grown equally strong. Though they might have preferred to serve together the rest of their lives, God had a more practical plan. He had other young preachers He wanted each man to train. As a result of their differing convictions, two preachers became four, and soon we'll see a fifth! Paul and Barnabas went their separate ways, two mentors, each with a new apprentice. The empty place in Paul's ministry left an appropriate space for a man named Silas to fill.

Scripture tells us most divisions are not of God, but our text today suggests that sometimes God wants to divide and multiply. Can you imagine how much simpler church life could be if we accepted that God could place two people under different convictions to multiply ministry? I've seen this phenomenon occur at my own church. Two very strong leaders in our church differed over whether we should have traditional worship or contemporary worship. Who was right? Both of them. God divided one worship service into two, and we now reach more people.

Often differences erupt due to less noble motivations—two opinionated people unwilling to budge. Unless we invite God to come to the rescue, the results can be disastrous. Ministries and partnerships often divide and dwindle rather than divide and multiply. On the other hand, when God leads two people who have walked together to a "y" in the road, He can do something wonderful IF they and their constituents are mature enough to deal with it!

Describe an occasion from your experience when God divided so He could multiply.

_____

_____

Were strong feelings involved? ❏ Yes ❏ No
Were the people involved ultimately able to give one another their blessings?
❏ Yes ❏ No

As long as we are part of church life, we will occasionally see good people disagree. Let's reiterate once again our best responses when godly people disagree:
- Resist the temptation to pass judgment.
- Resist the temptation to take sides.
- Resist the temptation to fuel the fire with unnecessary talk.

Unfortunately, sometimes we may be the ones involved in a dispute. We may find ourselves strongly differing with someone about matters related to church or ministry. Differing convictions don't have to become razor-sharp contentions. Let's conclude our lesson today by exploring a few ways we can avoid turning convictions into contentions.

1. Identify the real source of the argument. Job 16:3 asks a relevant question: "'What ails you that you keep on arguing?'" Ask the Holy Spirit to shed light on the true source. Sometimes we believe that conviction is the motivation for our differing views until we allow God to reveal our selfishness or unwillingness to change.

*R*ead the following Scriptures and identify underlying causes of some divisions and quarrels.

1 Corinthians 3:1-4 _____

James 4:1 _____

Sometimes, our strong feelings come from sources other than deep personal conviction. Part of spiritual maturity is risking our position in favor of the will and glory of God. Let's be willing to allow Him to shed light on any selfish or worldly motive.

*H*ow can Psalm 139:23-24 help with sharp differences between believers?

_____

_____

2. *Submit the issue to God.* James 4:7 exhorts, "Submit yourselves, then, to God. Resist the devil, and he will flee from you." A very important part of giving anything to God is taking everything from Satan. Perhaps you'll allow me to say it this way: Surrender the situation totally to God and ask Him to get the devil out of it!

*R*ead Ephesians 4:26-27. In what ways do you think Satan can get a foothold in arguments between two Christians?

_____

_____

Satan has a field day with our arguments and quarrels. What happens when we submit our disagreements to God, asking Him to remove all selfish, worldly motives and influence of the enemy? Issues often either disappear or downsize to a workable level.

3. *Resist the temptation to sin in your anger.* You read the exhortation in Ephesians 4:26 not to sin in your anger. Anger in and of itself is not sin. It is an emotion, and sometimes a very appropriate emotion. Unfortunately, anger heightens the risk of wrong actions or words. Each of us regrets something we've said or done in anger. Let's ask God's help when we are angry at another believer, so that our feelings do not turn into wrong actions.

4. *Pray for the other person involved and, if possible, with that person.* Prayer changes things and people! Philippians 4:6 invites us to pray about everything. Can you imagine how defeated the enemy would be if two divided church leaders or laymen got down on their knees together and prayed for God's glory? We don't have to be together on every issue, but we can be together in prayer!

None of these steps are easy for us, but God can keep differing convictions from becoming contentions if we let Him. Sometimes the fear of being wrong or having to relent will keep us from inviting God into the middle of a dispute. Today we've become more open-minded to the possibility that both people can be on the right track, even when they are feeling led in different directions. We've seen an occasion when differences ultimately brought gains rather than losses. If God could use a sharp disagreement between two of His faithful servants, then Luke 1:37 has been tried and proven under some of the most difficult human conditions: Nothing is impossible with God!

*H*ow does God want you to respond to what He showed you today?

_____

_____

_____

_____

_____

_____

The Birth of a Spiritual Son

Today's reading unfolds as Paul returns to Derbe and Lystra to check the temperature of the churches. Trace Paul's second missionary journey in a different color ink. Though he begins his second missionary journey in cities previously visited, God will soon adjust Paul's eyes to a wider vision.

*P*lease read Acts 16:1-5 and complete the following.

1. Scripture tells us Timothy's mother was a Jewish believer and his father was a Greek. Meditate on these facts for just a moment. What are a few ways you think parents' differences might have affected his upbringing?

_____

_____

2. After the decisions of the Jerusalem council in Acts 15, which of Paul's actions seem most peculiar? Choose one.

❑ He took Timothy.   ❑ He circumcised Timothy.
❑ He argued with Silas.   ❑ He did not preach to the Gentiles.

Before assuming Paul violated his own teachings, understand why he had Timothy circumcised. Jews recognized Timothy's Jewish heritage. His mother was a Jewess. They would have been terribly offended and refused to allow him into the synagogues to preach. Paul wanted Timothy to minister to both Jews and Gentiles. He had him circumcised so the Jews would not be offended and close their minds to his testimony.

I hope we can capture some insight into Paul's heart by observing how he loved and related to people. He must have been very endearing to many people. He had many close friends and associates. We rarely see him working alone. More than anyone recorded in all of Scripture, Paul taught believers to work together. He was both a preacher and a teacher, yet he was never a one-man show. He clearly enjoyed working with other servants and was quick to acknowledge their valuable contributions.

Perhaps a favorite part of this study may be exploring some of his friendships; yet as many as he had, one would differ from all the rest. Many years later, I'm sure his heart was washed with emotion as he recalled his return to Lystra and the risk he took on a young man named Timothy. From the very beginning, Timothy was special. Allow Scripture to shed some light on his distinctives.

1. *Timothy was a unique choice.* He differed from the others in a basic way.

*R*ead 1 Timothy 4:12. Why had people been looking down on Timothy?

❑ because he was young   ❑ because he was not circumcised
❑ because he was timid   ❑ because his father was Greek

The verse you just read came 15 years after Timothy joined Paul. Timothy was a unique choice because of his youthfulness. Paul's words in 2 Timothy 3:15 demonstrate that in spite of his youth, Timothy was fertile soil from which ministry grew: "from infancy you have known the holy Scriptures, which are able to make you wise for salvation through faith in Christ Jesus."

I believe Paul saw Timothy's tremendous potential for fruit bearing. The opportunity to train Timothy while he was still young and teachable was probably a benefit to Paul's ministry, not a hindrance.

Recently a fellow believer told me the wonderful news of his 12-year-old son surrendering to the ministry. These parents knew his heart and were overcome with joy and humility over their son's serious decision. The response of others was somewhat perplexing, however. People said things like "God is obviously going to use him someday" and "I hope he still feels this way when he is old enough for God to use him." A person doesn't have to turn 20 for the Lord to use him in ministry.

Anyone with the maturity to surrender entirely to God is mature enough for God to begin using him or her. What could be more important than a ministry by students for students on a junior high school campus? To this student and other girls and boys like him, I extend the words of the apostle Paul: "Don't let anyone look down on you because you are young, but set an example for the believers in speech, in life, in love, in faith and in purity" (1 Tim. 4:12).

*D*o you know any young people who are trying to be genuine servants of God? If so, they may be discouraged because no one is taking them seriously. Give yourself an extra assignment today: Make a point of encouraging a young servant through a note, a call, or a pat on the back.

2. Timothy had a unique upbringing. Earlier I asked you to explore any effects his parents' differences might have had on his upbringing. You may have greater insight into Timothy's childhood because of differences in your own parents' belief systems. Growing up in a home with one believing and one unbelieving parent is very difficult. In those days, having a Jewish mother who had accepted Christ and a Greek father who didn't believe would have been both different and difficult.

I have two daughters in high school. I am very concerned about a seemingly harmless belief system society has been shaping in children's minds. My generation was the first to be raised on movies and fairy tales in living color. Movies like *Cinderella*, *Snow White and the Seven Dwarfs*, and *Beauty and the Beast* redefine romance as two people from totally different worlds falling deeply in love. Typically, their only problem is their unyielding family. Ultimately, love overcomes and they live happily ever after.

We need to teach our children the truth about real romance and love that lasts. The sparks that fly from two different worlds converging in one couple usually end up burning someone!

*W*hat strong exhortation did the apostle Paul give in 2 Corinthians 6:14?

_____

_____

The Greek word for *yoked* is *zugos* which means "a yoke serving to couple any two things together and a coupling, a beam of a balance which unites two scales, hence a balance." In the next verse, Paul asks a question to make his point: "What harmony is there?" When two completely different belief systems are joined together, the result often is a lack of balance and harmony. You may have grown up in this kind of home, so you know how rocky this life can be. Perhaps you may presently be in a home where spiritual beliefs differ drastically. If so, I hope you receive some encouragement from today's lesson. God can prevail and bear wonderful fruit from an unequally yoked couple as we will see, but their lives often are more complicated than they had to be.

Keith and I have miraculously made it for 20 years, but we've had to work very hard to overcome many differences in our belief systems. We are both hoping our daughters find romance with young men reared with spiritual beliefs close to their own.

What could be more exciting than two people coming together and entrusting their uncertain futures to God's purposes, bound by a common love for His Son? Now, I call that real romance.

3. Timothy had a unique perspective. Timothy had been intimately exposed to three practices he and Paul would encounter in ministry:

- Agnosticism because of his father's unbelief,
- Judaism because of his mother's heritage, and
- Christianity because of his mother's acceptance of Christ as Messiah and Savior.

Even though he did not have the security of two believing parents, he gained an insight which would prove valuable in ministry.

*I*dentify differences between your primary caregivers as you were growing up. How has God used these differences?

_____

_____

God wasted nothing in either Paul's or Timothy's background. He won't waste anything in your background either, if you will allow Him to use you.

4. Timothy had a unique maturity. In our society, we've almost become convinced that bad influences are stronger than good. Timothy certainly is evidence to the contrary. We have a wonderful biblical precedent proving that godly influence can carry a much heavier weight than ungodly influence.

*R*ead 2 Timothy 1:5. How would you diagram Timothy's heritage of faith on the following family tree? Include his natural and spiritual family.

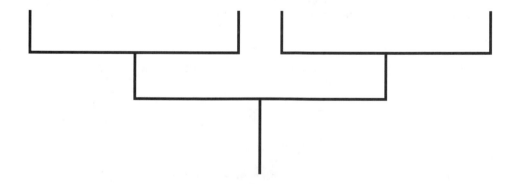

I hope 2 Timothy 1:5 and the family-tree visual aid are strong encouragements to anyone married to an unbeliever. You can rear godly children in spite of imperfect circumstances. One key to winning a child over to faith is found in the word *sincere*. Timothy's grandmother and mother both possessed a sincere faith. The original word is *anupokritos* which means "without hypocrisy or pretense." Originally the word meant "inexperienced in the art of acting." What a wonderful way to be inexperienced!

Lois and Eunice lived their faith. Timothy saw genuine examples of faithfulness. Their lives were devoted to God even when the company left. They were genuine—not perfect, but real. Their sincerity won Timothy to the Truth. I once thought Exodus 20:5, about the sins of the fathers being visited upon the children, was one of the scariest verses in the Bible. Then I looked up the word *visit* (KJV) and realized what it meant. The word is used for taking a census or a head count. When a parent practices sin and rebellion against God, adversely affected children, grandchildren, and great-grandchildren share some of the same tendencies. But sin and rebellion are not the only heritage passed down to future generations! Faithfulness has an even greater influence!

*C*ontrast God's promise in Deuteronomy 7:9. How many generations can love and faith affect?_____

Hang in there, parent! Let your children see the sincerity of your faith. Let them see you praying and trusting. Nothing carries the weight of sincere faith!

While Saul was on a mission of death, God brought him to his knees and broke his heart for Christ. As he followed his Savior in obedience, he sacrificed many things dear to the Jew: marriage, children, strong extended family. God honored Paul's willingness to forsake earthly expectations and honors by giving him other priceless gifts. Timothy was one of God's priceless gifts to Paul. He filled a void in Paul's life no one else ever matched. Years later Paul wrote of Timothy, "my dear son." Perhaps God thought a crusty old preacher needed a young whippersnapper as much as Timothy needed him.

Diagram your heritage of faith on the family tree below. You may have a heritage of faith from both parents. You may have a heritage of faith from one side of your family. Or you may be the first believer in several generations. Paul considered Timothy to be his son in the faith even though he was not his biological father. You've probably received a heritage of faith from a spiritual if not a natural mother or father. Find out who gave your spiritual parent his/her heritage of faith. Try to diagram at least three generations on the family tree below.

*H*ow does God want you to respond to what He showed you today?

_____

_____

_____

_____

_____

_____

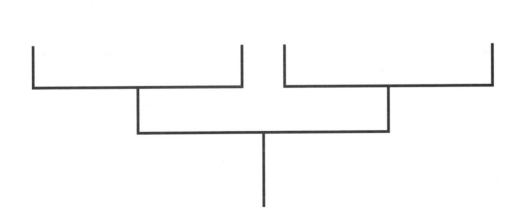

Meditate on your family tree. Thank God for your heritage. As you conclude today's lesson, pray for the generations which will follow you. Just think, if Christ tarries, your faithfulness could affect a thousand generations. Isn't God wonderful?

DAY 3

The Leadership of Christ's Spirit

Today's Treasure
"When they came to the border of Mysia, they tried to enter Bithynia, but the Spirit of Jesus would not allow them to. So they passed by Mysia and went down to Troas" *(Acts 16:7-8).*

Today's lesson takes us into new territory, both logistically on our map and spiritually in our understanding of a difficult concept. As they ventured farther from home, new challenges awaited Paul, Timothy, and Silas. These new challenges were not only in relationship to people and places, but also in relationship to Christ.

No matter how God has prepared us in advance, when we surrender our lives to serve God, we are not fully grown. In fact, the greatest challenges to learn and grow are ahead! Not coincidentally, Paul met Christ for the first time on a road and he would "meet" Him on every road he traveled for the rest of his life.

We probably did not see a light and hear a voice from Heaven as did Paul, but we met Christ somewhere on the road to our chosen destinations. Our lives took a detour at that point, and we've been sojourning ever since on the roads He's placed before us. Life is not only about receiving Jesus and one day seeing Him. Life also is about walking with Christ and learning from Him on the winding road.

Read Acts 16:6-10. What possible reasons might have existed for the Holy Spirit to keep Paul, Silas, and Timothy from preaching the word in the province of Asia?
- ❑ **He cared more for the people in Macedonia than those in Asia.**
- ❑ **He had another person in mind to minister to the people of Asia.**
- ❑ **The people of Asia weren't ready to hear at that time.**
- ❑ **Other** _____

How did God redirect Paul? Choose one:
- ❑ **through Timothy**   ❑ **through Silas**
- ❑ **through a vision**   ❑ **through a letter**

Before we explore our text, we have the privilege of adding Luke, the inspired writer of the Book of Acts, to the band of men on Paul's second missionary journey. Notice an important change in the references made to Paul and his men in verse 10. Suddenly, instead of *they,* which is used as recently as verse 7, the expression becomes *we.* Somewhere on this significant journey, Luke joined the growing band of missionaries.

Early church fathers identified Luke as being from Antioch.[1] In Colossians 4:14 Paul refers to him as a dear friend and a doctor.

A number of scholars believe Paul's thorn in the flesh, which we will consider later, might have been a physical illness. Perhaps Luke offered himself both spiritually and professionally to the service of Christ; then he traveled with Paul and his associates as a physician and record keeper. Whatever his original motivation for joining them, we are forever indebted to his obedience in providing vivid accounts of the life of Christ in his Gospel and the lives of the apostles in the Book of Acts.

Assuming Luke caught up with Paul, Silas, and Timothy on their journey, he was fortunate to find them at all after their sudden change in plans! The redirection God gave the disciples as they attempted to enter the province of Asia offers us several timely learning opportunities. We've learned from Scripture today that even the most noble plans of God's anointed servants sometimes differ from the plans of God.

Paul wanted to take the gospel to the province of Asia. He could not have imagined God having any reason to object, yet "They tried to enter Bithynia, but the Spirit of Jesus would not allow them" (Acts 16:7). Why would God object to the preaching of the gospel in the province of Asia? One reason may have been timing. Later God opened "a great door for effective work" for Paul and his associates in Ephesus, in the province of Asia (1 Cor. 16:9). A second reason may have been His plan to use Peter rather than Paul in Bithynia. The inclusion of Bithynia in 1 Peter 1:1 indicates that God gave Peter some level of access to the area. Whether the problem is the wrong place, the wrong time, or the wrong person, God exercises His right to redirect His children.

Today's Scriptures remind us that God can sometimes say no or wait, even when godly people have unanimously voted yes! Spiritual maturity does not mean we will never make the wrong plans. Spiritual maturity often means having the courage to admit we've made the wrong plans and seeking God for the new direction.

*H*ow did they know the Spirit of Jesus would not allow them to enter? List ways the Holy Spirit keeps Christians in tune with God's will.

_____

_____

How can we know when God is redirecting us? Let's see if we can discover how Paul probably recognized the closed door to Asia. Did God use opposition? Apparently not, because when Paul spoke of the door opening later in Ephesus, he said "a great door for effective work has opened to me, and there are many who oppose me" (1 Cor. 16:9). Opposition didn't seem to slow Paul down much. Did God use a supernatural means like the vision He gave him regarding Macedonia? I don't think so, because if He had, the vision probably would have been recorded just like the one several verses later.

I believe God hindered Paul in the same way He often will hinder us when we are heading the wrong direction or going ahead of schedule. He stopped them through the inner working of His Spirit.

*B*efore we consider what the leadership of the Spirit is, let's determine what it is not. Read Jude 1:18-19. Based on verse 19, obviously the leadership of the Holy Spirit is not mere _____.

We can't just rely on our feelings as we try to do God's will. The leadership of the Spirit is far more than "mere natural instincts." Read 1 Corinthians 2:12. What is one reason we have received the Spirit of God?

_____

Romans 8:9 tells us God has placed His Spirit within each person who has received Christ. One reason His Spirit takes up residence inside us is to tell us things only believers can understand, leading us in areas of obedience to Christ. The Holy Spirit always leads believers in Christ, but we don't always recognize His leadership. What are a few basics we can practice so that we can learn to follow the leadership of the Holy Spirit?

1. *Study God's Word.* God will never lead us any direction contrary to His Word.
2. *Yield to the Holy Spirit's control.* Being yielded to God's authority keeps us pliable and open minded to a possible change of plans.
3. *Pray for clear leadership in specific directions God wants you to take.*

83

You might consider adopting David's approach to prayer in Psalm 27:11. What two requests did he make of God?

_____

_____

4. Pray for wisdom and discernment to recognize specific directions.

In Ephesians 1:17 what did Paul ask God to give believers?

_____

Start asking God to give you the Spirit of wisdom and revelation!

5. Make plans, but hold on to them loosely!

I don't believe God intended for Paul, Silas, and Timothy to travel haphazardly through the countryside. Paul was a very intelligent man. He probably formulated a travel plan just like most of us would, but he kept his map in an open hand just in case God had different ideas!

How does James 4:13-15 say we should approach our plans?

_____

6. Learn to recognize peace as one of God's prompters.

Read Romans 8:5-6. Fill in the blank according to verse 6:
"The mind of sinful man is death, but the mind controlled by the

_____ is life and _____."

Peace is one of the most obvious earmarks of the authority of Christ. A sense of peace will virtually always accompany His will and direction—even when the direction might not have been our personal preference. On the other hand, a lack of peace will often accompany a mistaken path—even when the direction is definitely our personal preference. As we grow in Christ, we will learn how to appreciate peace over personal preferences. Remember, Christ is the Prince of Peace. His peace will accompany His authority.

Paul and his fellow servants were yielded to the leadership of the Holy Spirit. Therefore, they were pliable when God prompted them not to enter the province of Asia by removing their sense of peace and approval. Thankfully, they were willing to allow God to change their plans. More than any other disciple, God used the apostle Paul to teach about the activity of the Holy Spirit. Paul could not teach what he had never learned. He learned to follow the leadership of the Holy Spirit one day at a time, one city at a time—on-the-job training. Let's learn from his example and be willing to change our course when we sense God has different plans.

Has God ever redirected you away from a plan you formerly thought was His? ❑ Yes ❑ No

If so, how did you recognize the change in plans?

_____

_____

Paul and his small band of missionaries did not have to wait long for redirection. God used a vision of a man begging for help to lead them into uncharted territory.

_R_ead Acts 16:11-15 and trace Paul's travels into an exciting new territory on your map.

If you are like me, you probably completed your reading without much fanfare. Lydia seemed like a nice enough woman, but we've seen Paul have more thrilling encounters. Verse 14 simply says, "The Lord opened her heart to respond to Paul's message." Nothing outwardly dramatic happened. Almost seemed ho-hum, didn't it? But take a good look at your map one more time. After temporarily closing a door in the province of Asia, God strained their eyes to see a much wider vision and took them all the way to Philippi. The account we just read had monumental impact! The gospel of Jesus Christ went to Europe! Within a couple of hundred years, Christians numbered in the ten thousands in Europe. And it all started with a businesswoman named Lydia.

No one would ever suspect some of the feelings of spiritual inferiority professional Christian businesswomen harbor at times. They don't have some of the opportunities to serve and attend Bible studies that others do. For everyone who ever wondered if God could use a professional businesswoman, meet Lydia. She was a city girl, a salesperson. A homeowner with enough room to house a host of people. Yet her professional life was balanced by the priorities of her spiritual life. She worshiped God. She didn't see the Sabbath only as an opportunity to catch up on some sleep and straighten up the house. She gathered with other believers. She found a place of prayer (v. 13). She opened her home. She made herself available to God. Because she did, "the Lord opened her heart to respond" (v. 14). And God gave birth to the gospel in Europe. I'd say that business-woman had a pretty important ministry, wouldn't you?

Be encouraged, professional. Balance is never easy. But as Lydia has shown us today: it's possible. I believe the key is finding your own personal place of prayer. A place and a time for temporarily resigning all other roles to regain strength through worship and perspective through prayer.

_D_o you have a place of prayer? ❏ Yes ❏ No If so, where is it and how often do you normally retreat to it?

_____

Prayer is the key to many strides in our Christian lives. Today we've seen seasoned believers and new believers learn to respond to the leadership of the Holy Spirit. They would never have recognized God's leadership or known how to respond without prayer. Because they were completely surrendered to God's will, Paul, Silas, and Timothy did not fret when the Spirit of Christ hindered them from following through with their plans. They simply awaited new marching orders. We often hear people say "when God closes a door, He opens a window." Sometimes we might just be underesti-mating Him. We just saw Him close a door and open a continent.

_H_ow does God want you to respond to what He showed you today?

_____

_____

_____

_____

_____

The Midnight Song

Life seems to be drawn to the extremes like a magnet, doesn't it? As we look back over our own personal histories, the years may seem to fall into interchanging ups and downs, valleys and mountaintops. We sometimes feel we've lived no place but the ups and downs. We're left with a sense of having lived our entire lives in the extremes. Paul and his small band of missionaries only spent a matter of days in Philippi according to Acts 16:12. In that time, they were "guests" in only two places: a mansion and a dungeon. Let's meet Paul in the extremes today.

*R*ead Acts 16:16-40 and complete the following.

1. What was the actual reason why Paul and Silas were taken before the authorities? Choose one.
   ❑ They were blaspheming the Roman government.
   ❑ They were preaching in the marketplace.
   ❑ They insulted the Jews.
   ❑ They ended a very profitable exploitation of a slave girl.

2. How were Paul and Silas punished? Choose any that apply.
   ❑ They were stoned.   ❑ They were expelled from the city.
   ❑ They were stripped.   ❑ They were placed under house arrest.
   ❑ They were severely flogged. ❑ Their feet were placed in stocks.
   ❑ They were imprisoned.

3. Use your imagination. Suppose Paul and Silas knew the hymns familiar to us today. What hymns do you think they might have sung?

_____

_____

4. Compare the circumstances of Paul's miracle in prison with those of Peter's in Acts 12. Based on Acts 12:18-19, why do you think Paul's jailer was going to kill himself?

_____

5. A number of amazing twists occurred in the prison in Philippi. In your personal opinion, what is the most striking part of this account?

_____

Let's review why Paul and Silas landed in prison. Few of us have ever encountered a demon-possessed slave girl. But all of us have felt exactly like Paul when he finally had enough! I'm not sure patience was Paul's natural strong suit, so I find myself amused at his best attempts to control himself. As he and the others tried to preach, teach, and meet for prayer, this young, disturbed woman followed them and shouted incessantly. Obviously, the apostle had tried not to react; but after many days, he became troubled.

I can't help but grin as I share the original definition of *troubled* with you. None of us will have difficulty relating to it. The word *diaponeo* means "to be tired ... become wearied ... at the continuance of anything."

When was the last time someone continued an annoying habit until you wanted to scream? I recall a bumper sticker that read, "I have one nerve left and you're on it." Most of the time, our trouble is not an evil spirit. More often, it's one of our children getting on our last nerve!

The apostle had the power to do something about his frayed nerves, and he commanded the spirit to come out of the girl. As a result, her exploiters lost a source of income. They were more than troubled. They were incensed. Paul and Silas ended up being dragged into the marketplace to face authorities not because of the charges made against them, but because they had ruined a good scheme.

You may be wondering why four men preached the gospel in Philippi, but only two of them were punished. Where were Luke and Timothy when the sparks started flying? The Roman world had recently experienced a fresh surge of anti-Semitism, and Emperor Claudius had expelled all Jews from Rome. Because few things are more contagious than prejudice, Philippi (a Roman colony) quickly caught the virus. Timothy and Luke may have been considered Gentiles by the Roman authorities. Since the governors of Philippi knew virtually nothing about Christianity, Paul and Silas were dragged before a strongly anti-Semitic magistrate and persecuted because of their Jewish heritage. Imagine how the foursome felt: divided over their backgrounds, two were freed and two were carried away maliciously. I'm not at all sure which two had the easier sentence.

*H*ebrews 10:32-33 acknowledges the kinds of roles both pairs played in **Philippi that day. Read these verses and fill in the following blanks based on Hebrews 10:32.**

"Remember those earlier days after you had received the light, when you

stood your ground in a _____ in the_____."

Hebrews 10:33 describes two different kinds of roles in the face of suffering. What are they?
1. _____

2. _____

Do you see Scripture acknowledging the authentic pain a person experiences when a friend or loved-one suffers? God is very aware that standing close to someone who is hurting hurts! He does it every day. Whether we are the ones suffering or we're alongside another, His grace is sufficient for our need. Aren't you refreshed to see God validate in Scripture the experience of the deeply concerned bystander? You can cry out for help when you're hurting for someone else. He'll hear you and acknowledge your need!

Luke and Timothy deeply needed God's comfort as they watched the severe flogging of their partners. First, Paul and Silas were stripped—an incomprehensible humiliation to anyone with a Jewish background. Then they were mercilessly beaten with rods.

Paul probably suffered from both sides of the great contest we considered in Hebrews 10:32-33. He suffered his own blows, but he also stood by Silas as he was stripped and severely whipped. What a frightful initiation into ministry this must have been for Silas. Can you imagine how Paul ached for his new assistant? Did he wonder if Silas could take it? If so, he found that no one needed to underestimate Silas. Luke and Timothy strained for a last look at their partners as the authorities dragged them to prison. They probably wondered if they would ever see them again. Luke and Timothy's night may have been longer than Silas and Paul's. And much less eventful!

The two bloodied servants of God were taken to a dungeon and placed in stocks, unable to move, with pain wracking their bodies. Though they were bound in iron chains, they found freedom to sing. We cheat the faithful servants from showing us God's glory if we believe God anesthetized their pain. Death would have been a relief. The challenge of their moment was living until the pain became bearable. I don't believe Paul and Silas sang out of joy and gladness. They were lifting up a sacrifice of praise in its finest form. Paul and Silas were praying and singing hymns to God.

Pain is never more vivid than in the midnight hour. The night lacks the kindness of the day when demands and activities distract. Bound in stocks, every time their hearts beat every nerve ending throbbed with pain. In spite of their anguish, their prayers ascended before the throne and God gave them "songs in the night" (Job 35:10).

Prayers come naturally when we are distressed—but songs? To find notes is difficult when your body is gripped with pain. A few notes found their way into a melody and their melodies turned into hymns. Every stanza issued a fresh strength, and their voices were unchained—penetrating walls and bars.

The most difficult part of my service as a Sunday School teacher has been watching a number of my members bury loved ones. Several years ago one of my members lost her 15-year-old son in an automobile accident. I will never forget accompanying our friend to the funeral home and helping her choose a casket. All four of us walked to the car and took our seats without saying a word. Within a couple of blocks, one of us began to cry, and then the rest joined her without saying a word. After several minutes of silence, another leader began to sing with broken notes, "I love you, Lord … and I lift my voice … to worship You … O, my soul rejoice." I could hardly believe the nerve of my fellow member to sing at such a time as this. Before I could look at her with proper horror, the mother's best friend joined in, "Take joy, my King, in what You hear … may it be a sweet, sweet sound in Your ear."

The words fell from their lips a second time and to my shock, Bernard's broken-hearted mother began to sing. If she could sing, I knew I could not remain silent. We sang all the way home that day. Not one of us had a solo voice, and yet I wonder if I will ever hear a sound so beautiful again. I knew that day what God meant when He told us to lift up the sacrifice of praise. When praise is the last thing that comes naturally to us and we choose to worship Him anyway, we've had the privilege of offering a genuine sacrifice of praise.

Can you think of a time when you've had the opportunity to offer God a sacrifice of praise? ❑ Yes ❑ No

Can you sense any benefit from your willingness to praise Him at a difficult time? ❑ Yes ❑ No   If so, what benefit did you gain?

_____

When we sing a midnight song or speak praises in the darkest hours, the chains of hopelessness not only drop from our ankles, but sometimes from the ankles of those who listen. We can preach the gospel in many ways, but the message is never more clear than when God's people refuse to cease their praises during intense suffering.

In their bondage, Paul and Silas were free to sing. They were also free to stay. Finally their songs were eclipsed by the rumblings of an earthquake. The foundations of the prison trembled before an awesome God. The prison doors flew open, every chain was loosed, and the jailer drew his sword to kill himself. Paul's words penetrate my heart: "'Don't harm yourself!'" (v. 28). How many people have sought to harm themselves over hopelessness? The jailer knew he would be held responsible for their escape. "'Don't harm yourself! We are all here!'" shouted Paul.

Sometimes God frees us from chains so we can turn our backs on our slavery and walk away like Peter in Acts 12. He was free to leave. As a result, the church which was praying for his release was edified. Other times God frees us from chains so we can remain where we are to share the message of freedom with other captives. Paul was free to stay. Because he did, a man asked, "'What must I do to be saved?'" (v. 30). And an entire household found sweet liberty.

I met a young man who had experienced freedom from the bondage of homosexuality. Although he was a dedicated servant, God had never appointed him to share that part of his testimony nor minister to those still chained in that lifestyle. Like Peter, he had been freed to leave.

After God delivered me from the bondage of my childhood victimization, He called me to share my basic testimony and reach out to other survivors of abuse. I had been freed to stay. Both my friend and I experienced the glorious freedom of Christ. One was free to leave and one was free to stay, but we each trust God with His perfect plan for our lives.

What about you? Have you been freed from chains which bound you in the past? If so, at this point in your life, do you believe God has freed you to leave or freed you to stay? Explain briefly.

_____

_____

God reserves the right to use His servants and their experiences in different ways. Let's try to resist copying a blueprint from another person's ministry. God is very creative, and He always has purpose in the specific ways He chooses to use us. Be willing to allow Him to put some things to public use and other things to private use. Today, we've seen a slice of Paul's life in the extremes: a welcomed guest and a prisoner. Either extreme could have been a test. Paul passed. As life draws us to extremes, may we pass our tests as well.

How does God want you to respond to what He showed you today?

_____

_____

_____

_____

_____

DAY 5

The Noble Example of the Berean Believers

Today's reading takes us to the next two stops on Paul's second missionary journey. Be sure to continue tracing his travels on your map as you read your assignments. We know Luke accompanied the missionaries to Philippi; but his terminology suggests their paths parted for awhile, presumably for the sake of the gospel. Luke's references to "we" rather than "they" will pick up again several chapters later in the Book of Acts.

Today's Treasure
"Now the Bereans were of more noble character than the Thessalonians, for they received the message with great eagerness and examined the Scriptures every day to see if what Paul said was true" (Acts 17:11).

$\mathcal{R}$ead Acts 17:1-9 and complete the following.

1. Paul had been called by God to be a light to the Gentiles. Can you think of any reasons why he customarily went to the Jewish synagogues first?

_____

_____

2. What was the outcome of his preaching in Thessalonica according to verse 4? Choose any which apply.
   - ❑ Many Jews were persuaded. ❑ Some Jews were persuaded.
   - ❑ Few were persuaded. ❑ A large number of Greeks believed.

3. Why was Jason dragged before the city officials? Choose one.
   - ❑ He helped Paul and Silas escape.
   - ❑ He welcomed Paul and Silas into his home.
   - ❑ He abandoned Judaism.

We will consider Paul's experiences in Thessalonica only briefly in our present lesson. Later we will study the letters he wrote to them. His next stop will be today's focus. Before we proceed, let's highlight a few points from our first reading. Paul and Silas had traveled 100 miles from Philippi to Thessalonica without the benefit of a motorized vehicle. They seemed to know exactly where they wanted to go and certainly did not lack the stamina to get there! You may be wondering what criteria made one city more a priority than another. Obviously, the first criteria was the leadership of the Holy Spirit. If He did not lead, they did not go.

$\mathcal{P}$aul cites another criteria in Romans 15:20-22. What was it?

_____

God used the leadership of the Holy Spirit and Paul's desire to go into territories untouched by the gospel. In each new venue, not only did he customarily preach in the synagogues first, he employed the same method each time. He sought to prove that Jesus was the Christ with the Old Testament Scripture. I believe he used this method with them because God had used it so effectively on him in the desert of Arabia. He knew this technique could work on the hardest of hearts because he had once had one.

As a result of the message and the method, some Jews and many Greeks believed. Wherever there is an awakening, you can expect opposition. Soon the seed of jealousy was planted in other Jews, and they formed a plan to incite a riot.

$\mathcal{R}$ead Acts 17:10-15 and complete the following.

1. Take a good look at your map. Thessalonica is 100 miles from Philippi. How far would you estimate Paul and Silas traveled from Thessalonica to Berea? _____

2. What characteristics set the Bereans apart from the Thessalonians? Choose any that apply.
   - ❑ They were more noble. ❑ They eagerly accepted the message.
   - ❑ Many Jews believed. ❑ They examined the Scriptures daily.

Having narrowly escaped the Thessalonians in the night, the tenacious missionaries traveled approximately 50 miles to Berea. (Did you come close in your estimate?) Miles away from their destination, they saw a most imposing landmark: Mount Olympus rising high into the sky from the foothills of Berea. Only 20 miles from the sea, Berea had everything to offer: warm coastal breezes tempered by snow-capped mountains. What could be more inviting than a city set between the mountains and the ocean? Exceeding the noble sight, however, was the nobility of the people. The Bereans possessed characteristics that provide an excellent standard for church members today:

1. They were willing to receive. Acts 17:11 tells us the Bereans received the message. The original Greek word is *dechomai* which means "to accept an offer deliberately and readily." The Bereans accepted the offer to come and hear what Paul had to say.

Many churches work overtime to offer opportunities for Christian growth and encouragement through conferences, retreats, Bible studies, discipleship training, and other methods. Often, a relative few attend. Sometimes the ones who don't are the very ones who criticize the church for not doing enough. Many times we don't lack opportunities, we lack willingness. The Bereans accepted the offer to hear Paul teach and preach, and the fruit was bountiful.

*H*ow do you respond to opportunities to grow and be encouraged?
❑ I often accept opportunities.
❑ I sometimes accept opportunities.
❑ I rarely accept opportunities.
❑ I haven't accepted an opportunity in years.

2. They were ready to receive. The Bereans not only accepted the offer to hear Paul, they were eager to receive what he said. The original word for *eagerness* is *prothumia* which indicates a predisposition for learning (Strong's). Our experiences in Bible study, worship services, and other discipleship opportunities are greatly enhanced when we approach each one with a predisposition for learning. We need to prepare ourselves with everything we can to have a receptive disposition before we arrive.

*N*ame several ways we can be predisposed to receive from those who seek to disciple us.

_____

_____

3. They cross-examined the message with the Scriptures. Paul must have been a very effective communicator, yet the Bereans did not take his word for everything. They measured the accuracy of his message against Scripture through their own personal examination of the Word. The original word for *examined* in Acts 17:11 is *anakrino* which means "to ask, question, discern, examine, judge, search" (Strong's).

We all need to learn to study the Scriptures for ourselves. Every believer has the right to ask questions and examine the Scriptures to check the accuracy of the teaching they hear. Congregations can be easily misled if they do not feel or exercise the freedom to double-check teaching and preaching against the Word of God. A savvy communicator could use the Scriptures taken out of context to teach almost anything! Any portion of Scripture must be compared with Scripture as a whole.

Some years ago, a national forest had to close off a portion of the park to tourists. A number of bears starved to death during the time the park was closed. They had grown so accustomed to being fed by the tourists, they had ceased feeding themselves. We can likewise grow so accustomed to being spoon-fed the Word of God, we forget how to examine the Scriptures for ourselves.

We can also cease checking the nutritional value of what we're being taught! My most earnest prayer would be that this Bible study, and others like it, be a help in teaching you how to examine Scripture for yourself. Yet I plead with you not to accept my instruction without question. Always check my teaching against a thorough examination of the Word. I would never knowingly mislead you, but I am subject to human error just like every other teacher. I ask you to examine the Scriptures every day to see if what I'm saying is true.

The Bereans not only performed the right practices, I believe they possessed the right heart. They didn't examine the Scriptures to see if they could catch Paul in a wrong way he had dotted an "i" or crossed a "t." Their motive was not to argue. Some people double-check their pastors and teachers on every issue just to find an error so they can feel superior. The Bereans had no such motive. They were eager to believe, but they were wise to check Paul's teaching against the only standard of truth—the Scriptures. After careful study, they found his teaching sound and placed their faith in the Savior he preached. A wonderful and sometimes rare combination occurred in Berea: the best kind of preacher met the best kind of audience. And a great awakening of faith resulted.

As we conclude today's lesson, we can reap one last benefit from the Bereans' approach to teaching. Soon the Jews in Thessalonica found out Paul was preaching in Berea. They were vindictive enough to travel 50 miles to agitate and stir up the people! As long as congregations exist, there will always be someone ready and willing to stir up the people. The original word for *stir up* has an interesting meaning that provides proper closure for today's lesson. The word *saleuo* means "to rock, topple, shake, stir up" (Strong's). The enemy of our souls will use every means and every human agent he can to topple us and shake us up. If all we have going for us is the opinions of men through sermons or lessons, when life shakes us up, little is left. When we've learned to examine the Scriptures for ourselves, we have a few things nailed down when life starts to rock. I cannot express to you how studying God's Word has helped me when the earth around me seemed to quake. At times when everything seemed to fall apart in my life, the Word abiding in me kept me from falling apart with them.

*H*ow does God want you to respond to what He showed you today?

What is at least one Scripture or biblical concept you've nailed down that has kept you from toppling when everything around you seemed to rock?

_____

_____

_____

_____

_____

_____

As you continue to study the Word of God, one nailed down, personally discovered truth will turn into many; and you will be better equipped to face anything that comes your way. Nothing will profit you more than learning to examine the Scriptures for yourself. Let every preacher and teacher be a catalyst to your own personal journey through the Word. Spend time exploring. Invest in an exhaustive Bible concordance, a good Bible dictionary, and a sound set of commentaries. Accept more opportunities like this one to get into in-depth Bible studies and really get to know the Word. Be ready and willing to receive from the many opportunities available—but with the ability to discern truth from error through deep personal examinations of the Scripture. Imitating the noble practices of the Bereans will be your safety as teachers come and go—and your sanity when life rocks and rolls.

[1]Trent C. Butler et al., eds., *Holman Bible Dictionary* (Nashville: Holman Bible Publishers, 1991), 899.

Unexpected Sojourners and Wider Paths

1 Thessalonians 3:1-3; 4:13-18

Thirteen points Paul assures us in Scripture will give us hope.

1. Christians don't have to be _____ about other believers who have already died (1 Thess.4:13).

   Falling asleep means "to _____ _____ or to lie down" (2 Cor. 5:6-9).

2. Christians don't have to grieve without _____ (1 Thess. 4:13). The meaning for

   hope can be interpreted as anxious _____.

3. Our hope is in a glorious future _____ of all believers in Christ.

4. This future resurrection of believers who have died in Christ is as _____ as Christ's

   past _____ (1 Thess. 4:14).

5. We do not know the _____ this ingathering will take place (1 Thess. 5:1-3; Matt. 24:36).

6. God made a special provision for those who _____ before Christ's return for believers (1 Thess. 4:15).

7. The Lord _____ will come down from heaven with a _____ _____ (1 Thess. 4:16).

   Keleusma, the original word for *loud command* means:
   First, for the soldiers charging their _____.
   Second, for _____ inciting their _____ (2 Kings 2:10-13).

8. Christ's coming will be accompanied by the voice of the _____ (1 Thess. 4:16).

9. A _____ will sound the ingathering (1 Thess. 4:16).

10. The _____ in Christ will rise first; then those who are still alive will be _____ _____
    together with them (1 Thess. 4:16-17). *Meet* means a "meeting from every conceivable direction."

11. We will meet the Lord in the _____ (1 Thess.4:17).

12. All Christians will receive new imperishable forms or _____ at this ingathering (1 Cor. 15:51-54).

The original Greek word *atomos* means "_____."
The word *caught up* means "to rob, to seize."

13. All Christians will be with the Lord _____ (1 Thess. 4:17-18; Job 19:23-27).

WEEK 5

An Unfamiliar Road

Day 1
The Idols of Athens

Day 2
With Fear and Trembling

Day 3
The Tentmakers

Day 4
One Stick of Dynamite

Day 5
A Great Show of God's Glory

This week we will reach the mid-point of our journey with the apostle Paul. I feel like we just got started, don't you? Flip back through the pages preceding this one and take a look at all you've accomplished. You've worked too hard to stop now. Anyway, exciting adventures await us over the weeks to come! I'm not giving away a single clue. You'll have to stay aboard and discover them for yourself! We will conclude our study of Paul's second missionary journey this week. We will share a rare look at the apostle Paul. Believe it or not, he could be insecure and intimidated. Find out for yourself as you seek the answers to the following questions.

Principal Questions
Day 1: How was Paul's visit to Athens particularly unique?
Day 2: What was Paul's apparent state of mind when he came to Corinth?
Day 3: Why did Paul take extra measures to consecrate himself to God in Corinth?
Day 4: How would you describe Apollos?
Day 5: What are several extraordinary miracles God performed through Paul in Ephesus?

God is so awesome. He chooses to do extraordinary works through ordinary men—and women! Through our study, let's learn how we can develop a passion and perseverance that will enable us to be part of something extraordinary!

DAY 1

The Idols of Athens

Today we will have a lesson in contrasts. The next audience Paul encountered differed drastically from the noble Bereans. As we journey on with the tenacious missionary, we will meet the ancient Athenians and wonder how people who knew so much could understand so little.

*R*ead Acts 17:16-34 and complete the following.

1. According to verse 16 Paul reacted very strongly to the sight of a city full of idols. Imagine going on a mission trip to a city like Varanasi, India— a Hindu holy city filled with temples and images depicting hundreds of gods. What feelings would you have?

_____

_____

2. Which of the following terms seem to describe the Athenians? Choose as many as you think apply.

❏ open-minded ❏ argumentative ❏ intellectual
❏ closed-minded ❏ philosophic ❏ responsive

3. Reread verses 32-34. Paul's message was met by three distinct responses. What were they?

_____

_____

_____

4. As a witness have you also encountered a time when someone responded in any of these three ways? If so, briefly describe the responses.

_____

_____

_____

This stop on Paul's second missionary journey was unlike all the others. I observed four distinct facts about his visit. First, the city itself was so different. The preceding cities Paul visited were much smaller and less sophisticated. Although Athens was at least 100 years past her days of glory, she was still a sight to behold. Athens had maintained her reputation as the center of higher learning with one of the most sought-after universities in ancient history. She was full of philosophers and freethinkers.

Second, Paul encountered the imposing city all by himself. Presumably escorts left him at the gates, and Timothy and Silas never had a chance to join him before his depar-

Today's Treasure
"'For as I walked around and looked carefully at your objects of worship, I even found an altar with this inscription: TO AN UNKNOWN GOD. Now what you worship as something unknown I am going to proclaim to you'" (Acts 17:23).

ture. We have a tender opportunity to see the sincerity of Paul's heart. Acts 17:17 tells us "He reasoned in the synagogue with the Jews and the God-fearing Greeks, as well as in the marketplace day by day." He had no emotional or spiritual support and probably little physical support. None of the others would have known if he had simply been too intimidated to preach. No one would have blamed him anyway. Yet day by day he tried to reason with any Athenian who would listen, because he was so concerned that they needed Jesus Christ.

A third consideration making this trip peculiar was Paul's speech. I believe you just read one of the best sermons he ever preached. He used the perfect illustration (the unknown God) and drew them to the perfect invitation.

Yet my fourth observation about the uniqueness of this trip is the lack of response to the gospel. Acts 17:34 tells us that only a few people became believers in Athens. Paul never mentions a church resulting from his work. He never made contact with them again as far as we know. Based on the information in Scripture the few believers never multiplied into more. Paul's experience in Athens proves that the best of sermons will never change an unwilling person's heart. On the other hand, the weakest message can have a profound effect on a person willing to listen and be changed.

Why were the hearts of the Athenians as a whole so resistant to the gospel? As we explore a few possible answers to this question, let's allow God to shed light on any philosophies we might share with the Athenians. Their approach to Paul's message hindered the powerful work of the Holy Spirit among them, just as a similar approach will hinder His work today. Consider the following hindrances to a profound work of the Holy Spirit in Athens:

1. *Many did not accept God's uniqueness.* As Paul entered the city, he was completely overwhelmed by the sight of temples and idols. Paul's biggest struggle in approaching the Athenians must have been how to present the God of the Bible as the only true God! He must have felt so small against the monumental task.

Last year I sensed God's call to intercede seriously for the nations of the world. As long as I was preoccupied with my own little part of the world, I could feel fairly good about spiritual things. Then I discovered that such praying tested my faith in the effectiveness of the gospel. When God called me to pray for the nations, I started researching their spiritual health. My eyes were forced open. I was nearly overwhelmed by the odds stacked against Christianity by all the world religions.

We have been called to take the gospel to every nation. We must awaken to our responsibilities and our human inadequacies for the task. Only God can plow through the odds stacked against us, but as we pray and make ourselves available He can and will do it. Billions of lives hang in the balance. No matter how many false gods are worshiped around this globe, we must never lose heart and cease believing in the One True God. He is completely unique. Do not allow Satan to tempt you to believe that God is no different than the gods of the peoples of the world.

*R*ead Isaiah 46:8-11. **Cite every way these Scriptures attest to the uniqueness of our God.**

_____

_____

God is not intimidated by the gods of this world. Nor was He overwhelmed by the idols of the Athenians. Their disbelief did not keep Him from being the One True God. Paul spoke the truth, but most were unwilling to accept the uniqueness of God.

2. Many did not accept God's completeness. God needs nothing, yet He offers us everything. He stands in stark contrast to the petty gods of the Greek pantheon.

*L*ook back at Paul's message to the Athenians in Acts 17:22-31. Cite every way Paul attempted to share God's completeness or sufficiency.

_____

_____

Every breath we take, every move we make, every place we live, and even the time in which we live has been ordained by God. In His mercy, He set a stage in which "Men would seek him and perhaps reach out for him and find him, though he is not far from each one of us" (v. 27). He is complete. Nothing in your life is beyond His jurisdiction. Reach out for Him. He is there.

*H*ow do you feel about God's sovereignty today?
- ❑ Encouraged—I rest in the fact that He is the Lord of Glory.
- ❑ Puzzled—I don't understand how He can permit sin and suffering.
- ❑ Skeptical—I have difficulty believing God is ultimately sovereign.
- ❑ Awed—I am amazed that the Creator and Sustainer of the Universe cares about the details of my life.
- ❑ Other_____

We began today by reviewing several peculiarities of Paul's trip to Athens:
- The city was nearly overpowering.
- Paul courageously confronted the Athenians all by himself.
- Paul delivered one of his finest messages.
- Only a few responded.

As we conclude today, look at one final difference between this trip and many others in Paul's ministry. He was not persecuted nor was he forced to leave the city. Acts 18:1 tells us he simply left. Glance back over the previous chapters. Count the times he ran into very little opposition, or persecution. You will search in vain to find another experience exactly like the one he had in Athens.

Why didn't they lift a hand to persecute him? Because they were too cold to care. Paul's experience in Athens is a perfect example of a situation in which people were open-minded to a fault. Their motto was "anything goes." Everyone was welcome to their own philosophies. Live and let live! If it works for you, go for it! Athens was the birthplace of the tolerance movement. They tolerated virtually any belief, any lifestyle, any philosophy. Every new idea offered them the opportunity to have a good, healthy debate; and then go away virtually unchanged. All thinking was about the mind, not the heart—about challenge, not change. Notice the core of their curiosity in Acts 17:19: "'May we know what this new teaching is that you are presenting?'" They were only concerned about Paul's teaching. They had no concern for the Author of the Book from which he taught.

*H*ow does your practice of your faith resemble or differ from that of the

Athenians? _____
Is God more to you than a religious practice? ❑ Yes ❑ No
Are you allowing Him to really make a difference in your life? ❑ Yes ❑ No

Describe ways your life is different because He is your Lord and Savior?

_____

_____

Often persecution is not nearly the enemy that indifference is. The Athenians did not care if Paul stayed or left. They believed virtually everyone was entitled to his god. A few sneered. Others were polite enough to say they would be willing to listen to his strange teachings again. But most never realized Paul was escorted into town by the one True God. And most never cared.

Today's lesson will change the way I pray about the nations. I cannot count the times I've asked God to crumble the spirit of opposition and persecution in many nations where Christians are a small fighting force. I will still continue to ask God to strengthen and protect those facing opposition and persecution. However, I now find my heart drawn across the map to places where a quieter dragon of perhaps equal force has made his den—the spirit of indifference. Christianity can grow and flourish under some of the most difficult opposition, but it will prosper very little where people refuse to be changed by it.

Join me in praying for nations full of people like the Athenians:

- People who don't acknowledge the uniqueness and completeness of God
- People who see the True and Living God as just another philosophy

*U*se the space below to write a prayer of intercession for the apathetic nations. Ask God to break the barrier of unconcern. Someone may have the veil of indifference torn from his or her eyes today as a result of your prayers. Remember, we are not called to have faith in our ability to pray. We are called to have faith in God's ability to act.

_____

_____

_____

_____

*H*ow does God want you to respond to what He showed you today?

_____

_____

_____

_____

_____

D A Y   2

With Fear and Trembling

Today's Treasure
"I came to you in weakness and fear, and with much trembling" (1 Cor. 2:3).

Today we see Paul as a human being with our insecurities. I find encouragement in the normal emotions and human reactions of some of God's best. How could we ever have the courage to minister if we thought those who preceded us were superhuman? God used average men and women. Paul was not superman. He had the same feelings, fears, and insecurities we share. We gain a new insight into the mind of the apostle as we journey with him to the next stop on his second missionary journey.

*R*ead Acts 18:1-17. Paul had been in danger many times before, yet to our knowledge God never before used a vision to encourage him not to fear. Why do you think God encouraged Paul through a vision on this trip?

_____

_____

The passage offers a golden opportunity to gain a fresh insight into emotions and insecurities of Paul, and all who inhabit an earthly tent of flesh (see 2 Cor. 5:1). Let's look at Paul's state of mind after his departure from Athens and 50-mile hike to Corinth.

*P*aul described how he approached Corinth in 1 Corinthians 2:1-5. Read the passage. In the following columns record those things that were absent and those things that were present in Paul when he came to them.

ABSENT	PRESENT
_____	_____
_____	_____
_____	_____
_____	_____

Let me share what I believe about Paul. Admittedly, I am speculating based on the hints in the accounts. I suspect that Paul's visit to Athens affected him far more than we realize. Few people believed and received Christ. Paul was overwhelmed by the polytheistic beliefs of the residents. They wanted to argue philosophies rather than consider the Truth. The Athenians did not throw Paul from the city or persecute him in any obvious way. The few converts appear to have produced little fruit. Apparently no church was established. Paul spent most of his days in Athens alone. Although 1 Thessalonians 3:1 indicates Timothy and Silas might have come as he asked, they were quickly sent elsewhere. After a brief stay in Athens, he simply moved on in frustration.

Paul had plenty of time to think on his way to Corinth. He spent several grueling days alone. During those long hours, I believe he convinced himself that every effort in Athens had failed. As we often do, I suspect he became so focused on the negative that he lost sight of the positive.

Have you ever noticed how lengthy times of solitude affect us differently depending on our state of mind? Aloneness exaggerates our emotions and sensitivities. For example, we can sometimes sense the presence of God and hear His voice far more clearly when we have several days alone. Solitude can also exaggerate negative feelings. We find ourselves almost thinking too much! We look back on a situation and decide nothing good came from it at all. Insecurity can turn into virtual immobilization, and intimidation can turn into terror!

*H*ave you ever had a lengthy time alone in which your mind "ran away with you" with negative thoughts? ❏ Yes ❏ No   If so, briefly describe.

_____

_____

99

I believe what happened to Paul was similar to what we've experienced when carried away with negative thoughts. The more Paul thought about his experiences in Athens, the worse he felt. First Corinthians 2:1 may suggest that Paul felt intimidated by the Athenians, and those feelings accompanied him to Corinth. Athens attracted intellectuals who could debate eloquently and were very anxious to flaunt their knowledge. As he tried to preach to them, the Epicurean and Stoic philosophers disputed with him. Some sneered, "'What is this babbler trying to say?'" (Acts 17:18).

Paul was the pride of his graduating class—the child prodigy! You can imagine the beating his ego took in Athens. I think Paul felt like a failure. First Corinthians 2:2 says by the time he reached Corinth, he "Resolved to know nothing ... except Jesus Christ and him crucified." Thank goodness, he knew the only thing he really had to know! He determined to base his life and ministry on Christ—his one certainty!

*I*n 1 Corinthians 1:18-20 we see an insight Paul eventually gained from his experience. What evidence do you see to suggest he may have been thinking back on the Athenians?

_____

_____

Now read 1 Corinthians 2:14. How can Paul's insight help you when you feel like a failure because you were unable to persuade an unbeliever?

_____

_____

Paul ultimately gained the insights he wrote in 1 Corinthians; but as he traveled to Corinth he was still in turmoil. On the miles between Athens and Corinth Paul probably hashed and rehashed his experiences. He wished he had said this or that. Sometimes we can't explain exactly what we believe. Other times, we think of just the right answer when it's too late. We end up feeling foolish because we weren't persuasive.

*H*ave you ever felt like you babbled instead of answering intelligently when someone tried to argue with you about your beliefs? ❑ Yes ❑ No If so, describe the situation.

_____

_____

What kind of impact did your experience have on your next opportunity?

_____

Obviously, Paul's experience had a great impact on his next opportunity. He entered Corinth "in weakness and fear, and with much trembling" (1 Cor. 2:3). The word *weakness* comes from an original word used for a sickness. The word suggests that Paul was so scared he was physically ill. The word for *trembling* indicates something we've all experienced: hands shaking from nervousness. The opposite word is *confidence*. By the time Paul reached Corinth, he had lost his confidence. Possibly he wondered if the fruit he had seen in other cities had come from God's blessings on Barnabas or Silas.

*W*hen was the last time you lost your confidence? Or when did you last have to do something that made you so nervous your hands shook and you were physically ill?

_____

You probably didn't know the apostle Paul shared the same feelings. Neither did I. How can you find encouragement in his experience?

_____

_____

The enemy would have enjoyed preventing Paul from ministering in Corinth because of feelings of inadequacy, but Satan was unsuccessful. God used Paul's feelings to give a great "demonstration of the Spirit's power" (1 Cor. 2:4). The word for *demonstration* in this passage is *apodeixis* which means "proof." What a wonderful term! Do you see what Paul meant? He was so intimidated by the time he reached Corinth, the abundant fruit ultimately produced through his preaching was proof of the Holy Spirit's power!

What about you? Has God ever used you at a time when you felt weak, with little to offer? ❑ Yes ❑ No If so, when? What happened?

_____

_____

God often proves Himself when we feel we have the least to offer. In 1 Corinthians 1:26-31 Paul explains why God sometimes uses this method. Perhaps Paul's words will mean more to you now that you know how he felt when he left Athens.

*A*ccording to 1 Corinthians 1:26-31, why does God sometimes use us most powerfully when we feel the least adequate?

_____

God has proved Himself faithful so many times when I felt inadequate or like a failure. Just before the filming of my first video series God allowed me to go through a very difficult time. My confidence took a severe beating. I was so emotionally exhausted over a situation that I did not know how I would get through the taping. I sat before the Lord very early the morning we were to begin taping, and I told Him I did not think I was going to make it. I had worked so hard in preparation; yet as the time arrived, I had nothing to offer. I was too tired to even sob! The tears simply ran down my cheeks.

I wearily said to the Lord, "You're on Your own here. I have nothing to give." The skies did not open that very second with a divine outpouring of strength. I walked on the set three hours later completely in faith. Thousands of dollars worth of equipment had been shipped to Houston. An amazing number of personnel worked to prepare. Six cameras were strategically set in place. An audience had gathered. Everything and everyone was ready—but me. I walked out on that set with only enough strength to get on my knees in front of them and pray.

When I got up off my knees to teach, a stream of strength seemed to pour from Heaven. Not in buckets. It was more like an intravenous drip. Just enough for me to know He was sustaining me minute by minute. I never felt a rush of adrenaline. I never felt a sudden gust of mighty wind. All I know is that many demanding hours of work took place over the days of that taping, and never did I lack the strength necessary to complete the task. Never in my adult life have I had less confidence, yet He gave me enough of His to keep my knees from buckling.

You may wonder why God allowed me to go through such a difficult season of inadequacy just before this task. I wondered myself until I received the first letter from a viewer of the video series. I wept as I read her words of thanks; and I whispered back, "It was God. Not me." With the second taping came another set of circumstances through which God proved Himself. I laughed with my assistant when I was asked to do a third series and we both said, "I wonder what's going to happen this time!"

Perhaps God has opened a door for you, but you have no confidence. Is insecurity holding you back from the ministry God has for you? Each of us struggles with insecurities and the loss of confidence. No one has ever been used more mightily than the apostle Paul, yet he was so scared at times he made himself sick!

*H*ow does God want you to respond to what He showed you today?

_____

_____

_____

_____

_____

I don't ask you to write an entire Scripture unless I am convinced that by concentrating enough to write it on paper, God will write it on your heart. Please write the following Scriptures in the space below.

Proverbs 3:26 _____

_____

Jeremiah 17:7 _____

_____

Oh, beloved, God is faithful. Even when the enemy tries to batter us and make us lose confidence, God can steal the victory with a demonstration of the Spirit's power. In those times God sometimes produces a harvest of fruit unlike any other. Those who have been touched are encouraged in a faith that does "not rest on men's wisdom, but on God's power" (1 Cor. 2:5). They end up seeing God instead of us. Hallelujah.

D A Y   3

The Tentmakers

Today's Treasure
"Because he was a tentmaker as they were, he stayed and worked with them"
(Acts 18:3).

We will be using the same text in Acts today, but with a completely different emphasis. Your reading will take you one verse further than day 2. Dr. Luke seems to have included a sentence of pure trivia; in it we will discover a hidden treasure.

*R*ead Acts 18:1-18 and complete the following.
1. Why did Paul stay with Aquila and Priscilla?

_____

2. Who joined Paul in Corinth? Choose any which apply.
   ❑ Timothy   ❑ Barnabas   ❑ Silas
   ❑ Luke   ❑ John Mark   ❑ Jason

3. What influential person believed in the Lord? _____
What fruit resulted from his salvation?

_____

4. How long did Paul stay in Corinth? Choose one.
   ❑ 2 years   ❑ 18 months   ❑ 1 year

5. What bit of trivia does Dr. Luke seem to be sharing with the reader in
verse 18 about Paul's activity in Cenchrea? Choose one.
   ❑ He dropped in on old friends.   ❑ He got a haircut.
   ❑ He ate a good meal.   ❑ He bought a new suit of clothes.

Some verses seem so strange—even out of place at times. At first glance, Acts 18:18 seems one of those. Luke's writing is so tight, so succinct, his inclusion of Paul's quick stop by the barbershop is almost comical. Why in the world would we need to know Paul got a haircut? Actually, this verse holds a primary key to understanding Paul's visit to Corinth. The point is not Paul's haircut. The point is the reason for Paul's haircut.

Verse 18 tells us Paul's haircut resulted from a vow he had made. Remember, Paul was a Jewish Christian. His Jewish heritage was deeply rooted. He understood Christ did not save him to make him forget but to complete that heritage. At times he still applied some of the former practices of the Jew, not as legalities but as wise choices. Virtually without a doubt, the vow to which Luke was referring was the Nazirite vow.

$\mathcal{R}$ead Numbers 6:1-8. The second verse perfectly explains the nature of this vow. Fill in the following blanks according to the NIV. "Speak to the Israelites and say to them:

'If a man or woman _____ to make a _____ vow, a vow of

_____ to the Lord as a Nazirite.'"

Your first blank called for the word *wants*, demonstrating the first crucial element of the Nazirite vow—it was voluntary. You filled in your second blank with the word *special*. The Nazirite vow was special because of its voluntary nature, and because it was offered to men and women alike (v. 2)—unusual in ancient Judaism. The purpose of the vow is found in the final blank: *separation*. The original Hebrew word is *pala* indicating something consecrated to God, distinguished from others, and something marvelous and even miraculous often coming from something difficult (Strong's).

Now let's see if we can put that definition into understandable terms. If an Israelite man or woman was going through a time when he or she felt the necessity to be extraordinarily consecrated to God, the person would voluntarily take this vow. Usually they would choose to take the vow when experiencing difficult circumstances or temptations. To be victorious or obedient they needed extra help and concentration on God.

Paul's recent experiences in Athens were not the only problems he faced in coming to Corinth. He must also confront incredible depravity in this very cosmopolitan city. Even by today's standards, Corinth was extremely sexually explicit. The most significant

103

pagan practice was the cult of Aphrodite. An imposing temple for the worship of Aphrodite was perched right on the top of the Acropolis. More than the goddess of love, she represented lust and every kind of sexual perversion. Her followers literally worshiped her through acts of immorality—often in plain sight. Paul had never seen anything remotely similar to the perversion he must encounter in Corinth.

The haircut in verse 18 is not the beginning of the vow. The haircut signaled the end. Before he entered Corinth's gates, Paul wisely committed himself to the vow of the Nazirite so he could maintain consecration to and concentration on Christ, the only One who could lead him to victory (see 2 Cor. 2:14).

Paul's actions teach us an important lesson. We need to avoid temptation, but when we must face it, we can prepare ourselves.

When you must face temptation, how can you take extra measures to remain consecrated to God?

Numbers 6:3 commands anyone taking the Nazirite vow to abstain from wine or strong drink. Why would abstaining from alcohol be wise for someone trying to have an extraordinary amount of consecration to God?

I have chosen to abstain from alcohol not because I believe alcohol is forbidden, but because I believe it could become a distraction to me. No one told me to abstain from alcohol. I voluntarily made the decision after an honest self-evaluation. I do not believe I could deal with both alcohol and the serious devotion God has asked of me. I can think of too many ways Satan could use it to trap me.

Another practice of the Nazirite is our clue to understanding Acts 18:18. Those who took the Nazirite vow were to allow their hair to grow long as a physical sign of special devotion to God. If they temporarily forgot their vow, the quickest glance in a mirror would remind them. Others would also ask why they let their hair grow so long, and they would have an opportunity to testify about their devotion to God. Once Paul's need for extraordinary consecration to God was over, he went to Cenchrea and got a haircut!

I am impressed with Paul at this point. How about you? His weaknesses, insecurities, and temptations were the same as ours; but he was wise in dealing with them.

Matthew 10:16 is one of my favorite verses. How did Paul exhibit this Scripture while he was in Corinth?

In Matthew 10:16 innocence does not mean naiveté. In fact, had Paul approached Corinth naively, he could have gotten into serious trouble. The kind of innocence Christ described was righteousness in spite of reality!

Paul intended to keep his head on straight while in Corinth. He did not want to be enticed into any kind of trouble. He applied another bit of wisdom which offered him further protection while he was there. He purposely did not take money from the Corinthians. He was careful to avoid the temptations which sometimes accompany money and ministry. A Macedonian church sent him some money so he would be free to preach, but he supported himself by a far more typical method—he got a job!

*I*n Acts 18:2-3 we meet a couple who became good friends and coworkers with the apostle Paul. What were their names?

_____

Those names sound good together, don't they? Like Beth and Keith, you might say. Paul stayed with this godly couple because he was a tentmaker as they were. What wonderful opportunities we've had to see the human side of Paul! The more we view him as a person not so different from us, the more we will see ourselves with the potential for his kind of godly passion. Paul's deep spirituality did not keep him from getting hungry at supper time or needing a new pair of sandals after a 50-mile hike! Have you ever noticed God never lets our heads get so lofty that our feet leave the ground?

Paul sometimes had to support himself through the trade he learned as a boy. I wonder if he saw this necessity to return to the secular workplace as a hindrance to ministry or an opportunity to minister.

*H*ow could God use Paul's return to secular work to benefit the kingdom?

_____

_____

Often, those who labor in the secular work force have opportunities preachers and Bible teachers will never have. Week 4, day 3 touched briefly on the contribution Lydia (a professional businesswoman) made to Paul's ministry. She was able to balance her work life and her spiritual life in a remarkable way. Today we have an opportunity to focus on another way God can use people in the work force. They are sometimes His only means of getting into environments where Christianity is otherwise unwelcome.

Through one of the handbooks I use as a guide to pray for the nations, I've learned to appreciate the term *tentmaker*. This term is based on Paul's example. It identifies a person using a secular skill or profession as a platform for sharing the gospel where Christianity is prohibited. Many workers have left the comforts and financial benefits of the United States to go into hostile environments for the specific purpose of ministry. These tentmakers are so worthy of our respect.

According to *Operation World,* "There are about 60 nations in the world where [tentmaking] is the major means for gaining entry into a country and in 33 of these it is the only way."[1] Tentmakers need our prayers as badly as any missionaries. They are surrounded by those of entirely different belief systems. They have no means of public worship. They are often isolated and lonely, and long for Christian encouragement. They are also in great danger of imprisonment or death for witnessing. They must think of creative ways to share their faith. They take great risks in slipping a few pages of Scripture to those who are interested. Their calling is very difficult.

These tentmakers make great sacrifices because they do not want people to die without Christ. In many nations, tentmakers are the only light in the darkness. We will frequently stop and pray during these 10 weeks. I am praying right now that God will burden your heart for the difficult calling of tentmakers all over the world—especially in parts of the Middle East, Asia, and Africa.

How does God
want you to respond
to what He showed
you today?

_____

_____

_____

_____

_____

Pause now and intercede for tentmaking missionaries. Pray for their safety, for opportunities to witness, for their encouragement. Pray for influential people to be saved.

Crispus in Corinth was such an influential person. His salvation led to the salvation of many other Corinthians. We serve the same God who was active in Paul's day. If He could save people in a cult-driven society spewing with depravity like Corinth, He can save anywhere. He's just looking for a few willing tentmakers.

We can also be tentmakers without going to a foreign destination. Many ways exist for us to be effective tentmakers on the job. We can demonstrate excellence in our work. We can show humility. We can apologize when we're wrong. We can display a Christian calendar, a Christian book, or Bible on our desks. Believe me, these characteristics will draw attention in our present society. After work hours, we can witness with all our hearts as God leads and provides opportunities. Tentmaking is a very noble profession, my working friend, as long as you don't hide under the tent! Stay visible. Maintain integrity. God is using you more than you know.

D A Y   4

One Stick of Dynamite

Today's Treasure
*"Meanwhile a Jew
named Apollos, a
native of Alexandria,
came to Ephesus. He
was a learned man,
with a thorough knowl-
edge of the Scriptures.
He had been instructed
in the way of the Lord,
and he spoke with
great fervor and taught
about Jesus accurately,
though he knew only
the baptism of John"
(Acts 18:24-25).*

Continue tracing Paul's travels on your map. He concluded his second missionary journey in Antioch (see Acts 18:23); but practically before he could unpack his suitcase and wash his clothes, he was traveling through Galatia and Phrygia. When you reach his brief stay in Antioch be sure and change pens to a third color. The subsequent travels constitute his third missionary journey. As you mark your map, when Scripture tells us he traveled from place to place throughout a region, simply assume he stopped in the major cities.

Today we work through the end of Acts 18, but consider the Scriptures in sections. Begin by reading Acts 18:19-23 and complete the following.
1. How do you know the Jews were obviously receptive to Paul's messages at the synagogue? Choose one.
  ❏ They asked him to stay longer.   ❏ They were baptized.
  ❏ They took him into their homes.   ❏ They didn't persecute him.

2. How did Paul respond to their invitation?

_____

3. When Paul departed Ephesus, Priscilla and Aquila remained. What does 1 Corinthians 16:19 tell us they did in Ephesus, a city in Asia?

_____

People who use their homes for ministry must make sacrifices in frequently opening their homes to others. Perhaps you're like me. I'm around groups of people so much, I sometimes resist opening my home. I want to maintain my own quiet sanctuary. What blessings we miss when we do not open our homes to the fellowship and discipleship of other believers.

*P*aul remained in Antioch for a brief furlough. Then he returned once again to the churches in Galatia and Phrygia. What was his purpose?
- ❏ to appoint elders
- ❏ to strengthen the disciples
- ❏ to find Barnabas
- ❏ to discipline the churches

Recall Paul's last experience with the Jews in the synagogue of Corinth. He became so frustrated with them, "he shook out his clothes in protest and said, 'Your blood be on your own heads! I am clear of my responsibility. From now on I will go to the Gentiles'" (Acts 18:6). I thought he had finished preaching to the Jews altogether. But in Ephesus he made a beeline to the synagogue and reasoned with them again. Paul's ministry was far more productive among the Gentiles, so why did he continue to return to the Jews in virtually every city he visited?

In Romans 9:2-5 Paul answers that question. He so desperately wanted his fellow Jews to know Christ that, if possible, he would have died for them. He could hardly bear for the Jews to miss Christ. He must have been ecstatic over the favorable response of the Jews at the synagogue in Ephesus. They were open enough to his messages to ask him to spend more time with them.

Again we see why Paul was such an effective minister and servant. He had surrendered his life to the leadership of the Holy Spirit. He was not driven by his own desires and rationalizations. In his position, I might have convinced myself I was supposed to remain in Ephesus at least for a while based on two criteria:
- my own desires to see God do a work among a people I loved, and
- an apparent open door.

They were begging for more! Yet Paul resisted making assumptions based on those two influences. Instead, Acts 18:20 tells us he declined. The original word is *ou* which means "no, expressing direct and full negation, independently and absolutely." Paul firmly and lovingly said no.

I have a difficult time saying the word *no*. Do you? Why do you think we have such a difficult time saying no?

_____

_____

Paul probably had a difficult time saying no, but he was careful to remain focused on God's priorities for him. Paul's example teaches us a timely lesson today. The fact that a need exists does not mean God has called me to meet that need.

Can you think of a time when an opportunity to serve seemed so rational for you, but you realized later it was not God's will for your life?

_____

_____

107

You probably learned from the experience just like I have when I realized my rationalizations had misled me. When was the last time you said no to a great opportunity because you were convinced the open door was not meant for you?

Recently I saw a sticker which said, "There is a God and you're not Him." A good reminder, isn't it? We are wise to trust Him when He seems to be leading us contrary to those things we want to do or those things which seem to be so rational and fitting.

*W*e now get to discover one reason God did not lead Paul to remain in Ephesus. Read Acts 18:24-28 and complete the following.

1. Which of the following sentences accurately describe Apollos? Choose any which apply.

❏ He taught about Jesus accurately.   ❏ He was an educated man.
❏ He knew the Scriptures thoroughly.   ❏ He spoke with passion.
❏ He knew about John's baptism.

2. In what way do you see Priscilla and Aquila opening their home once again for the sake of the gospel?

_____

_____

3. To our knowledge, Paul never met Apollos, but what evidence of his influence can you find in verse 28?

_____

_____

I love studying the Word of God to get to know new people in Scripture. Just think how much fun we'll have meeting some of them face-to-face in Heaven! Several characteristics make Apollos a servant worthy of our attention:

1. His way with Scripture. The NIV says Apollos "was a learned man, with a thorough knowledge of the Scriptures" (Acts 18:24). In this verse, the KJV packs a better punch. It says he was "mighty in the scriptures." The original word for *might* is *dunatos* which means powerful (Strong's). From it we derive the word *dynamite*. When Apollos spoke, he was dynamite with the Scriptures. His teaching could blow your wig off!

*T*hink of someone you've heard preach or teach who was dynamite with the Scriptures. What made the teaching so dynamic?

_____

_____

Now, perhaps you have a picture of what Apollos might have been like.

2. He was passionate about God. Verse 25 tells us he spoke with great fervor. Anyone can be loud, boisterous, and demonstrative, but I don't think passion for God is easy to fake. Some of the most passionate people I know are those who are soft-spoken but deeply moved by God and His Word. I am so blessed and drawn to people when I sense a passion for the Lord Jesus in the things they say or do. In today's society, we don't lack passion. Passion constantly invades our television screens by way of advocates for numerous causes from animal rights to political parties. Even as believers in Christ, we can be more passionate about some cause than we are about God. Not Apollos. The word picture drawn by the Greek term for *fervor* is a boiling pot of water.

*L*uke 6:45 perfectly explains Apollos' speaking ministry. What is the basis of the words which come out of a person's mouth?

_____

_____

You see, Apollos couldn't help but speak. God had so much cooking in him, he was about to boil over. He spoke because he was compelled!

3. He was faithful with the little he knew. All Apollos knew was John the Baptist's message about Jesus and John's baptism unto repentance (the practice of confessing and repenting of sin so there will be a readiness to receive Jesus, Matt. 3:1-3,11). Apollos was faithful with everything he knew; he just didn't know the rest of the story!

4. He was teachable. Most of us don't like to be told we don't know everything! When corrected, we can be shocked and insulted like we've just heard an unwanted news flash! Not Apollos. Priscilla and Aquila brought him into their home and told him the rest of the story. And guess what? He listened!

In this account God allows us to see at least one reason Paul did not stay in Ephesus. He didn't know it, but the void left an opening for a dazzling preacher named Apollos. When we can't say no even when God does not give His approval, two unfortunate repercussions often result: We don't do a good job, and we don't leave an opening for God's chosen person to fill.

Like me, when someone asks for a volunteer, you may feel you must raise your hand if 15 seconds pass. We think, "If no one raises her hand, I guess it has to be me!" God may be wanting to raise up that timid person who has never said a word. She may have to go home and let God work on her for a few days before she has the courage to volunteer; but if someone jumps forward just to fill the gap she will remain uninvolved.

The account of Apollos lends us one more lesson before we close today. He traveled to Achaia to preach. Corinth was the capital of Achaia, so he walked into exactly the same audiences the apostle Paul had. With his new-found knowledge, Apollos even preached the same kind of message but with his own style.

*T*ake a good glimpse into human nature as Paul later addressed the believers in Corinth in 1 Corinthians 1:12-13 and 1 Corinthians 3:3-9. How did the believers respond to those who came and preached to them?

_____

_____

We tend to compare Christian leaders and fall into camps behind our choices. We must make a concerted effort to avoid doing so. Each of us could cite an example, but one readily comes to my mind. Every branch of in-depth Bible study has loyal supporters who swear by that particular method or teacher, as if it were the only one anointed by God. Some would rather fight than switch. God is wooing people to His table for the meat of His Word like never before. He is joyfully using many different methods and styles to accomplish His goal of equipping His church to be effective and holy during difficult days.

God has raised many fine teachers and preachers for our day. Let's reap the benefit of as many as possible and value their contributions whether they are magnetic like Apollos, analytical like Luke, forthright like Paul, or warm like Priscilla and Aquila. Paul's style may have been one reason some of the Corinthians preferred Apollos: Paul didn't mince words. His answer to camping around certain speakers? Oh, grow up! (1 Cor. 3:3-4). I've ended with a snicker today. Hope you did, too.

*H*ow does God want you to respond to what He showed you today?

_____

_____

_____

_____

_____

_____

109

DAY 5

A Great Show of God's Glory

Today's Treasure
*"God did extraordi-
nary miracles through
Paul" (Acts 19:11).*

My oldest daughter, Amanda, was very frightened of storms when she was little. Loud peals of thunder sent her into near panic, even when we were in the safety of our home. One day when the sky seemed to be falling, I held her in my arms and said, "Honey, the heavens are just displaying the glory of God (see Ps. 19:1). They are showing us how mighty He is." Her little forehead furrowed as if she was really thinking over what I had said. Some weeks later, she was upstairs playing when a storm hit. I heard her feet scurry like lightening down the stairs. Then she yelled at the top of her lungs, "Mommy! God's really showing off today!"

God seemed to work "overtime" on Paul's next stop as He revealed His power in extraordinary ways. God used special demonstrations of power to authenticate His ambassadors and persuade belief. As we accompany Paul on the next lap of his third missionary journey, we will witness some pretty exciting events. We might end up agreeing with Amanda: "God's really showing off today."

*R*ead Acts 19:1-23 and complete the following.
1. Consider verses 1-7. What was the purpose of John's baptism?

_____

_____

How did John's baptism differ from Christian baptism?

_____

_____

2. Read verses 11 and 12. What does the word *extraordinary* (NIV) or *special* (KJV) say to you in regard to the miracles God performed in Ephesus?

_____

_____

3. The seven sons of Sceva used the name of Jesus to try to cast out demons. Why do you think they were unsuccessful?

_____

_____

4. Jews and Gentiles alike responded in awe to the events happening around them and ultimately held the name of the Lord Jesus in high honor. In what two ways did their awe turn into action? (vv. 18-19)
   ❑ Many fell on their faces.　　❑ They worshiped Jesus.
   ❑ Many confessed evil deeds.　❑ Many burned the sorcery scrolls.

5. What was the result of virtually an entire city highly esteeming the name of Christ and cleansing their homes of evil materials? Choose one.
   ❑ God performed more miracles.
   ❑ The Word of the Lord spread and grew in power.
   ❑ People were baptized.

I told you God was showing off! He was showing off His Son! In the verses below, you will discover two general purposes for miracles in the New Testament. How does each purpose ultimately center on Christ?

Acts 2:22 _____

Hebrews 2:3-4 _____

Paul was not confused about the extraordinary powers displayed through his ministry. What reason did he cite in Romans 15:17-19 for God doing signs and wonders through him?

_____

_____

God works in countless ways we cannot see. He remains active in our lives even when we are unaware. Sometimes, however, He makes Himself entirely obvious so that what we see will strengthen our faith in what we cannot see. The early church was learning concepts completely new to most. God purposely showed His visible handprints so many would place their lives in His invisible hands. Let's reflect on a few ways He made Himself or His work obvious in Ephesus.

1. God made His Holy Spirit obvious. The original converts knew virtually nothing about the Spirit. Even their knowledge of the Old Testament didn't help much, because His activity was so different after the coming of Christ. Remember, in the Old Testament, only about 100 people were ever described as having the Holy Spirit in or on them. Prior to Christ and the birth of the New Testament church, the Holy Spirit's purpose was not to mark salvation, but to empower certain individuals for designated tasks. Since the birth of the church, the Holy Spirit takes up residence in every believer in Christ (see Rom. 8:9). John's baptism was a sign of repentance in anticipation of the coming Christ. Christian baptism is a mark to demonstrate the salvation Christ has given and the receipt of the Holy Spirit.

God knew the concept of the Holy Spirit would be difficult for new believers to understand as He raised up His church. Therefore, He sometimes accompanied His Spirit with a sudden physical evidence like speaking in tongues. Few topics have caused division like speaking in tongues. No matter what you believe about tongues, during his ministry Paul was clear on at least two points concerning the activity of the Holy Spirit:

- All believers are baptized by the Holy Spirit. The Spirit resides in all believers equally (see 1 Cor. 12:13).
- Not all spoke in tongues (see 1 Cor. 12:30).

Many believe God never uses the gift of tongues today. Many others believe God always gives the gift of tongues to every true believer. I believe we are wise to avoid words like always and never. He told us to love one another, not judge one another.

2. God made obvious His blessing on true discipleship. Interestingly, the same group who previously asked Paul to spend more time with them (see Acts 18:20) quickly got over him when he returned! "Some of them became obstinate," and Paul took a group aside and began discipling them daily (Acts 19:9). Can you imagine being part of that Bible study? Don't miss the bountiful fruit produced from Paul's discipleship group: within two years "all the Jews and Greeks who lived in the province of Asia heard the word of the Lord" (Acts 19:10). The churches of Laodicea, Colosse, and Hieropolis were all founded as a result of this great and supernatural movement of God.

Like Gideon's army (see Judg. 7), a few well-trained soldiers in the Lord's service can be more effective than hundreds who have never been discipled. God honors His Word and often overtly blesses discipleship with fruit far beyond human effort.

*R*ead Acts 19:9 once again. What was one of the methods Paul used to disciple?

❑ parables   ❑ miracles   ❑ discussion   ❑ debate

In your opinion, why would teaching followed by discussion be an effective form of discipleship?

_____

_____

Yes, Paul was an effective teacher; but God still produced fruit far beyond his efforts. When a few seeds produce a huge crop, God's up to something supernatural! Acknowledge it and praise Him!

3. God made His ambassador obvious. God clearly tells us through His Word that the method He used to mark authenticity in the apostle Paul was rare. God meant to draw attention to the apostle Paul because He knew the apostle could be trusted to bring attention to Him. In one way, Paul was no different than the handkerchiefs. God used the ordinary to do the extraordinary.

4. God made His power over the occult obvious. We now have the opportunity to discover one reason why God was showing His marvelous power to such a degree in this particular city. Ephesus was a renowned center for magical incantations. In his book *Paul the Traveller,* Ernle Bradford wrote, "Ephesus was the centre of occult studies, indeed it has been called 'The Home of Magic.'"[2] He also tells us, "Ephesus was full of wizards, sorcerers, witches, astrologers, diviners of the entrails of animals and people who could read one's fortune by the palm of the hand or the fall of knucklebones."[3] Many of the Ephesians were neck deep in the occult, but virtually the entire population was extremely interested in supernatural phenomena and the powers of the unseen world. This is one reason Paul was most outspoken to them about spiritual warfare in his letter to them, the Book of Ephesians. While Paul was in their midst, God intentionally got their attention by surpassing anything they had ever seen. Even the articles that touched the apostle were used by God to cure illnesses and remove evil spirits.

I see humor in the scene of the seven sons of Sceva who didn't realize that the power of Jesus' name is for the people of Jesus' name. The evil spirit responded to their efforts by saying, "'Jesus I know, and I know about Paul, but who are you?'" (Acts 19:15). What a slap in the face! People would rather be insulted than insignificant! Actually, the encounter turned into more than a verbal slap in the face. The last we saw of the seven sons of Sceva, they were flying through the door one by one naked and bleeding. Their pride wasn't the only thing that took a beating.

5. God made true repentance obvious. This activity of the Holy Spirit is perhaps my favorite of those God performed in Ephesus. Some works of God are more subtle but not necessarily less supernatural.

*W*hat is one of the most important activities of the Holy Spirit according to John 16:8?

_____

Now read Matthew 3:8. What do you think this verse means?

_____

_____

How does Scripture demonstrate the fruit of repentance in Acts 19:17-19?
- ❏ People publicly confessed their evil deeds.
- ❏ Many joined the church.
- ❏ People were baptized and spoke in tongues.
- ❏ Many people burned their books of witchcraft.

From the beginning of our lesson today, we established that God can reveal Himself through natural means or supernatural means. Both are at His complete disposal. Although God also worked in subtle ways, He apparently chose to reveal Himself through several phenomenal means while Paul was in Ephesus. Why did He make His activity so obvious among the Ephesians? Because Satan had made his work so obvious there. Satan is powerful, but he is no match for the Almighty God.

Sometimes I am completely perplexed by God's willingness to humor man. His mercy knows no bounds. When He wanted to lead the Magi to the Christ Child, He did not lead them by a mark in the sand. He led them through a star because they were star gazers—then He went beyond anything they had ever seen. In the same way, when God wanted to lead the Ephesians to the Savior, He did not lead them through a cloudy pillar. He got their attention through supernatural phenomena, because that's where they were looking. God wants to be found. He does not will for any to miss Him; and He is so gracious to show up right where we are looking—so He can take us beyond anything we've ever seen.

God sometimes reveals Himself to a homeless man hiding under a bridge through a blanket brought to him by a caring minister. He sometimes reveals Himself to a drunk through a servant who cares for him and offers him Living Water. He sometimes reveals Himself to a prostitute through a godly policeman who tells her Christ can set her free. If we're waiting for the needy to simply walk through our church doors, we may wait a long time. God doesn't just wait for people to come to Him. He goes to them and desires to intervene right at the point of their need. He's just looking for a few brave people, like the apostle Paul, who are willing to go rather than wait for them to come. He's not looking for show-offs. He's looking for people through whom He can show off His Son. May we be some of those people.

As you conclude today, can you think of a time when God intervened and met with you right at the point of your concern? Describe briefly.

_____

_____

_____

How does God want you to respond to what He showed you today?

_____

_____

_____

_____

_____

_____

[1]Patrick Johnstone, *Operation World* (Grand Rapids, MI: Zondervan Publishing House, 1993), 614.
[2]Ernle Bradford, *Paul the Traveller* (New York: Barnes & Noble, 1974), 196.
[3]Ibid., 197.

An Unfamiliar Road

Lessons Paul learned from hardships in Asia

2 Corinthians 1:8-11

1. We sometimes face the most _____ when we're being used most powerfully (v. 8).

    Acts 19:8-12, 17-20; 1 Corinthians 15:30-32

2. The enemy can't squelch the _____ of God so he tries to disable the _____

    of God (v. 8). *Hardship* means "to be _____ on every side."

    Great pressure means "to be _____."

3. Even the most devoted believers can encounter hardships _____ _____ our ability to

    endure (v. 8; 1 Cor. 10:13). *Huperballo* means "to throw beyond, to surpass."

4. Believers can experience _____ (v. 8). The original Greek word for *despair* means

    "to be wholly without _____."

5. Believers can experience feelings of _____ (v. 9). *Sentence* means "answer."

6. God wants us to _____ on Him (v. 9). *Rely* means "to be _____" (1 John 4:16).

7. When our hardships surpass our ability to endure, God wants us to discover His …

    • Surpassing _____ (2 Cor. 4:7). *Power* actually means "achieving power."

    • Surpassing _____ (2 Cor. 4:17). *Glory* means "to recognize."

    • Surpassing _____ (2 Cor. 1:3-5).

8. God has a special _____ in mind when His children suffer hardships (2 Cor. 1:10).

    The original Greek word for *rescue* means "to draw to oneself."

Travel Ties and Hard Good-byes

Day 1
The Riot in Ephesus

Day 2
A Long-Winded Preacher

Day 3
A Tender Heart

Day 4
From the Mouths of Prophets

Day 5
A Prophecy Fulfilled

The apostle Paul's experiences afford the observer with golden opportunities to laugh and cry. This week's studies may deliver both. No one could charge the apostle Paul with aloofness and unavailability among those he served. He got completely involved as you will see. Our present journey will prove that Paul gave his heart and strength as he ministered to each flock. Even though he knew farewells were inevitable, he still formed deep relationships which would make departures painful. He chose to follow the will of God even when his coworkers begged him not to go. Look for the answers to the following questions as you study this week.

Principal Questions
Day 1: What prompted Paul to leave Ephesus?
Day 2: What prompted an eye-opening miracle during one of Paul's long-winded sermons?
Day 3: How would you describe the farewell between Paul and the Ephesian elders?
Day 4: Who was Agabus and how did God use him?
Day 5: How did Paul fellowship in Christ's sufferings in Jerusalem?

How I pray God is having His way in your life. May God enable you to hear Him speak directly to your heart and allow you to sense His tender touch as you study each lesson. He is worthy to be our first priority—our heart's desire.

DAY 1
The Riot in Ephesus

I wonder, do you share my emotions as we reach week 6 of our journey? Time passes so quickly. After anticipating our time together, desiring to savor every moment of the expedition, these 10 weeks will whirl through our lives like every other. I pray that God will set this time apart to bring lasting change, unparalleled service, and a passion for Him. May He never cease using the things we learn as we walk on the apostle's road.

I am going to stop right now and commit myself afresh to God as we journey through the second half of our study. I want to be fully available and completely teachable. Would you join me and use the space below to write a prayer of commitment?

_____

_____

As we begin our study today, please take another look at several Scriptures I purposely did not emphasize on week 5, day 5.

*R*ead Acts 19:21-22.

Paul surely knew the heights and depths in Ephesus. Satan attacked the apostle relentlessly, but he was no match for the power of God. Righteousness prevailed, repentance fell, and Paul had never been more greatly used. About the time the word of the Lord spread widely and grew in power, Paul's missionary heart began to quicken and draw him elsewhere. For the first time, we see the apostle set his sights on a destination unparalleled in his ministry. Much of the remainder of our series will involve his approach and activity in this priority place.

*F*rom the words carefully employed in the text, we receive insight into Paul's motivations:
Paul decided to go to _____ but then felt he must visit _____ also.

While Paul was in Ephesus, the Emperor Claudius was poisoned and the Roman kingdom fell into the hands of a 17-year-old boy named Nero. Christians soon suspected he was the antichrist. God had no intention of Paul missing Rome. He used Paul's reasoning to draw him back to Jerusalem, but He seemed to compel him by a much greater force to set his sights on Rome.

*R*eread verse 21.

The word *decide* seems to indicate the weighing of pros and cons, the consideration of personal desires, rationale. The word definitely indicates choice. In essence, Paul chose to go to Jerusalem, but he felt he must go to Rome. Both examples are valid ways in which God leads His children in service. Let's think about the difference between the two for a moment.

$\mathcal{N}$ame something you decided to do for the sake of the Kingdom based on your own reasoning, personal feelings, and choices.

_____

Now think of something you've felt compelled to do in service for Christ. What has burned within your soul? Perhaps completing this sentence will help you discover the answer to this question: God has allowed me to decide to do a number of things for His sake, but beyond all other

things I feel I must... _____

_____

Paul was flesh and blood just like you and me. We have seen God lead him by many of the same methods He uses in our generation. Today we discover that God directed Paul through wise decisions, as well as burdens that became musts in Paul's life.

Like Paul's decision to go to Jerusalem, I have chosen to do some things for the sake of the Kingdom based on reasoning and personal desires. God sometimes uses our ability to make sound decisions. But like Paul's burden to go to Rome, I feel I must do some things. God compels me to do those things. Teaching is one of those things. People have asked me if I like to teach. I have no idea how to answer. I don't like or dislike teaching. I must do it. If I didn't have a class to teach, I would have to hit the nearest coffee shop with my Bible and a handout! Perhaps you can relate on the basis of a burden God has placed on your heart.

Rome will ultimately be an important part of Paul's life. God did not want him to miss it, so He placed a virtually irresistible compulsion in Paul. Just in case the motivations of wisdom and burden were not enough, we are about to see a third—trouble—lots of trouble.

$\mathcal{W}$e will read the remainder of Acts 19 in brief sections followed by questions and commentary. First, read Acts 19:23-28 . In our study so far, Paul has been opposed only twice by the Gentiles. One opposition is recorded in this text while the other is recorded in Acts 16:16-19. In both examples, what motivated Gentiles to oppose Paul?

_____

Obviously, a person does not have to be entirely genuine to be effective! Demetrius appealed to the people of Ephesus both financially and spiritually. He apparently reasoned that one of those two needles would surely hit a vein in everyone. He may have lacked integrity, but he didn't lack intelligence. His approach worked better than he could have dreamed. The people began shouting, "Great is Artemis of the Ephesians!"

In Greek mythology, Artemis was believed to be the daughter of Zeus. The temple the Ephesians built in her honor was so mammoth, it was "one of the Seven Wonders of the Ancient World."[1] The Ephesians exceeded the size of Artemis' temple, however, with their ability to make a buck in her name. The silver craftsmen were making a fortune off silver charms and statuettes of her likeness. You can be fairly certain most of the merchants cared very little about robbing Artemis of her majesty. You can also be certain the outspoken apostle had assured them she had none.

$\mathcal{N}$ow read Acts 19:29-31. Complete the following.
1. Why did the disciples not want Paul to appear before the crowd?

_____

2. Carefully reconsider verses 30 and 31. Based on the information given in these two verses, cite every assumption you can make about Paul:

_____

_____

I've made my own list of assumptions. In all probability, our lists are similar. Based on verse 30, we may assume that Paul sometimes had more courage than sense! He was going to speak out in behalf of Christianity no matter what! The theater in Ephesus held 25,000 people! When God gives us good sense, He expects us to use it. I believe the only time we are to walk into a dangerous or very risky situation is when we have crystal clear leadership from God.

Also based on verse 30, I believe Paul's disciples were not afraid to disagree with him. He was not a religious dictator who surrounded himself with yes-men. Times obviously existed when his colleagues said no. Remember, he was not only a preacher and teacher, he was a discussion leader (see Acts 19:9). Leaders who are afraid of others disagreeing with them usually don't leave much room for discussion.

I am fairly impressed by a third assumption we can make: Paul sometimes let the wisdom of others dictate over his own desires. We read that they would not let him go. If I know anything at all about the apostle, he had to let them not let him! Short of being physically tied down, I can't imagine how they could stop him from going unless he submitted to their wisdom. He could have rebuked them for not believing that speaking up was worth the risk of dying. Instead, he obviously listened to them and relented. I am refreshed by leaders who do not think they always have to be right.

You may have listed other assumptions, but one more I would like to make is based on verse 31. Paul obviously had many good friends. When we began our journey together 5 weeks ago, I'm not sure any of us pictured him as friendly. Although he possessed a passion for Christ and a perseverance in servitude, I never really thought of him being genuinely gracious. I assumed he was respected far more than he was liked! Paul obviously had good friends from every walk of life: Jews, Gentiles, rich, and poor. Aquilla and Priscilla did not leave their home and travel with Paul because he was unpleasant! Obviously, he possessed a genuinely likable personality. Many people surrendered to serve Christ as a direct result of Paul's influence. Had he been an ogre, people would not have been so anxious to follow his example.

Verse 31 describes another group of people who were extremely fond of Paul: officials of the province. They loved him enough to beg him not to venture into the theater. Let's learn something about judging others. We tend to describe people in brief phrases: he's always funny, she's always so bossy, he's such a controlling person, she never fails to be upbeat. God created human beings to be the most complex creatures alive. None of us can be wrapped up in a single phrase. Yes, Paul could be unyielding, but he could also be persuaded. He could be unlikable, and he could be very gracious. He was not so different than the rest of us, perhaps, on any given day!

$\mathcal{N}$ow read Acts 19:32-41. Complete the following.

1. What does verse 32 tell us about most of the people? Choose one.
   ❏ They did not know why they were there.
   ❏ They did not know Paul.
   ❏ They did not know why Paul had come.

2. Why do you think most of the people came? _____

_____

The Jews probably pushed Alexander to the front to provide a disclaimer for them. They wanted him to tell the crowds that Paul's teaching was separate from theirs and they were not responsible for the financial harm done to the silver craftsmen. The Jews knew without a doubt that the silver craftsmen were profiting off the ignorance and sinful practices of pagans.

$\mathcal{R}$ead Exodus 20:3-4. Briefly, what are the first and second commandments?

First: _____

Second: _____

The Jews certainly had a stake in confronting idolatry. Keeping their beliefs to themselves meant harming their Gentile neighbors. Because of their opposition to Paul, they violated their own consciences and belief system.

$\mathcal{H}$ave you ever violated your own conscience or beliefs because you were angry or opposed to something? ❏ Yes ❏ No If so, describe an example.

_____

Finally, take one last look at verse 35. The Ephesians believed the image of Artemis fell from heaven. Some scholars assume they were describing a meteor which hit Ephesus, and the people imagined it looked like a multi-breasted woman. Therefore, they assumed it was the goddess Artemis and hailed her as the deity of childbirth. I am sometimes amazed over the things people believe.

About seven years ago, I prepared to teach the Book of Genesis in Sunday School. In an attempt to be prepared for questions and rebuttals, I thought I'd study the theory of evolution in preparation to teach creationism. I was somewhat intimidated by the prospect, but I checked out a few books and started my research. I only had to flip a few pages before my chin dropped to the ground. At times I even laughed out loud. I couldn't believe the theory taught as fact in many public schools. After a fairly in-depth comparison, I decided it took far more faith to believe in evolution than creationism!

When Paul came to Ephesus, he brought the message of a Messiah sent from God who offers eternal life to every individual who believes.

I'm no rocket scientist, but I find Paul's message far more believable than a goddess falling out of heaven in the form of a meteor. Yes, God requires faith—but not as much as a number of other belief systems falling out of the skies today. Go ahead and believe Him. He's very believable.

$\mathcal{H}$ow does God want you to respond to what He showed you today?

_____

_____

_____

_____

_____

_____

A Long-Winded Preacher

Today's Treasure
"Seated in a window was a young man named Eutychus, who was sinking into a deep sleep as Paul talked on and on" (Acts 20:9).

I am so amused by today's text. God used my desire to be like Paul to motivate me to write this series. So far, I've noticed that most of the characteristics I share with him are those of his human nature rather than his spiritual nature. A common colloquialism states, "If the shoe fits, wear it." I don't know what size shoe you wear; but I can tell you in advance, this lesson is a size 7 medium. Just my size. Read on. It just may come in your size, too. If it doesn't, at least you'll get a chuckle out of it at my expense.

Read Acts 20:1-12. Trace Paul's travels carefully on your map; then complete the following.

1. Reread verse 3 and use your imagination for a moment. Since Paul was about to set sail for Syria when the Jews were plotting against him, what might have been their plans? Write a brief description of what the Jews might have plotted against Paul.

_____

_____

2. Notice the use of the words *us* and *we* in verses 5 and 6 after the writer of the Book of Acts has used the word *they* for the last several chapters. What assumption can you make over the sudden change in pronouns?

_____

3. Counting Luke, how many people accompanied Paul back through Macedonia? _____

4. Why do you suppose Paul was so long-winded when they met together to break bread?

_____

_____

5. Luke wrote meticulously without inclusion of unnecessary details. What bearing do you think the lamps mentioned in verse 8 had on the account of the midnight meeting?

_____

_____

6. Can you think of any reasons why God made certain Luke joined Paul in time for this strange set of circumstances?

_____

Only God could mingle the typical and the entirely atypical the way we've seen today! Without a doubt, this was an evening when the mundane gave way to the miraculous. Let's take a look at the fairly typical side of this account first. Like many other preachers and teachers, Paul preached longer than his audience was prepared to listen!

We want to grasp the kind of man Paul was as accurately as possible. Paul was so compelled by Christ that his energy seemed to have no bounds. We will do his memory no harm, however, by pointing out that sometimes his energy exceeded that of his audience.

Figuratively speaking, at this point I am pulling this size 7 shoe out of the box and putting it on my guilty foot. I recall a woman saying to me after one of my speeches, "I'm going home and taking a nap. You've worn me out." On behalf of every listener, allow me to make a statement to those of us in teaching, preaching, and speaking positions. Sometimes we talk too long. Mind you, we can have the best of intentions. I can entirely relate with the apostle on his reasoning for being so long-winded: "He intended to leave the next day" (v. 7). This was his last chance, and he was determined to say everything he could before he departed.

In Paul's defense, I must explain one of the pitfalls accompanying the gift of teaching. Teachers often feel that whatever they learn, they must teach—every last word of it! I have 45 minutes on Sunday mornings. I often try to teach everything I learned in hours of preparation. Sometimes I've tried to teach all I knew, and a lot of things I didn't know! Paul obviously didn't always know when to wrap up a message either. Because I tend to be so long-winded, a few reminders often help me. If you find yourself making a presentation, see if these guidelines can help you too.

1. Listeners are far more likely to retain a few succinct points. While preparing, I like to ask myself, "If asked the following day what the message was about, will my listeners be able to state an answer in one sentence?" If I've saturated them with too much information, they will retain very little of it. Better to make one point well, than 10 points poorly. Listeners tend to judge a message according to its ending. Even if the first 45 minutes are interesting but I talk on and on, their frustration will cause them to regard the message unfavorably. As a listener, have you found this to be true?

2. Listeners today tend to listen in short time bursts. With all our computer technology, we've grown accustomed to drive-through data. We look for quick and highly stimulating information. As you watch television, try to count every time your mind is switched to a new stimulus while on the same channel. For example, almost all situation comedies have at least two story lines going at once with a commercial break every eight minutes. As speakers, we may have all sorts of important information to share; but if our presentations aren't stimulating, we lose our audience. We must never compromise our message, but we are wise to choose stimulating methods. I am not proposing dog and pony shows, but I am suggesting studying our target groups and praying about ways they can best be reached for the sake of the gospel.

In what ways have you noticed people today having a shorter attention span than people in the past?

_____

_____

What new methods are you using to mature spiritually?

_____

_____

You might consider such options as Christian videotapes, instead of TV sitcoms, and Bible-teaching audiocassettes rather than listening to the radio while driving.

3. Most listeners will hear other preachers and teachers. I am not in charge of teaching everything a listener needs to know! When Paul preached in Troas, he may have forgotten what he taught the people of Corinth: one person often plants and another waters (see 1 Cor. 3:6). As preachers, teachers, and speakers, sometimes we tend to think of ourselves as planters, waterers, and weed pickers! I don't think God often raises up one-man shows. We are wise to leave a few points for the next messenger to make!

I believe God purposely gave us the opportunity to giggle over a fairly typical event: a preacher or teacher outlasting the audience. However, God provided a very effective eye-opener by doing something quite atypical. He gave Paul a chance to raise the dead!

Picture the scene with me a moment. In ancient homes, the largest room was typically on the top story. A large group of people were gathered in one room and the lamps provided just enough heat to make the atmosphere cozy and warm. Most of the listeners had awakened with the rising sun, and the time was now approaching midnight. A young man by the name of Eutychus was sitting in the windowsill trying to stay attentive. The young man's eyelids would drop; then he would force them open. He finally fell into a deep sleep, probably had a dream which caused him to jump, and out the window he flew. This story would not be humorous without the happy ending. Since you know God raised Eutychus from the dead, wouldn't you have loved to see Paul's face when the boy fell out of the window? He ran downstairs as fast as his spindly legs could carry him. "Paul … threw himself on the young man and put his arms around him. 'Don't be alarmed,' he said, 'He's alive!'" (Acts 20:10). What a relief! A wonderfully rare phenomenon took place that day.

Scripture records two other times when God's servants raised someone from the dead by a similar method. Read both of the following accounts and record the participants and the general circumstances.

Text:	Participants:	Circumstances:
1 Kings 17:7-24	_____	_____
2 Kings 4:8-37	_____	_____

God did not often empower human agents to raise the dead; but, strangely, He allowed three of his ambassadors—Elijah, Elisha, and Paul— to bring someone back to life by similar methods. Of course, there was absolutely no magic in the method. The power was God's alone. Note that Peter also raised Dorcas from the dead (Acts 9:36-42), but he did not employ the method used by the other three.

The similar procedure invites us to see if any other similarities exist. Compare the three accounts for a moment. Can you think of a way they resemble one another? If so, explain.

_____

_____

You may discover a similarity I did not see, but what stands out to me is the potential for the servant of God to be blamed for a tragedy. Elijah, Elisha, and Paul were the most influential men of God in each of their generations. People were forming their opinions about God based on the characteristics they found in His servants.

*H*ere is a thought question. How many people are basing their opinion of God on how they see you act in time of stress or trouble?

They did not have an entire Bible on which to base their beliefs about God. Their opinions of God were based almost entirely on their impressions of His servants. None of the three servants were responsible for the deaths that could have been linked to their ministries. God graciously made sure their messages were not stained by tragedy. God desires for people to associate Him with life not death. He gave them a vivid reminder of His power over the grave, and reaffirmed the authenticity of each servant.

*R*eflect on your concept of God. How do you think you would react if your child were suddenly killed by accident or disease? Would you want to blame God? Why or why not?

*H*ow does God want you to respond to what He showed you today?

_____

_____

After a moment of seriousness, I find myself amused once again as the scene ends. Paul went back to business as usual. He climbed three flights of stairs, broke bread with them, and talked until daylight. All in a day's work. I have a feeling no one fell asleep this time. In fact, they may have been wide awake for days! Here is my moral to the story: may God bring back to life whom man hath put to sleep.

For some strange reason, I feel particularly led to be brief today. Just make me one promise as we conclude: never sit close to a window when working on one of my lessons. Meanwhile, I'll see if I can get this size 7 shoe off my foot and back in the box where it belongs.

D A Y   3
A Tender Heart

Already I am being tested on our previous lesson! Today's text is so rich that I could keep talking until midnight. May God help this long-winded teacher set a short but meaningful sail with you today.

*R*ead Acts 20:13-38. Be sure to mark Paul's travels on the map. He is still on his third missionary journey. Notice that Paul purposely sailed past Ephesus because he needed to be on his way to Jerusalem, yet he summoned the elders to come to Miletus and meet with him. What do you think he accomplished through this plan?

Today's Treasure
"They all wept as they embraced him and kissed him. What grieved them most was his statement that they would never see his face again. Then they accompanied him to the ship" (Acts 20:37-38).

_____

_____

Paul had little time; so he left them the basic necessities. Like a father with moments left to share his heart with his children, Paul shared things that were priority to him. He reminded them of his attention to them. He shared his assumptions, his ambition, his heartfelt admonition, and his deep affection. Let's look at each of these priorities. Notice first his attention to them.

*P*aul summarized his conduct among the Ephesians. Based on verses 18-21, write words or phrases that describe Paul's ministry to them.

_____

_____

I believe Paul was personally attentive to the Ephesians because he became involved with them emotionally as well as spiritually. Remember, he remained among these people for several years. I believe he poured himself out among them as much or more than any other group to whom he ministered. They saw his humility. The original word is *tapeinophrosune* which involves "the confession of his sin and a deep realization of his unworthiness to receive God's marvelous grace." He was very open with them about his past sin and his feelings of unworthiness in the ministry God had given him.

*I*n verse 24, Paul stated the task God had given him: "the task of testifying to the gospel of _____."

Who better to testify than one who admits how much he has received? They not only saw his humility, they saw his heart. He did not hide from them his tears or the pain of his hardships. The Ephesians knew Paul was genuine. He approached them withholding nothing. He did not hesitate to preach anything that would be helpful. He loved them enough to teach them anything and everything that would be of benefit, even if they didn't like it. He was willing to hurt their feelings momentarily, if it would help their hearts eternally.

Paul's kind of teacher is not always who we prefer, but is who we usually need. I don't need a teacher or preacher to simply tell me what I want to hear. Sometimes God's most helpful lessons hurt even when delivered through an earthly agent.

*C*an you remember a challenging, painful, or difficult message that helped you in the long run? Explain briefly.

_____

_____

Paul had given them everything he had while he was there. In verse 27, he restated: "For I have not hesitated to proclaim to you the whole will of God." He didn't just teach them the many wonderful things God wanted to do for them. He also taught them the truth about hardships that would inevitably come and the calling of the crucified life.

In his attentiveness, Paul withheld nothing from the Ephesians. Next he told them of his assumption for the future.

*R*eread verses 22-25.

124

First, notice that Paul's decision to go to Jerusalem (see Acts 19:21) had now turned into a compelling of the Holy Spirit. His decision had turned into a must. God sometimes shows us His approval over a decision we have made by fueling our desire until it is a complete compelling. Paul shared with the Ephesians several important assumptions he had made. He assumed he was bound to have difficulties in Jerusalem because the Holy Spirit had warned him of hardships in every other city. He couldn't imagine Jerusalem being an exception. In fact, he probably assumed he would have more problems than ever as he returned to Jerusalem.

*W*hy do you suppose difficulties might be awaiting Paul in Jerusalem?

_____

_____

He also assumed he would never see the Ephesians again. I have a feeling he might have feared he would be put to death in Jerusalem. Some scholars believe he did see the Ephesians once more. Others believe he did not. At this point, he spoke to them as if he would never see them again.

Next Paul shared with them his chief ambition: "If only I may finish the race and complete the task the Lord Jesus has given me" (Acts 20:24). He was so determined to be faithful to the task God had assigned him, his certainty of suffering could not dissuade him. Fear is a very powerful tool. Don't think for a moment Satan did not try to use fear to hinder the apostle from fulfilling God's purposes, and don't think Paul was not terrified at times. Of course he was. To think otherwise would minimize his faithfulness. Paul was afraid, but his love for Christ exceeded his fear of suffering and death. His primary ambition was finishing his task faithfully. Notice the phrase in verse 24: "the task the Lord Jesus has given me." Paul felt no responsibility to complete the task Christ had given Peter, or Barnabas, or Timothy. He believed and taught that God has specific plans for each believer.

*I*n the margin, write Paul's words in Ephesians 2:10.

God has a task for you. One He planned very long ago and suited for our present generation. Remember you are not responsible for completing anyone else's task, just yours. God desires for us to encourage one another in our tasks (see Heb. 10:24-25), but we are only responsible for completing our own.

These words might evoke one of two responses from you today: You could sense a fresh responsibility for discovering and fulfilling God's tasks for you, OR you may feel a fresh wave of relief that you are not responsible for someone else's task. Which is your response today and why?

_____

_____

Believing he would never see the Ephesians again, Paul not only shared with them his attentions, his assumptions, and his ambitions, He had an urgency to share with them an admonition.

*R*eread Acts 20:25-31. In your own words write what Paul admonished his hearers to do.

_____

_____

Paul warned the Ephesian elders about the vulnerability of the young church. He told them to expect savage wolves to try to devour the flock. He considered the warning so vital, he repeated it over and over during the three years he was among them.

*D*on't miss a very important part of his admonition. In verse 28, what two groups were they to keep watch over?

1. _____   2. _____

What an important message Paul's words send to us! We can hardly keep watch over a group if we don't keep watch over ourselves! The original Greek term for *keep watch* is *prosecho.* "As a nautical term, it means to hold a ship in a direction, to sail towards … to hold on one's course toward a place." Many leaders have seasons when their lives seem temporarily out of control. Most people who have served God for decades have had a season in which they got off course. Those who never depart from the course in many years of service deserve our highest commendations; but they are rare.

I do not believe a leader who temporarily veers away from the course should never be allowed to lead again. I can't find a biblical precedent for such thinking. On the other hand, we are wise leaders to step out of leadership when we are having a difficult time staying on the course. We simply cannot lead others to a place to which we are not steering our own lives. Yes, leaders must watch over their own lives very carefully; but Paul also told them they must act like shepherds keeping watch over their flocks.

*G*od issued strong words concerning shepherds who care nothing about their flocks in Ezekiel 34:1-5. How had the shepherds failed their flocks?

_____

_____

According to verse 5, what can happen when a shepherd is not properly keeping watch over the flock? Choose any which apply.
- ❏ The flock can turn to an evil shepherd.
- ❏ The shepherd will be killed.
- ❏ The flock can scatter.
- ❏ The flock can become food for wild animals.

We don't have to be church elders for these words and warnings to apply to us. If God has assigned you a flock, you have a serious responsibility to keep a close watch over your own life and to care deeply for theirs. A crucial part of keeping watch over our flocks is knowing the Word of God! Look back at Acts 20:30. Paul warns that "men will arise and distort the truth." The word *distort* denotes an action of twisting or turning. Satan is a master at twisting and turning the Word of God. He's been honing his twisting skills since his first successful attempt in the garden of Eden. He subtly twists the Word in hope that we won't realize we've been misled until after he reaps havoc. Paul had very little time to address the Ephesian elders, yet the warning to watch over themselves and their flocks was an absolute priority.

Let's take a look at one last element Paul shared with the Ephesians. He shared his sincere affection for them. The final picture painted at the end of Acts 20 tenders my heart so much. Paul was a man of many words, but the priority message of his affection for the Ephesians came more in action than in words. Any man as beloved as Paul had most assuredly loved. He was the very one who taught others "Love never fails" (1 Cor. 13:8). I wonder if at this moment he thought love also never fails to hurt. He committed them to God, said a few last words, then knelt with them and prayed.

Don't quickly pass by this moment. Let it take form in your mind. Imagine a group of men, replete with all the things that make them men—size, stature, strength, controlled emotions—on their knees praying together. Thankfully, this is not a picture I have trouble imagining. My pastor often asks the men of our church to join him at the altar down on their knees in prayer. As a woman in the church, nothing makes me feel more secure. To me, a man is his tallest when he is down on his knees in prayer.

Imagine the next scene between Paul and the elders. "They all wept as they embraced him and kissed him" (v. 37). One by one each man hugged him and said good-bye. With every embrace, I'm sure he remembered something special—a good laugh shared, a late night over a sick loved one, a baptism in a cold river, a heated argument resolved. He had been their shepherd. Now he would leave them to tend their flocks on their own. In the midst of painful good-byes, perhaps Paul thought what I have a time or two when my heart was hurting. Perhaps he thought, *I will never let myself get this involved again.* But, of course, he did. And so will we, if we continue to walk in the footsteps of our Savior. To extend hands of service without hearts of love is virtually meaningless.

The chapter concludes with Paul and his friends walking side by side down the path to the docks, beards still wet with tears. Had I been Paul, I would have gotten on that ship as quickly as possible and dared not look back. That's not what happened. Luke opens the next chapter with the words, "After we had torn ourselves away from them, we put out to sea and sailed straight to Cos" (Acts 21:1). I think Luke, who was waiting at the boat (see Acts 20:13), literally had to go and tear the apostle away from them.

Obviously, the Ephesians had some idea how blessed they were to have the kind of leader Paul was to them. He was a leader who kept watch over himself and his followers. In nautical terms, the best kind of captain. One who kept the vessel on course even if his compass took him far from those he loved. He had given them all he had. The best kind of good-bye is the kind with no regrets.

*H*ow does God want you to respond to what He showed you today?

_____

_____

_____

_____

_____

_____

DAY 4
From the Mouths of Prophets

Today's Treasure
"Then Paul answered, 'Why are you weeping and breaking my heart? I am ready not only to be bound, but also to die in Jerusalem for the name of the Lord Jesus'" (Acts 21:13).

Today we will board so many ships with Paul, we may develop sea legs. I have decided women can be a touch too practical. I find myself wondering how Paul and his associates washed their clothes. I wonder if Paul suffered in ways he deemed too ordinary to share with us. For example, did he experience seasickness? I would almost rather be beaten than be seasick. Our protagonist probably suffered in big and small ways more times than he could recount (see 2 Cor. 11:26).

Look at your map for a moment. In the last lesson, we walked with Paul and the Ephesian elders to the docks of Miletus where Paul set sail with Luke and the others. Paul's immediate goal was Jerusalem. Ultimately he felt compelled to go on to Rome. As you can see, Miletus is quite a distance from Jerusalem. Based on today's text in Acts, several weeks had to pass between the time Paul departed Miletus and the time he entered Jerusalem. Like us, Paul probably wished he could skip the tiring travel and miraculously show up at his destination. As usual, God had far more important plans. He had meaningful encounters and peculiar preparations for Paul on his journey to Jerusalem. You see, to God, our journey is as important as our destination. As we seek to know His will and go where He sends us, God doesn't just wait for us at our next stop. He travels every mile right beside us.

*R*ead Acts 21:1-16.

Although Paul had the opportunity to stretch his legs at several different ports on his way to Jerusalem, he disembarked twice for a number of days. His first lengthy stop was not by choice. Because the first boat made so many stops, the traveling preachers sought out a vessel going straight across to Phoenicia (v. 2), hoping to save time. To their dismay, the ship docked in Tyre for seven days to unload cargo. Have you ever noticed how often God has a blessing on the unscheduled stops along our way? God had a blessing waiting for Paul and the others on their unscheduled stop.

*N*otice Acts 21:4 indicates Paul sought out the Christian disciples in Tyre so he and his men would have a place to stay. Look back at Acts 11:19. How had Christians originally been planted in Phoenicia, the region in which Tyre was located? Choose one.
   ❏ Paul had preached the gospel to them.
   ❏ They had been scattered by persecution.
   ❏ Barnabas was a Phoenician.
   ❏ Paul had sent Timothy to minister to the people of Phoenicia.

Don't forget how deeply involved Paul, then known as Saul, had been in the persecution which caused these same believers to scatter. Had they heard about the amazing convert, or did they believe he was still a terrible threat? Either way, they were surprised to lay eyes on the sea-weary travelers. I never cease to be amazed at the hospitality of believers in the New Testament church. Even in my grandmother's day, she and many others often opened their homes to total strangers who needed a place to rest for a night on their long travels. I am saddened about our loss of hospitality today. The disciples in Phoenicia took the risk and opened their homes to Paul and his fellow travelers. Their hearts were so instantly bound with his, they begged him not to go to Jerusalem.

Paul had been "compelled by the Spirit" (Acts 20:22) to go on to Jerusalem. Yet Acts 21:4 says, "Through the Spirit they urged Paul not to go." Don't let this expression confuse you. I don't believe they were saying the Holy Spirit did not want Paul to travel to Jerusalem. I believe the Holy Spirit burdened their hearts with an awareness that trouble lay ahead. Therefore, they concluded the apostle should certainly avoid it. To Paul's honor, once he determined the will of God, no amount of flesh and blood could stop him. When the ship was ready to set sail, he was ready to board it.

*T*his time, who accompanied him to the harbor?

Can you imagine what a sight this scene must have been for others to behold? Men, women, and children kneeling in the sand praying with one heart and mind for the apostle and his beloved associates. Just picture what the sand must have looked like after Paul boarded the ship and the crowd went back home. Footprints leading to and from the shore. Then nothing but knee prints clustered together in the damp sand. A sight for God to behold. Long after the tide washed away every print, the power of those prayers was still at work.

*P*aul's second lengthy stop is the one on which we will focus. Acts 21:8 tells us Paul and the others disembarked in Caesarea and stayed in the house of a man named Philip. In what two ways is he identified in verse 8?

❏ a wise man of many years ❏ an evangelist
❏ one of the Seven ❏ a strong disciple

We can learn volumes about this mighty man of God from these two expressions. Philip is first mentioned in Acts 6:5 in the list of the seven. What were the qualifications of the seven according to Acts 6:3?

_____

_____

Not only was Philip a Spirit-filled Christian and a very wise man, he was an extremely effective evangelist. Let's see him in action so we can picture the man who hosted the apostle Paul during his stay in Caesarea.

*R*ead Acts 8:26-40. Based on these verses, list as many descriptions of Philip as you possibly can:

_____

_____

Based on all the descriptions we can compile from collective verses concerning Philip, is it any wonder he had four daughters who prophesied? In a previous unit, we had a wonderful opportunity to consider the rich heritage a son received from his mother and grandmother. Timothy's ministry was profoundly affected by the sincere faith of those two women. Today we get to see four daughters also obviously affected by the faithfulness of their father.

Young people are far more likely to surrender their lives to serve God when they have seen genuine examples firsthand. Many are touched by the faithfulness of youth ministers, Sunday School teachers, and pastors, but what can match the lasting impact of a faithful parent? If my children don't think I'm genuine, no one else's opinion matters to me. On the front page of my Bible I've written a reminder I'm forced to see every time I open my Bible: No amount of success in ministry will make up for failure at home.

Right about now you may be wondering if Paul had to be resuscitated when he met four women who prophesied. In his defense, I would like to say that Paul was the first to recognize women with the gift of prophecy (when he taught spiritual gifts in 1 Cor. 11). A study of the entire life and ministry of Paul reveals an interesting fact. He had a vastly different outlook and attitude toward women than we might have first supposed. Unfortunately many people have based their thinking about him on a couple of excerpts from his writings. If Paul had disapproved of Philip's four daughters, he would have been the first to tell him!

What exactly were Philip's daughters doing anyway? What does prophesying mean? The original word for *prophesying* is *propheteuo* which means "to declare truths through the inspiration of God's Holy Spirit....To tell forth God's message." A prophet is a "proclaimer, one who speaks out the counsel of God with the clearness, energy, and authority." In ancient days, prior to His completed revelation, God often used prophets or "proclaimers" to warn people about the future. Virtually all God wanted foretold, He ultimately inspired in His written Word, the Bible; so the gift of prophecy is most often used today as the proclamation of God's truth. Whether or not they foretold any part of the future, Philip's four daughters—in today's terms—were Christian speakers!

Believe it or not, this concept is not new. Both the Old and New Testaments speak of prophetesses. Although the concept is not new, I believe with all my heart God is using something old to do something new. Recently I've had the strangest feeling God is up to something unique in the Body of Christ. We have concentrated so heavily on all the negatives in our society, we may be missing something good. In my opinion God seems to be pulling out all the stops as He desires to equip His people in these last days. Never before has Bible study been more accessible and applicable. He seems to be raising up a strong remnant of well-equipped servants. We see great movements of God among both men and women not only in this nation but around the world. Yes, many who are not serious are falling away. At the same time a wonderful remnant of godly people are hitting their knees in repentance, then standing up to fight the good fight around the globe.

*U*pon whom did God say He would pour out His Spirit in Acts 2:18?

_____

I believe the growing numbers of strong Christian men and women speakers are examples of God's fulfillment of His promise. I am convinced we are living in the midst of a very significant work of God on His kingdom calendar. We are simply so involved we can hardly see what's happening. Indeed, there is war in the heavenlies. Satan is pulling out all stops, but so is God. And as a dear pastor says, "It's a fixed fight."

*L*et's turn our attentions now to another prophet Paul encountered at the house of Philip. His name was Agabus. Reread Acts 21:10-11. What did Agabus predict through his dramatic interpretation?

_____

Agabus must have been extremely convincing, because his actions had a far greater impact than the disciples' words in Tyre. Notice on his last stop, although Luke and the others accompanied Paul to Tyre, only the Phoenician disciples urged him not to go to Jerusalem (see Acts 21:4).

*I*n Caesarea, after Agabus' prophetic performance, who urged Paul not to go according to Acts 21:12?

_____

In turn, Paul also responded with strong emotion. Though he could hardly tear himself away from the Ephesian elders in Acts 20:37, he never wavered in his resolve. He also remained unmoved when the disciples in Tyre urged him not to go. Yet we see him respond with enormous emotion when his beloved associates—Luke, Timothy, and the others—wept and pleaded with him not to go. Let's try to capture an accurate picture. These men were not just crying. The original word for *weeping* is the strongest expression of grief in the Greek language. These men were sobbing. Paul responded tenderly, "'Why are you weeping and breaking my heart?'" (Acts 21:13). The original Greek word for *breaking* is *sunthrupto* which means "to break, crush together into pieces, ... take away one's courage." The root word means "to crumble."

Have you experienced a time when someone desperately wanted you to do something that you could not do? ❑ Yes ❑ No **If so, describe your feelings at the time.**

_____

Paul's beloved friends were so crushed over what awaited Paul, their strength dissolved, their noble sense of purpose disintegrated, and they begged him not to go. Had he not been so convinced of the Spirit's compelling him to go, he surely would have changed his mind. He voiced his determination to each of them: "'I am ready not only to be bound, but also to die in Jerusalem for the name of the Lord Jesus'" (v. 13).

Have you begged and pleaded with God for something you are realizing you're not going to get? Do you sometimes feel you must give up and just let the Lord's will be done? We sometimes feel as if we're playing tug of war with God. In bitter tears, we sometimes let go of the rope, tumble to the ground, and cry, "Have your way, God! You're going to do what You want anyway!"

Please recognize that God is not playing a game. He wants to say yes to us so badly. He knows how desperately we want some of the things for which we are asking. God doesn't jerk on the rope just so He can win. In fact, He doesn't want us to let go of the rope at all. Rather than see us drop the rope and give up, He wants us to hang on and let Him pull us over to His side.

God's will is always best even when we cannot imagine how. Surrendering to His will does not mean you lose. Ultimately, it means you win. God does not want you to feel defeated when you realize He's overruled a desire of your heart. God is not asking you to give up. He's leading you to give over. Keep hanging on to that rope and let Him pull you over to His side. One day you'll understand. And you'll see His glory.

How ow does God want you to respond to what He showed you today?

_____

_____

_____

_____

_____

DAY 5

A Prophecy Fulfilled

In the Old Testament God often used proclaimers to foretell the future. He gave the people a rule of thumb by which they could judge a true prophet: "You may say to yourselves, 'How can we know when a message has not been spoken by the Lord?' If what a prophet proclaims in the name of the Lord does not take place or come true, that is a message the Lord has not spoken. That prophet has spoken presumptuously. Do not be afraid of him" (Deut.18:21-22). You will quickly discover in today's reading that Agabus was a true prophet. Some prophecies take centuries to fulfill. Others, like the visible return of Christ, may even take millennia. Unfortunately, scarcely a week passed before a belt around Agabus' wrists became a chain around Paul's.

Today's Treasure
"The whole city was aroused, and the people came running from all directions. Seizing Paul, they dragged him from the temple, and immediately the gates were shut" (Acts 21:30).

131

$\mathcal{R}$ead Acts 21:17-36. Be sure to mark Paul's crucial entry into Jerusalem on your map, then complete each of the following.

1. Which of the following words best describes Paul's initial reception in Jerusalem? Choose one.

❑ hostile ❑ unconcerned ❑ ecstatic ❑ warm ❑ suspicious

2. For what reason did Paul come to Jerusalem according to Acts 24:17?

_____

_____

3. Why were the believing Jews upset with Paul?

_____

_____

4. Name as many reasons as you can why Paul might have followed James' advice.

_____

_____

5. Which Jews stirred up trouble against Paul in Jerusalem?

❑ Asian Jews   ❑ believing Jews
❑ unbelieving Jews   ❑ hypocritical Jews

6. These Jews were in the city because of the observance of a particular Jewish custom. Refresh your memory by reading Acts 20:16. What was obviously being observed around the time of Paul's arrival?

❑ the Passover   ❑ the Feast of Unleavened Bread
❑ the Year of Jubilee   ❑ the Day of Pentecost

7. Do you see any irony in who God chose to intervene so that Paul was not beaten to death? If so, explain briefly.

_____

_____

Had Paul's arrival in Jerusalem been a performance, he certainly would have received mixed reviews. The apostle encountered three distinct responses to his coming: acceptance, apprehension, and accusation. Let's consider each one separately.

1. Paul met acceptance. After such imminent expectation, what blessed words: "When we arrived at Jerusalem, the brothers received us warmly" (v. 17). Don't miss Luke's terminology, "When we arrived." After being unsuccessful in their attempt to plead with Paul to avoid Jerusalem, if they had said, "You go ahead if you want. The rest of us refuse to be so foolish," who would have blamed them?

Nearly 30 years earlier, Christ's disciples also tried to talk Him out of going back to Judea when they knew trouble awaited Him. When He could not be dissuaded, Thomas said, "'Let us also go, that we may die with him'" (John 11:16). Neither group was called to give their lives in association with their leader at this point, but surely God acknowledged their willingness.

What a sigh of relief must have come when Paul and his associates were greeted with warmth and approval by the believers in Jerusalem. Only one verse attests to Paul's testimony to James, the elders, and the others (v. 19), but you can assume he talked for some time. "Paul reported in detail what God had done among the Gentiles." The hearts of James and the others are evident in their reception of his testimony: "they praised God" (v. 20).

*N*otice, they did not praise Paul. They praised God. When was the last time you shared a testimony, whether one-on-one or in a group, which was met by praise to your God?

_____

How did the response make you feel?

_____

_____

God was gracious to allow Paul to be encouraged by the praises James and the others gave to God for his faithful work. Unfortunately, acceptance was not the only response Paul met.

2. Paul met apprehension. After hearing Paul's wonderful news, James and the elders had good news of their own, and a little bad news. They gave Paul the good news first: "'Many thousands of Jews have believed'" (v. 20). What glorious words! What could Paul have wanted more? According to Romans 9:3, absolutely nothing! He would have agreed to be cursed forever if the Jews would accept Christ. I wonder if Paul immediately began shouting hallelujah and dancing and praising God; regardless, they jumped quickly to the bad news. They almost seemed to be sparing his dignity. Yes, many had believed in Christ, but "'all of them are zealous for the law. ... [And] They have been informed that you ... [tell] them not to live according to our customs'" (v. 20-21). In other words, they're saved—but they're mad. Talk about throwing a bucket of ice water on a warm reception. So much for the punch and cookies.

This dilemma draws compassion from my heart for both James and Paul. I feel compassion for James. We have all been in his position. He was caught in the middle of anger and disagreement between people he cared about. Just imagine the gnawing in James' stomach as Paul was giving a detailed account of all God was doing among the Gentiles. James knew he would have to tell Paul about the Jews.

*W*hen was the last time you were stuck in the middle of a situation involving Christians on both sides?

_____

_____

Like James, you may have felt responsible for the resolution of the entire issue. He was the leader of the Jerusalem Christian Church. He understood how both sides felt. Even though the text uses the word *they,* you can appropriately assume that James was ultimately responsible for bearing the difficult news.

I also feel compassion for Paul. He expected opposition from unbelievers, but to be hit immediately in Jerusalem by the disapproval of fellow believers must have drained his energy and excitement. Furthermore, much of what they were saying about him wasn't even accurate. He never told Jewish Christians not to circumcise their children. He told them not to insist Gentile Christians circumcise theirs! He was trying to make the point that circumcision had nothing whatsoever to do with salvation.

*P*erhaps you know how Paul felt when he met disapproval among his own and found he had been misunderstood. Have you ever thought, *I expected this kind of thing from unbelievers, but I wasn't expecting this from my own fellow believers*?   ❑ Yes ❑ No If so, how did you feel?

_____

The response of the Jerusalem Christians probably knocked the wind from Paul's sails so quickly that he would have done most anything they asked him to do. James and the elders immediately insisted he join four men in their purification rites, so all would see he still respected the customs. Were James and the others right in their insistence? Only God knows as He looked on the situation and the hearts of those involved. We do know, however, that Paul submitted to their authority and did as they asked. Remember, he had formerly taken a similar voluntary vow (see Acts 18:18). His point regarding the ancient Hebrew customs was to practice them when wise or observe them as a reminder, but not to live under them as a burden and a means of salvation.

*S*everal times in Paul's ministry he was placed in a similar position with both Jews and Gentiles. He explained his actions in 1 Corinthians 9:19-23. Read these verses and explain how Paul's actions in Acts 21:26 were indicative of this philosophy.

_____

_____

How do you need to apply Paul's philosophy of becoming "all things to all men" to save some?

_____

_____

We can respond legalistically and shun harmless practices. However, we would risk alienating the very people we want to reach. What do people win with their strict legalism? Sometimes only the right to be right. Something far more important stands to be won: a precious human being. One of the most crucial elements foreign missionaries are taught is cultural sensitivity. Such sensitivity means, when possible, do not put obstacles in the way of reaching others for Christ. Of course, we have a plumb line. We obviously cannot sin to win.

*K*nowing how to apply Paul's standard of "all things to all men" requires both spiritual maturity and sensitivity. Ask the Holy Spirit to guide as you build witnessing relationships while maintaining appropriate standards.

3. Paul met accusation. Paul first met acceptance, then apprehension. Now we see the apostle meet another response in Jerusalem. Imagine capturing the moment Paul and the Asian Jews, who had given him trouble in Ephesus, saw each other. I have a feeling Paul thought, *Oh, no,* and the Asian Jews thought, *Oh, yes!* (See Acts 19:8-9, 33.) They couldn't seem to avoid a good riot, could they? The entire city fell into an uproar, and they grabbed Paul and tried to beat him to death. Can you imagine what the apostle was thinking? Sequestered in such a mob, I'm sure he thought he was about to draw his last breath. I can hardly imagine being beaten by one person. I certainly cannot empathize with being beaten by a gang.

I am sobered when I see God used pagans or unbelievers to rescue one of His own. Psalm 47:8 (KJV) says, "God reigneth over the heathen." That day in Jerusalem God used a godless government to intervene in the unjust persecution of His servant. The Roman commander was not trying to protect Paul. He was trying to protect himself. Order was a top priority in the more respectable echelons of Roman government. Uprisings could result in an immediate dismissal. We don't even have to wonder what Paul was thinking when he was bound in chains. I'm sure the image of the prophet Agabus tied up with his belt was indelibly engraved in his mind. Yes, Paul had expected to be seized, but I'm not sure expectation and preparation are always synonymous.

I don't think Paul was prepared to be carried by Roman soldiers. I also don't think he was prepared for a mob to keep shouting, "Away with such a *fellow*" (Acts 22:22, KJV). He had said, "'I am ready not only to be bound, but also to die in Jerusalem for the name of the Lord Jesus'" (Acts 21:13). But was he ready for hatred and wholesale rejection? I'm not sure how adequately a person can prepare for such pain.

*I*n his letter to the Philippians (3:10), Paul made a reference to wanting the fellowship of sharing in Christ's sufferings. In what ways was Paul's experience so far in Jerusalem a vivid fulfillment of his heart's desire?

_____

_____

*H*ow does God want you to respond to what He showed you today?

_____

_____

_____

_____

_____

_____

Paul received Christ by faith. He knew Christ by name. He came face-to-face with Christ through experience. He spoke to Him through prayer. He grew in Him through the Word. But this particular day, Paul experienced a fellowship in His sufferings unlike any he had ever encountered. Both Christ and Paul knew suffering was inevitable. Both Christ and Paul knew they would end up giving their lives: One as the Savior of the world, the other as His servant. Both Christ and Paul grieved over Jerusalem. Both Christ and Paul felt compelled to return. Both Christ and Paul knew the horror of being swept up in an angry mob. Both Christ and Paul experienced the "newness" of every rejection.

No matter how many times it comes, one can hardly prepare for people who wish you dead. Paul did not know what would happen to him, but he knew Christ. As the apostle fellowshipped in His sufferings, he had never known Jesus better.

---

[1]*Ephesus*, Infopedia, (Funk and Wagnall's Encyclopedia, 1994).

Travel Ties and Hard Good-byes

1 Corinthians 12:1-11, 27-30; Romans 12:3-8; Ephesians 4:11-13

Understanding of Spiritual Gifts

1. We do not need to be _____ by the subject of spiritual gifts (1 Cor. 12:1).

2. Scripture seems to suggest we should resist being overly _____ about spiritual gifts.

3. Spiritual gifts are products of _____. *Charisma* means "a gift of grace, an undeserved benefit."

4. God gives _____ _____ of spiritual gifts (1 Cor. 12:4).

   Different means "_____, distribution, classification, apportionment." God purposely divided the

   gifts among us so we would be compelled to be _____ in order to function properly as a

   church (1 Pet. 4:10). *Various forms* means "variegated, _____-_____!" (1 Cor. 12:4).

5. Spiritual gifts are _____ of the Spirit (1 Cor. 12:7).

   Manifestation means "to make _____ or _____."

6. God gives spiritual gifts to _____ believer (1 Cor. 12:11).

7. Your spiritual gifts are given _____ you but not primarily _____ you (1 Pet. 4:10; 1 Cor. 12:7).

8. Spiritual gifts remind us how much we _____ each other (1 Cor. 12: 21).

9. Spiritual gifts can be _____ or exercised "in the flesh" (1 Pet. 4:11; 1 Cor. 13:1-3).

10. Our spiritual gifts accompany the residence of the Holy Spirit in us when we _____ Christ,

    but they are developed through _____ _____ and _____.

    Paul told Timothy to "_____ _____ _____ the gift of God" (2 Tim. 1:6).

    1 Corinthians 2:9-10

A Walk of Faith

Day 1
A Willing Witness

Day 2
In All Good Conscience

Day 3
A Peculiar Deliverance

Day 4
An Inconvenient Gospel

Day 5
Man Alive!

This week we see Paul under very stressful circumstances. God ordained the apostle's ministry before he was born. He prepared Paul with certain assets for ministry under the influence of the Holy Spirit. Paul was a traveling man. Most of us prefer one consistent place of service. The apostle's soul burned for the next assignment and the next venue. Few men would have found imprisonment more difficult than the apostle Paul. I am sure he did not enjoy having his ministerial wings clipped, yet he maintained his testimony. We will witness a man of integrity this week as we search for the answers to the following questions.

Principal Questions
Day 1: What were several elements of Paul's powerful testimony in Acts 22?
Day 2: What did you learn about the conscience?
Day 3: How and why was Paul transported to Caesarea?
Day 4: What subjects did Paul preach to Felix?
Day 5: How can a person investigate whether or not Christ is alive today?

As we study this week, let's try to imagine being on trial for our faith. Work hard and stay teachable; then bring your imaginations to week 7 as we discuss a faith that endures trials and prospers as a result. Stay sensitive to times this week when your faith may be tried.

D A Y   1

A Willing Witness

Today's Treasure
"You will be his wit-
ness to all men of what
you have seen and
heard" (Acts 22:15).

The Spirit compelled Paul to go to Jerusalem. Along the way, God went to great lengths to warn him of tribulation he would encounter. Thus the apostle was not surprised nor did he assume he had stepped outside God's will. Years earlier, God sent Paul away from Jerusalem. He now compelled him to return. We might assume timing was the issue, yet the people didn't appear to accept Paul's message this time either.

Throughout the seventh week, we will consider Paul's experiences in Jerusalem. On a human scale, we cannot judge his visit as a success. Perhaps Paul's experiences in places like Athens and Jerusalem will teach us to think differently about success and failure. Hopefully, we will come to understand that, in our Christian lives, success is obedience to God, not results we can measure.

*H*ave you ever been in a situation where you desperately wanted to be used of God to reach a person or a group of people? If so, explain briefly.

_____

_____

Were the apparent results less than you hoped? If so, explain how you felt.

_____

_____

Remember Paul's deeply rooted connections to Jerusalem. There he received his education and made many friends. He wanted to bear fruit in Jerusalem more than any place on earth. Yet we see him face greater opposition and struggle in Jerusalem than virtually anywhere in his ministry. In the holy city Paul was forced to take every step by faith. He had to measure his ministry strictly on his obedience to the Spirit, not outward results. May Paul's example teach us to testify when God provides opportunity and learn to look at obedience as success.

*R*ead Acts 21:37–22:30. Consider carefully Paul's testimony to the mob. List every way Paul attempted to relate to his audience.

_____

_____

What had God told Paul the first time he visited Jerusalem? Choose one.
- ❑ Leave Jerusalem immediately. ❑ Preach in the synagogues.
- ❑ Shake the dust from your feet. ❑ Go only to the Gentiles in Jerusalem.

Based on 22:19, what was Paul's reason for believing he might have an effective testimony among the Jews?

_____

Why do you think the Jews listened to Paul until he talked about his ministry to the Gentiles?

Why was the order to flog Paul overturned? Choose one.
❏ Several men came to his defense.
❏ The commander believed in Christ.
❏ Paul was a Roman citizen.

The commander mistook Paul for an Egyptian terrorist and ordered him taken to the barracks. Earlier, an Egyptian who claimed to be a prophet persuaded four thousand people to follow him and commit acts of terrorism. He led them to the top of the Mount of Olives, promising that the walls of Jerusalem would collapse at his command. Of course, no such miracle occurred. Instead, the Roman army surrounded them killing some and capturing others, but inadvertently allowing the Egyptian leader to get away.

Paul was an ambassador of reconciliation (see 2 Cor. 5:19-20). We will never know how he felt when mistaken for a leader of terrorists. We do know that he boldly asked for an opportunity to speak to the people. Moments earlier these people beat him with their fists. Paul did not ask God to rain down fire from Heaven to consume them. He did not ask God to open the earth and swallow them. He asked nothing but a chance to give his testimony. He desired to overcome their hardened hearts by the word of his testimony (see Rev. 12:11).

I often sing the old hymns of our faith, and one of my favorites is "Blessed Assurance, Jesus Is Mine"! My voice never fails to quiver when I sing the chorus, "This is my story, this is my song." *My story. My song.* Whether or not anyone would trade testimonies with me, I have my own story with Christ. I have my own song. My personal testimony is the way I can illustrate the relevance of Scripture and the power of an invisible God in today's world. We must always be willing to give our testimonies.

I resist abiding by a formula in sharing our testimonies, but Paul's approach contains several elements that build a powerful testimony. Let's take a look at each one.

1. He communicated simply and clearly. Notice Paul spoke in Greek to the commander and in Aramaic to the Jews. Few of us are fluent in several languages, but we can apply his example in more general terms. We can learn to communicate our testimonies more effectively by speaking the language of our hearers.

*B*efore I make further explanation, what do you think "speaking their language" would mean in terms of our everyday opportunities?

I grew up in Sunday School and church. I spent much of my early social life with other Christians, so I had a difficult time learning to speak language an unchurched person could understand. My speech was so laced with church terms that those unacquainted with church life could hardly understand me. I practically needed an interpreter!

I still have to remind myself to resist assuming every listener knows the lingo. I'm learning to use figures of speech and expressions lost people will more likely understand. I'm also learning to use more contemporary expressions when speaking to youth.

Of course, learning to speak understandably does not mean adopting any level of vulgarity. It means speaking with a greater level of clarity.

2. He honestly described his former conduct. We lose our listeners the moment they sense an attitude of superiority in us. Paul spoke with honesty and humility in verses 1-5. As he explained his background and his persecutions of the church, in effect he was saying, "You know I'm not judging you. Anything you've done wrong, I've probably out-done!" He did not adopt a condemning approach. He related with them as one who had been exactly where they were. Not all of us have a background as dramatically different from our present lifestyles as Paul did, yet we have all been lost. Lost is lost. We have all been in the same lost state as those who presently do not know Christ.

Think of someone to whom you really want to witness. What similarities exist between the person and your present or past experiences?

_____

_____

How might you use those similarities to build a bridge to the person?

_____

_____

Are you careful not to condemn when you share Christ? ❑ Yes ❑ No

Depending on your answer to the previous question, John 3:17 may either be affirming or convicting. What does this wonderful verse say about God's approach to the lost through Christ?

_____

_____

Remember an important principle about sharing our former conduct. Generalizations usually are best. I try to avoid becoming specific about ungodly actions in my past. I want the listener to focus on my Savior, not my behavior. Sometimes we glorify ungodly behavior by boasting how *bad* we were. This method can dishonor God, and it can dishonor the listener by stirring unnecessary mental images of sin. Share past conduct with caution!

3. He related his experience of conversion. Few of us have experienced the dramatic conversion Paul described in Acts 22:6-16, but we can tell how we accepted Christ. Don't think your testimony is meaningless if you didn't have a dramatic conversion that ushered you from a life of drug abuse or crime. Don't assume your conversion means something less than Paul's because a light from heaven didn't engulf you. Every conversion cost the same amount of Christ's blood shed on the cross. Every conversion was worth the loss of God's only Son to Him. Yours is just as meaningful as the most dramatic conversion ever told.

In the parable of the prodigal son, the elder brother felt insulted because the father accepted his brother after a season of wild living (Luke 15:29-30). He didn't understand the biggest difference between the two brothers was that the prodigal son had to live with the personal loss and suffering. If your conversion was less sensational than others, praise God for less drama! With it probably came less pain!

You don't have to see a bright light from heaven to have a story to tell. The determining factor is not how exciting your conversion *was* but how excited you *are* now about your conversion. The simplest testimony from a person thankful to be saved is more powerful than the most dramatic testimony from someone who has told it so methodically that it has lost its fervor.

Have you lost your excitement over your personal conversion? Don't despair if your candid answer is yes. With sincerity, pray the prayer of David: "Restore to me the joy of your salvation and grant me a willing spirit, to sustain me. Then I will teach transgressors your ways, and sinners will turn back to you" (Ps. 51:12-13).

4. He shared how he received his commission. Paul was very clear in verses 17-21 that God had a purpose for his life. Our listeners need to know there is life after salvation! Salvation is not only about eternity. Salvation is also the open door to a rich earthly life in which we enjoy the love and direction of a very active God. If His only agenda were our salvation, once we accepted Him He would immediately usher us to Heaven. Each one of us is saved by grace to do good works prepared in advance for us (see Eph. 2:10). Many unbelievers are repelled by Christianity because they are afraid they will have to give up so much. As we share our testimonies, we can help them see all we've gained.

*D*escribe one way God has given you a sense of purpose. _____

_____

Make your sense of ongoing purpose a part of your testimony. We often have no idea how much people are struggling to find reason to live and persevere through difficulty.

Unfortunately, the Jews didn't think much of Paul's purpose on this earth. Once he acknowledged the importance of the Gentiles to God, he lost his audience. Sadly, their personal need to feel superior exceeded their spiritual sensibilities.

Paul desperately wanted the Jews to receive Christ. Was he a failure because they rejected him? Was his personal testimony shared in vain? Absolutely not. God compelled Paul to go to Jerusalem. He warned him of hardships. He gave Paul an opportunity to give his testimony to the very people who just tried to kill him.

Did they hear Paul's message? Oh, yes. Otherwise, they would not have responded so emotionally. Few of those in hearing distance that day forgot Paul's testimony. We cannot judge effectiveness from immediate results. According to John 14:26, the Holy Spirit can remind a person of truth taught long ago. When we obey God, we find great comfort in leaving the consequences up to Him.

Paul's experiences in Jerusalem were just beginning. Our reading today concluded as Paul avoided a flogging. God equipped him with Roman citizenship even before his birth! God used every ounce and detail of Paul's past, even his unique citizenship.

I want God to use every ounce of me, too. We will see Paul pour himself out like a drink offering in Jerusalem. He received little encouragement to preach while he was there—but he continued. Paul's certainty of what he had been called to do was exceeded only by his certainty of Who called. Paul considered Him who called worth it all.

Do you have a tendency to rate your own testimony or read your own results? Your personal story about Christ is worth telling. If you are excited about it, others are likely to find your testimony exciting, too. However, their reactions are not your responsibility. Sometimes I have to remind myself that I was never called to be the Holy Spirit. He will convict. He will remind. Don't do His job, but faithfully do yours. Go tell your story. No one can tell it like you.

*H*ow does God want you to respond to what He showed you today?

_____

_____

_____

_____

_____

_____

DAY 2
In All Good Conscience

Today's Treasure
"'My brothers, I have fulfilled my duty to God in all good conscience to this day'" (Acts 23:1).

During his stay in Jerusalem Paul had no need to make a living. God had already booked him a room in the city jail. Interestingly, his imprisonment was clearly the shield God used to keep Paul from being torn limb from limb by his adversaries. God did not allow the apostle to be jailed to his harm but to provide a temporary means of safety for him, all the while allowing him to share his testimony in the highest courts. In an attempt to discover the reasons for the accusations the Jews were making against Paul, the commander ordered all the chief priests and the Sanhedrin to assemble so Paul could stand before them. Our reading in the Book of Acts will be brief today, but it will introduce a pertinent topical study.

*R*ead Acts 23:1-11. What do you think Paul meant when he said he had fulfilled his "duty to God in all good conscience"?

_____

_____

The Pharisees and Sadducees disagreed on which of the following issues?
❏ resurrection ❏ angels ❏ spirits ❏ soul sleep

Who took up for Paul in verse 9? Choose one.
❏ Sadducees ❏ Pharisees ❏ the commander ❏ Ananias

These verses suggest that Paul could spar with the best of them! Take a good look at the scene. It unfolds with Paul addressing the chief priests and Sanhedrin with the words, "'My brothers, I have fulfilled my duty to God in all good conscience to this day'" (Acts 23:1). After which he was immediately struck in the mouth!

Why was Ananias so insulted? Was it because Paul referred to them as "brothers"? Or could it have been because Paul was indirectly suggesting a conscience check for everyone listening?

Unfortunately, we don't have the benefit of hearing Paul's voice inflections which would certainly have given away his attitude as he spoke. His response instantly following the slap suggests he might have been anxious for an altercation. "'God will strike you, you whitewashed wall!'" (Acts 23:3). I'm quite sure the temperature in the room rose dramatically.

*C*hrist also called the religious leaders of His day "whitewashed walls." **Read Matthew 23:27-28. What did He mean?**

_____

_____

After Paul called Ananias a whitewashed wall, those standing close to him said "'You dare to insult God's high priest?'" Don't miss Paul's response. "'I did not realize that he was the high priest.'"

If we could have heard Paul's voice, I believe his inflection might have contained a little sarcasm. No doubt Paul knew he was insulting the high priest. He was far too knowledgeable not to have recognized Ananias' robes and obvious position of honor. I believe he knew he was insulting the high priest and probably offended him further by saying, in effect, "Sorry, but I never would have recognized this guy as a high priest."

I'm suggesting Paul may have been in an interesting mood, if I may be so bold, even a touch of an insolent mood. Interestingly, history records this Ananias (not to be confused with the man by the same name in Acts 9) as a very insolent and hot-tempered man. Have you ever noticed our occasional tendency to adopt our foes' tactics? If they lose control of their mouths, sometimes we follow suit.

I mean absolutely no disrespect to the apostle, but I believe he sometimes struggled with a temper. The sight of the false piety of the religious leaders probably made his stomach turn—especially because he had been one of them. I have one more reason for believing Paul might have been in a mischievous mood.

*W*hy did Paul say he was on trial? _____

_____

Paul carefully voiced the reason he was on trial as his "hope in the resurrection of the dead" (Acts 23:6). Actually, the greater issue was his belief in someone far superior to Moses. His hope was in the One who had fulfilled all obligations to the Law—the promised Messiah who had died and risen from the dead. Paul had a very distinct motive for bringing up the volatile subject of life after death. He knew the resurrection of the dead was the biggest point of contention between the Pharisees and the Sadducees. Paul manipulated the spotlight *off* their grievances with him and *on* their grievances with each other. He accomplished two goals:
- he divided his enemy, diminishing their strength, and
- he caused the Pharisees to suddenly side with him.

Whether or not Paul planned an altercation, the disagreement got out of hand. The commander was so afraid they would tear Paul "to pieces" that he rushed the apostle back to the barracks. Once again, God used Paul's incarceration as protection.

Whether or not I am right about Paul's mood and motive, one point is unarguable: he wanted the religious leaders to know that his conscience was clear. As we study the life of the apostle, we will learn volumes by noting his priorities. A clear conscience was no doubt one of them, as he spoke often of it in his letters. How important is a clear conscience? Peace of mind cannot exist without it!

We'll explore the conscience for the remainder of our lesson today. First of all, let's consider the biblical definition. The original Greek word for *conscience* is *suneidesis* which means "to be one's own witness, one's own conscience coming forward as a witness. It denotes an abiding consciousness whose nature it is to bear witness to one's own conduct in a moral sense. It is self-awareness." The conscience is a marvelous recorder of both our beliefs and our behaviors.

*W*hy could the conscience be considered a "recorder"?

_____

How did Paul's conscience bear witness to his conduct (see 2 Cor. 1:12)?

_____

In layman's terms we might say the conscience is an inner constituent casting a vote about the rightness of our behaviors. God's Word helps us compile several facts concerning the conscience:

1. People without a spotless past can enjoy a clear conscience. What wonderful news! Paul spoke of possessing a clear conscience numerous times, yet he considered himself one of the worst possible offenders. His conscience was clear even though he had wronged many people in the past. A clear conscience is possible for those of us who have sinned.

2. Good deeds cannot accomplish a clear conscience. Have you ever tried to worship or serve God when your conscience was bothering you after an unsettled argument with your spouse or a coworker? Or perhaps after telling a lie to someone?

*R*ead Hebrews 9:9. What two things were unable to clear the conscience of the worshiper?
❏ gifts   ❏ apologies   ❏ tithes   ❏ sacrifices   ❏ prayers

We've all probably tried to soothe our consciences with good works. God's Word tells us we cannot offer enough gifts or sacrifices to clear a guilty conscience. Take heart! Before we conclude today's lesson we will discover steps to a clear conscience.

3. The Holy Spirit works with the believer's conscience. The Holy Spirit plays a critical role in creating and maintaining a clear conscience.

*R*ead Romans 9:1. Describe the relationship between the Holy Spirit and the believer's conscience?

_____

_____

The Greek word for *confirms* is *summartureo* meaning "to witness with another, to witness together." In other words, once we have received Christ and the Holy Spirit resides within us, the Holy Spirit will work with our consciences. The Spirit works both to confirm a clear conscience, as in Romans 9:1, and to convict a guilty conscience.

We all naturally prefer to ignore our sin. The one part of us that does not ignore sin is our conscience. For that reason the Holy Spirit deals with conscience first, not with our intellect or emotions. You might think of the relationship this way: the Holy Spirit plants conviction in the soil of the conscience. If ignored, that conviction will usually grow and grow.

4. The conscience is an indicator, not a transformer. Only the Holy Spirit can change us and clear our consciences. By itself, all the conscience can do with a guilty person is condemn. My conscience may lend an awareness of what I ought to do, but it supplies little power to do it. The believer possesses something far greater than a conscience. The Holy Spirit who resides in us supplies abundant power not only to recognize the right thing, but to do it!

*D*o you remember a time when your conscience bothered you, but you felt powerless to change your behavior? Explain briefly.

_____

_____

144

Have you discovered a difference since the Holy Spirit became active in your life? ❏ Yes ❏ No If so, describe that difference?

_____

_____

Can we really have clear consciences? The Bible says we can. Considering Paul's past, if he can have a clear conscience any of us can. Like me, you may have discovered that asking God for forgiveness doesn't always make you feel better. Sometimes we know we're forgiven, but we still feel a load of guilt. How can we discover the freedom of a clear conscience?

I believe Hebrews 10:22 holds several vital keys. Read this verse one phrase at a time out loud. Then consider these steps to a clear conscience.

1. Bring your heavy conscience to God. When we have a guilty conscience, we shy away from the presence of God. We tend to resist what we need most: an awareness of God's love! Draw near to God!

2. Approach God with absolute sincerity. Come entirely clean before Him. Spill your heart and confess everything you feel. Tell Him about the guilt that continues to nag at you. You'll not only clear your heart and mind, you'll tattle on the evil one who has no right to keep accusing you after repentance.

3. Ask God to give you full assurance of His love and acceptance. In His Word, God tells you over and over how much He loves you. He assures you of forgiveness. He also tells you He forgets your confessed sin. Ask God to give you faith to take Him at His Word. You need not fear rejection or ridicule. Let Him reassure you of His love and forgiveness.

Picture the cross of Christ once more. Really take a good mental look at it. Was Christ's death on the cross enough to cover your sin? Enough to take away your guilt? Yes. He gave everything He had for everything we've said, done, or thought. Then picture yourself at the foot of His cross, close enough to have your heart sprinkled by His redemptive blood. No sin is too grievous. No load is too heavy for Christ to carry. Walk away free, and leave with God that old condemning tape you've been playing over and over on your mental "recorder"!

One remaining issue could still bother the conscience. In Acts 24:16, Paul spoke about having a clear conscience before God and man. If my sin has only been against God and no one besides me has been hurt, I should be able to enjoy a clear conscience based on the steps in Hebrews 10:22. If I hurt someone else and I have not tried to make things right with the person, my conscience may still bother me because God wants me to make restitution. If I can possibly make amends, I should try. Caution: Never confess anything which will devastate another person just to unload your conscience; but if the person already knows we have wronged them, we should try to make amends (see Matt. 5:23-24).

Like the apostle Paul, we can enjoy a clear conscience even after a guilty past. Don't wait another moment. "Draw near to God" (Heb. 10:22).

*H*ow does God want you to respond to what He showed you today?

_____

_____

_____

_____

_____

_____

DAY 3

A Peculiar Deliverance

Today's Treasure
"Then he called two of his centurions and ordered them, 'Get ready a detachment of two hundred soldiers, seventy horsemen and two hundred spearmen to go to Caesarea at nine tonight. Provide mounts for Paul so that he may be taken safely to Governor Felix'"
(Acts 23:23-24).

Prisons can take many forms. Paul was physically imprisoned in Jerusalem. Yet he savored a certain freedom which flowed from a clear conscience. His accusers stood behind no bars. No chains rubbed their wrists raw, for we see them in a different kind of prison. A guilty conscience lived beneath their righteous robes. Outwardly, they were free men. Inwardly, they were in a prison of rage and resentment. I have purposely over-lapped your reading today to include the last verse in your previous reading.

*R*ead Acts 23:11-35 and complete the following.

1. Where was the Lord when He spoke to Paul in verse 11?

_____

2. How do you know these men were serious about their plot to kill Paul?

_____

3. Who told Paul about the plot against him? Choose one.
   ❑ Timothy   ❑ his sister   ❑ a Roman guard   ❑ his nephew

4. On what basis could Paul have known their plans would be unsuccessful?

_____

5. Who escorted Paul away from Jerusalem? Choose all that apply.
   ❑ two hundred spearmen   ❑ two hundred soldiers
   ❑ seventy horsemen   ❑ Paul's associates

6. Whose jurisdiction was Paul under in Caesarea? Choose one.
   ❑ Ananias   ❑ Emperor Nero   ❑ Governor Felix   ❑ King Agrippa

If we base our impressions of Paul solely on the Book of Acts, we could be tempted to think few things unsettled him. Luke gave many facts in his writing, but he did not elaborate on many feelings. Understandably, Paul's own writings tell us far more about his struggles and his temperament. Sometimes we must read between the lines in the Book of Acts to read the man and not just his travels. Acts 23:11 offers us a perfect opportunity to read between the lines without stretching the text. Read the verse again.

I hope Christ's tenderness toward His willing captive touches you. He stood near Paul and said, "Take courage!" We have no idea if Paul saw Christ near him or heard His voice so that he knew He had to be close.

Why did the Lord "stand near"? In earlier instances He directed Paul through visions. He also steered him through the leadership of the Holy Spirit. Why did Christ draw so physically close to Paul at this particular moment? I believe Paul was overcome with fear and may have been convinced he would not live much longer. In verse 10 the dispute between the Pharisees and Sadducees grew so violent even the commander feared Paul would be torn to pieces. Paul had looked straight into the eyes of rage. He was separated from his friends. He was imprisoned by strangers. I believe he was terrified.

146

The apostle's writings tell us volumes about God. The abundance of information Paul shares about God is so rich because he wrote from experience and inspiration.

What did Paul say about God in Philippians 4:19?

_____

This verse is beautifully illustrated in Acts 23:11. God looked on His chosen servant Paul imprisoned in Jerusalem, and He didn't just see emotions. He saw the need they represented. Paul was afraid. He needed courage. Just like Philippians 4:19 said, God literally met his need in Christ Jesus. That day in Paul's prison cell, Christ stood near—whether visible or invisible—and said, "Take courage!" God didn't mean for Paul to dig deeply into himself and muster up some courage. He wasn't suggesting Paul pull himself up by the bootstraps. When Christ stood near Paul and said, "Take courage," He meant "I'm right here. Take courage from Me!"

The Lord gave Paul great motivation for courage. He said, "'As you have testified about me in Jerusalem, so you must also testify in Rome'" (Acts 23:11). Paul received his confirmation: he was going to Rome. He did not know how or when, but his life could not be taken until the mission was complete. Paul surely knew that Christ's confirmation did not mean Paul wouldn't suffer or be greatly persecuted. He simply knew he could not be killed until he had testified about Christ in Rome.

Read Revelation 11:7. Based on Paul's experiences and the experiences of the two witnesses described in Revelation 11, what possible assumption might we make about servants of God and the timing of their deaths?

_____

_____

Although exceptions may exist for reasons beyond our understanding, I believe God allows His servants to live out their testimonies. The life of a committed servant which appears to have ended prematurely may have been fully completed to God. Jim Elliot, one of God's most passionate and devoted missionaries to Ecuador, is an example. His young life ended abruptly at the hands of the very people he tried to serve. To us he seems to have died prematurely, yet the testimony of his sacrificial love for God and belief in the gospel continues to speak today. Paul also could have easily been killed by people he loved and wanted to serve, but God was not finished with his earthly ministry. Christ came to him and assured him he would go to Rome.

God timed Paul's injection of courage perfectly because "the next morning the Jews formed a conspiracy and bound themselves with an oath not to eat or drink until they had killed Paul" (Acts 23:12). The original Greek word for this _conspiracy_ is _sustophe_ meaning "a turning or spinning together, as in a whirlwind, a gathering together of people, ... a public tumult." Let the definition help you draw a mental image of the force which gathered against Paul.

Not long ago, winds gathered into a terrible twister in my hometown and wreaked untold havoc. My siblings and I have grieved the loss of many of our childhood landmarks. The kind of conspiracy we're studying today can be pictured like the winds of rage gathering as one with a frightening capacity to destroy anything in its path.

Overnight in Jerusalem, Paul became the center of a dangerous whirlwind of rage which rapidly gained force. By morning, 40 men bound themselves with an oath to kill him. The original terminology tells us they were binding themselves to a curse if they didn't carry out their plans. They may not have realized they had bound themselves to a curse already!

*R*ead Micah 2:1-3 and consider all the similarities. According to these verses, how can God respond to evil conspiracies?

_____

_____

God did not allow the conspiracy against Paul to be successful. He delivered him from his persecutors. Paul's nephew brought him the news of the conspiracy. Don't miss Paul's response. He sent him to explain the plot to the commander. Remember, God had told Paul he was going to Rome. Paul knew somehow he would be delivered. Notice he didn't sit in his cell and expect another miracle like he and Silas experienced. When his nephew brought the news, he knew God might be planning his escape through natural means. He was right. Paul was escorted out of town by 200 soldiers, 70 horsemen, and 200 spearmen! God delivered him in style, didn't He? Surely Paul had moments when he was rather amused at the entourage. I wonder if he thought things like, *If my Daddy could see me now* or *Timothy would love this!* Paul's immediate destination was a cell in Caesarea, but he knew it had to be temporary. The same God who delivered him from death would deliver him to Rome.

*W*rite Psalm 3:8 in the space below.

_____

_____

God is the Deliverer (see Ps. 140:7). He can deliver us *through* peril, or He can deliver us *from* peril. Like Paul, during the courses of our lives we can probably expect both. We are challenged constantly not to measure God by our limited expectation. We can't put God in a box. We cannot assume He will deliver us by the same methods over and over again. God has a wonderful way of keeping things interesting, doesn't He? Remember, deliverance through a natural means is no less the work of God than deliverance through a supernatural means. Through Paul, He has shown us He can supernaturally shake the foundations of the prison to deliver; or He can employ the Roman cavalry to accompany a servant out of town.

Deliverance *through* and *from* peril is undoubtedly one of the themes of Paul's life. We have already had a number of occasions to consider God's creativity in His methods of delivery. When the apostle Paul wrote his second letter to the Corinthians, he had stated his hope to see God *continue* to deliver him and his associates.

*R*ead his words in 2 Corinthians 1:10-11. According to Paul, how could the Corinthians help?

_____

We must never underestimate the effects of intercessory prayer lifted for our deliverance. Nor must we underestimate the effects of our prayers for others. Last year my heart was torn to pieces over a devastating loss. For several months no one outside our family and friends knew we had suffered a loss; because the wound was so fresh, we were not yet able to tell the story. Letters poured in from all over the nation saying something like this: "God has placed a heavy burden on my heart for Beth and her family. I do not know what is wrong, but I'm praying for them." I could hardly believe it. Once we shared more openly about our loss, we learned that literally thousands of people were praying for us. I am absolutely certain those prayers delivered my family and me from the pit of despair. Many times my soul would sink in grief, and I would feel like I was about to descend into depression. Each time I began to slip, I sensed something like a supernatural net disallowing me to descend another inch. I know without a doubt intercessory prayer helped keep me out of the pit.

Have you ever realized the impact of intercessory prayer for your own deliverance? If so, when? Who was praying for you?

_____

_____

Do you think God can deliver us whether or not anyone is praying for us? ❏ Yes ❏ No Assuming your answer was yes, what role do you think prayer plays in someone's deliverance?

_____

_____

You may have cited a role other than Paul mentioned in 2 Corinthians 1:11, but look at his reasoning. What would Paul's intercessors have occasion to do if God granted such "gracious favor"?

_____

With great thanksgiving let's acknowledge God as the Deliverer today. He can deliver anyone from anything at anytime. He doesn't need any help. Yet He invites us to be part of His great work through prayer. If we don't intercede for one another, we miss opportunities to see His deliverance and thank Him for His faithfulness. I like to call this God's profit sharing plan. When we pray for one another, we share the blessings when deliverance comes because we've been personally involved. Their thanksgiving becomes our thanksgiving.

Many scholars believe Paul wrote 2 Corinthians on his third missionary journey, prior to his arrest in Jerusalem. If so, the Corinthians' prayers were involved in Paul's deliverance. He rode in style to Caesarea, surrounded by soldiers, horsemen, and spearmen. Surely the Corinthian Christians gave many thanks on his behalf.

A thankful heart is not the only result of helping someone be delivered through intercessory prayer; our faith in what He can do in our own lives is also strengthened. The believers in Corinth were babes in Christ. Can you imagine how blessed they were to know their prayers helped deliver Paul? They realized God could do the same for them. God's glory and power does not waver from one child to the next. He can just as surely deliver you as He delivered the apostle Paul. Today as you conclude this lesson, may you sense Him near you saying, "Take courage, child—My courage."

How does God want you to respond to what He showed you today?

_____

_____

_____

_____

_____

_____

D A Y 4
An Inconvenient Gospel

Today's Treasure
"As Paul discoursed on righteousness, self-control and the judgment to come, Felix was afraid and said, 'That's enough for now! You may leave. When I find it convenient, I will send for you'"
(Acts 24:25).

As we begin today's lesson, my mind drifts back over the many stops we've made with the apostle Paul. I suppose none of us want to trade times, places, and lives with him; but each of us must admit his tenure on this earth was extremely fascinating. He could write about "the breadth, and length, and depth, and height" (Eph. 3:18, KJV) because he experienced each of those extremes. The man we're studying in God's Word was flesh and blood. He bruised. He cried. He got angry. He made mistakes. But he was extraordinary. After preparing today's lesson, I am astounded by Paul's courage; yet, from our previous lesson, we know just where he got it: from a nearby Savior. Today's reading unfolds with Paul incarcerated in Caesarea after being escorted by a grand cavalry.

*R*ead Acts 24:1-27 and complete the following.
In verses 5-7, of what crimes did Tertullus accuse Paul?

_____

_____

Describe Paul's incarceration in Caesarea based on verse 23.

_____

_____

Write the three-point outline of Paul's sermon to Felix and Druscilla.

1. _____

2. _____

3. _____

How long was Paul incarcerated in Caesarea under the authority of Felix? Choose one.
❑ 2 months   ❑ 6 months   ❑ 2 years   ❑ 5 years

Few things are more disgusting than a political spiel that bears no resemblance to the truth. Based on Tertullus' description, Felix deserved his own holiday for being a peacemaker, a reformer, a tireless officer, and a noble man! Tertullus knew better. We can't fully appreciate the smoke Tertullus was blowing the governor's direction until we learn more about Felix. He was vile and incompetent. Nero had him recalled only two years later. He was a former slave who had cunningly gained favor with the imperial court. "Felix was known for his violent use of repressive force and corrupt self-aggrandizement."[1]

Felix obviously viewed the conflict between Paul and the Jewish leaders as a no-win situation. The size of the Jewish community and the Roman citizenship of Paul left Felix in a dilemma. He lacked the wisdom to make an appropriate decision, so he did nothing. God, however, was clearly up to something. I believe one reason God allowed Paul to be held under the authority of Felix for two years was to reach out to him with His Word. The more I see, hear, and experience, the more dumfounded I am over the lengths God will go for one soul. Second Peter 3:9 tells us God doesn't want anyone to perish. He wants all to come to repentance. God loves the most vile offender. He loved Felix, and He sent him a man who was unwilling to curtsy to him like Tertullus. He sent Paul: a man unafraid to preach the truth.

Let's focus on Paul's message to Felix several days after the hearing. God gave Paul an interesting opportunity. He sent the preacher to a congregation of two: Felix and Drusilla. Drusilla was the third wife of the governor, and both of them had deserted previous spouses to marry. God equipped Paul with a tailor-made lesson for the two. Verse 25 tells us Paul "discoursed" which means "to speak back and forth or alternately, to converse with." Paul didn't just give a sermon. He led Felix and Drusilla in an interactive study! Let's dig a little deeper into his personalized message by filling in the triangle below. The core of Paul's message was "faith in Christ Jesus" (Acts 24:24).

𝓛abel each point of the triangle with the three points of Paul's message listed in verse 25. Make your own choice for which you would place on the top, and briefly explain the reason for your choice in the margin.

_____

_____

_____

_____

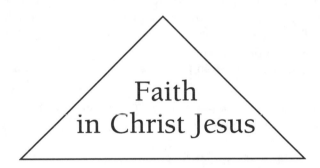

Take a moment to study the diagram of Paul's message to Felix and Drusilla. We know his topic and his three points. Now let's try to imagine what some of his content might have been. What do "righteousness, self-control, and the judgment to come" have to do with "faith in Christ Jesus"? In my preparation, God led me to several passages Paul later wrote to Titus. These passages can help us tie all three points to the central focus of Paul's message in Acts 24:25.

𝓡ead Titus 2:11-14 carefully. Verse 11 corresponds with faith in Christ Jesus in the center of the triangle above. In order to receive the salvation God brought to man, we must have faith in Christ. Now write any applicable phrases from Titus 2:12-14 beside the corresponding points of the triangle above. After you have completed this exercise, read Titus 2:15.

Which one of the following statements would apply to the comparisons we've drawn between Paul's words to Titus and his message to Felix and Drusilla?
  ❑ Salvation by grace has nothing to do with behavior.
  ❑ Salvation by grace is a matter of self-control.
  ❑ Salvation by grace teaches us to live self-controlled lives.

Paul risked bodily harm when he preached such a forceful message to Governor Felix and his wife. Christ had assured the apostle he would go to Rome, so he knew he wouldn't be killed; but torture can be a more difficult prospect than death! You can be relatively sure Paul didn't bring the message Felix was expecting. He and Drusilla, a Jewess, most likely expected a message of mystical divinity. Instead they got a message of practical clarity, and every point stuck.

Felix was not amused by the outspoken preacher. Meditate on his reaction once more. "Felix was afraid and said, 'That's enough for now! You may leave'" (Acts 24:25).

*D*escribe what you think Felix might have been thinking and feeling.

_____

_____

_____

At least Felix took the message personally enough to be afraid. The word *phobia* is related to the original Greek word *phobos* which means "to flee from." If only Felix had run to Christ rather than from Him. Christ would have received him as readily as the most noble convert. Instead, Felix dismissed Paul. I see some irony in his choice of words. History describes him as a man with a gross lack of self-control.[2] I have a feeling he rarely applied the words, "That's enough for now," to himself. Felix told Paul he would send for him at a more convenient time.

I'm not sure confrontation with personal sin is ever convenient. Some of the messages I've needed to hear most were those I wanted to hear least. Like Felix, we in our human natures often resist what is best for us. Unlike Felix, we can dare to accept a truthful but confrontational message and find freedom.

Can you think of a time when you heard a very confrontational message which God ultimately used to bring about freedom in your life? What was the general message?

_____

_____

*H*ow does God want you to respond to what He showed you today?

_____

_____

_____

_____

_____

You may have noticed no reaction is given for Drusilla. We might surmise she was also convicted and frightened, but Scripture only tells us Felix was afraid. I would like to offer a different theory. Perhaps Drusilla simply did not humble herself enough to be afraid. She had quite an interesting heritage—one plagued with pride.

*R*eview Acts 12:19-23.

This Herod was Agrippa I. He was also Drusilla's father. You might think having a father who was eaten alive by worms for receiving glory due only to God would have some impact. Instead, Drusilla led an adulterous life in spite of all she knew about morality and reverence for God from her Jewish heritage. The generational bondage of pride could have been broken with her father's dreadful demise. Instead, she resisted the message, willingly picked up the chain of pride, and carried on.

In His great mercy, God reaches out to the immoral, ill-tempered, and boastful. Many hear but run the other way. Others hear but never apply. But some listen, really listen, and they are set free. God not only sent Felix and Drusilla a fitting message, He sent them a fitting messenger. Paul could not stand before them as one who had never experienced a terrible lack of self-control. He was once puffed with pride. His only righteousness was in the law. Then one day Jesus confronted him in the middle of his sin. He'd been running straight to Him ever since.

D A Y   5
Man Alive!

As today's scene unfolds in the Book of Acts, at least two years have passed since Paul was incarcerated in Caesarea. Acts 24:26 tells us Felix sent for Paul many times after his discourse but solely in hopes Paul would offer him a bribe. No further word suggests he became frightened again. We only see the one glimpse of his awareness of sin and its possible consequences. Felix may have resisted the Holy Spirit repeatedly until conviction finally passed. I believe the governor was under great conviction of sin when Paul first preached to him. If only he had responded at that time.

Today's Treasure
"It is because of my hope in what God has promised our fathers that I am on trial today" (Acts 26:6).

*R*ead Hebrews 3:7-13. **How might God's message to the Hebrew people also speak to people like Felix?**

_____

_____

Today we will see the apostle Paul give his testimony before a new audience. They may not accept Christ, but they will not escape playing their part in the will of God. We will read two full chapters today, because we have previously considered Paul's testimony which is repeated in Acts 26.

*R*ead Acts 25 and 26 and complete the following. **Can you think of any reasons why the Jewish leaders were still so anxious to kill Paul two years later? No right or wrong answer exists. Just offer your conjecture.**

_____

_____

Why Paul appealed to Caesar rather than return to Jerusalem to be tried remains a mystery. Name as many possible reasons as you can think of why Paul made the decision to appeal to Rome.

_____

_____

_____

Reconsider Acts 25:19-21. Throughout our lives we will meet others who are not convinced that Christ is alive. How do you know He's alive?

_____

_____

How would you tell an interested but unbelieving person to investigate the living Christ? Name as many ways as you can.

_____

_____

_____

Based on our previous lessons, why was Festus' decision to send Paul to Rome (v. 25) so important?

_____

_____

You've read about Paul's background and his testimony several times at this point in our study. Did you learn anything new about Paul's past in Acts 26 or did anything stand out to you afresh? If so, what?

_____

_____

Can you find any evidence suggesting Paul cared about the souls of those who opposed him or stood in judgment over him?

_____

_____

_____

An interesting word emerged in today's reading: *investigate*. In Acts 25:20, Festus "was at a loss how to investigate" Paul's claims that a dead man named Jesus was alive. I asked you to consider the matter in spiritual terms. I wish I had the privilege of hearing you testify how *you* know Christ is alive. I know I would be so blessed.

Not long ago I shared with a loved one how *I* know Christ is alive. I'll never forget our conversation. He said, "I *believe* in reincarnation" and "I *believe* a spiritual presence exists rather than a certain God." He continued by repeating the words "I *believe*" over and over. Suddenly God gave me such a strange insight, and I was overwhelmed at the difference between my loved one and me. He *believed* the things he had been taught through New Age philosophers and their materials. I didn't just believe. I knew. With tears in my eyes, I gently said to him, "My God is not just Someone I believe in. He's Someone I know. I've felt His presence. I've seen His activity. I've experienced His deliverance. I've been touched by His healing. I've witnessed answered prayer. I've 'heard' Him speak straight to me through His Word. Yes, I believe. But more than that, I **know**." My loved one said nothing more, but I knew he heard my heart. Dead prophets don't save, guide, heal, deliver, answer prayers, nor speak through an ancient text like this morning's newspaper. My advice to anyone else investigating the matter would probably be two-fold:

- Open your heart to the possibility of Christ's authenticity by coming to church and getting to know Christian people.
- Ask Christ if He's real; then be honest and open enough to watch for Him to reveal Himself.

*A*ccording to Jeremiah 29:13, why might an investigation like this work?

_____

I may *know* Christ rose from the dead from personal experience, but plenty of other things exercise my faith! Good investigators ask certain questions: *Who? What? Where? When?* and *How?* Today's text shows *what* we may know: *Who* is in control and even *what* He's doing and *where* He's leading—but we'll rarely guess *when* and *how!* Let's take the Jewish leaders and Paul as an example of our inability to know *when* and *how.*

1. Neither Paul nor the Jewish leaders understood WHEN. Paul didn't know when God would fulfill His promise.

- Paul knew Who had called him—Christ.
- He also knew what Christ had called him to do—preach to the Gentiles.
- He even knew where—God was going to send him to Rome.

Paul might never have guessed he would still be sitting in jail two years after the promise. He probably asked God many times—When? Time means so much to you and me. When God sheds light on ministries He wants us to fulfill or promises He plans to keep, we usually assume He means right now! A study of the Jewish patriarchs will easily prove that years may separate God's promise and its fulfillment. Not one minute is wasted, but God seems to rarely fulfill His revealed plan when we expect.

*C*an you think of something God revealed to you but that took years to fulfill? ❏ Yes ❏ No Briefly describe the circumstance.

_____

_____

Likewise, the Jews didn't know WHEN God would fulfill His promise.

*R*eread Acts 26:6-7.

The Jews believed God would send the Messiah. The Messiah was the answer to Who. They also knew what He would come to do—bring salvation. They were certain where—Israel, then to all parts of the world. But, you see, they didn't understand *when.* They were still looking for a Messiah who had already come. Sometimes we can keep asking when God is going to do something He's already done!

I have a good friend who kept asking God when He was going to introduce her future husband to her. She later married her boss to whom God had introduced her five years earlier! Neither Paul nor the Jewish leaders understood the when of God's promise.

2. Neither Paul nor the Jewish leaders understood HOW. God had assured Paul He was sending him to Rome, but Paul would never have guessed how. You may have considered Festus' words in Acts 25:25 to be just as pivotal as I did. Festus announced to King Agrippa, "I decided to send him to Rome." Actually, God had decided to send Paul to Rome, but He was about to use Festus as the vehicle. Paul may have wondered over and over how he would ever get to Rome while under arrest. He probably asked his associates many times to pray for his release, so he could fulfill his calling in Rome. I wonder if Paul ever imagined his arrest would be the tool God would use to give him an all expenses paid trip to his destination.

Recently, I heard an award-winning actor tell his testimony before a secular audience. He said when he was a boy, God revealed to him that he would reach out to thousands and thousands of people. All his life he had waited for God to call him to preach. God never called him to a pulpit. Instead, the young man developed into an Academy Award winning actor. He was thankful for his opportunities to act, but he couldn't understand what happened to his calling. The evening he was honored he said to thousands that he realized God had fulfilled His promise. The young boy never would have guessed how God would do what He said.

On day 3 we learned that God is the Deliverer, but we never know how He might deliver us. Today the precept is underscored as we see that God always fulfills His promises, but not always the way we imagine.

$\mathcal{E}$arlier I asked you to recall a time when you wondered when God would do what He had revealed to you. Using your same example, would you have ever guessed how He was going to fulfill His promise? Explain briefly.

_____

_____

$\mathcal{H}$ow does God want you to respond to what He showed you today?

_____

_____

_____

_____

_____

If Paul was occasionally shocked by how God fulfilled His promises, he was not the only one. God had assured the Jews He would send the Messiah, but they never would have guessed how. They were expecting great pomp to accompany their king's arrival. They were not expecting someone who looked so ordinary, so common. They unfortunately wanted a prestigious king more than a servant Savior.

Praise God, He gives us what we need, not what we want. If Christ had come to immediately wear His crown, we would be hopelessly lost. A crown of thorns and a splintered cross had to precede a crown of jewels and a hallowed throne. If they hadn't, Christ would still have a throne but no beloved earthly subjects to approach it.

God calls us to be good investigators. We don't have to be at a loss on *how* to investigate such matters. When we don't know *what, when, where,* or *how,* we can trust in *Who.* We won't always find our answers, but we can always find our God when we seek Him with all our hearts. And He will love and comfort us until all other answers come.

[1]John F. Walvoord et al., eds., *The Bible Knowledge Commentary New Testament* (Wheaton, IL: Victor Books, 1983), 421.
[2]Ibid., 422.

A Walk of Faith

Acts 22

Faith That Stands Up Under Trial

1. A belief system beyond simple _____ (Acts 22:3-5; Rom. 9:3-5).

2. A belief system beyond personal _____ (Acts 24:13-16; 26:7; Rom. 10:2).

3. A belief system which stands the test of _____ rather than preferences or philosophies.

What are several criteria which help determine whether or not a claimed belief system is:

Preference or Genuine Conviction?

- True convictions are _____ _____ to daily living.

- True convictions have a _____ (Acts 26:19-23; Rom. 10:17; 14:1).

- True convictions are _____ (2 Tim. 4:16-17).

- True convictions are _____ against the pressure to _____
  (Rom. 12:1-2; 14:2-3).

- True convictions are _____ regardless of _____ (Acts 24:27).

WEEK 8

The Pathway to Rome

Day 1
An Anchor in the Storm

Day 2
An Umbrella in the Storm

Day 3
Island Wonders

Day 4
Brothers Among Strangers

Day 5
Ears, Eyes, and Hearts

Tighten your life jackets because the voyage ahead of us this week could get a little rocky! Storms in life are inevitable, but how we weather them is always optional. We have quite an adventure ahead of us. Allow God to completely capture your imagination and involve you in the experiences we will study this week. God is full of surprises—and some of them appear in the worst of storms. God is our refuge: the one plank still floating on the water when the ship around us sinks. This week, look for the answers to the following questions like a person on a deserted island looking for a treasure.

Principal Questions
Day 1: How would you describe Paul's voyage toward Rome?
Day 2: Why do you think all the passengers' lives were spared?
Day 3: What did the shipwrecked crew discover while in Malta?
Day 4: What ties bind Christians together as brothers and sisters?
Day 5: According to the original language, how can a person hear but never understand?

We may never leave our native land or travel by air or sea; but, if we love and serve God, our lives will be a great adventure. He'll never take you anywhere He has not already prepared for your arrival. Keep trusting Him.

DAY 1

An Anchor in the Storm

God promised the apostle Paul He would send him to Rome. Paul had no idea when or how. Following his hearing before King Agrippa, both questions were answered. Today we'll set sail toward Rome with the apostle Paul for a most unpleasant journey. Day 1 and day 2 provide biblical proof that excitement is not synonymous with fun!

*R*ead Acts 27:1-26. Trace Paul's travels to Rome on your map in a fourth and final color of ink; then complete the following.
List all the identified passengers on the same vessels with Paul.

_____

_____

What season of the year can you assume it was? _____

Considering the first day of the storm as Day One, match the desperate actions of the crew to the coinciding day.

Day One	They threw cargo overboard.
Day Two	They let the ship be driven along.
Day Three	They threw the ship's tackle overboard.

Describe the circumstances under which they finally gave up all hope.

_____

_____

When was hope obviously restored to Paul? Choose one.
❑ the weather changed ❑ God spoke to him through an angel
❑ Luke encouraged him ❑ they could see the shore

And you thought going on vacation with three children in a mini-van was rough! Give me the air or give me the road, but I think I'll pass on the sea! You no doubt noticed when you traced today's travels on your map that sea travel was the only practical means of making a voyage from Caesarea to Rome. At least Paul had a few good friends with him. We know Luke joined him because the terminology turns once again from *they* to *we*. Another associate by the name of Aristarchus was also named among them. Both these men were no doubt a tremendous support to Paul. Even though God allowed His faithful servant to be in chains for the gospel, He often provoked favor in the hearts of Paul's captors. Julius, a centurion in the Imperial Regiment, showed great kindness toward the apostle during the trek to Rome. Acts 27:3 tells us Julius "allowed [Paul] to go to his friends so they might provide for his needs."

*W*hat do you imagine some of Paul's *needs* might have been?

_____

Paul's *needs* obviously didn't diminish his sensibilities. We ordinarily think of the apostle Paul as deeply spiritual, but today's text reminds us he also could be rather practical. Take another look at Acts 27:9-10. In ancient days, few vessels risked the sea during the winter months.

Although Paul was no expert seaman, he also wasn't a man to keep his opinion to himself. He warned them in verse 10, "'Men, I can see that our voyage is going to be disastrous.'" The original word for *see* is one which denotes a "gaze" and a "careful observation of details." Can you picture this little bearded man licking the end of his index finger and holding it up to check the direction of the wind? Paul might have been perceived as a *know-it-all* at times. This was one of those times when someone probably should have listened. Paul had never steered a ship, but he had been a passenger many times. He probably stood next to the captain on many voyages and asked questions.

The pilot and owner of the ship insisted on sailing regardless of difficulty. They let their ledgers eclipse their good sense. The Alexandrian ship serviced Rome with expensive grain. They took advantage of the first gentle breeze and "sailed along the shore of Crete" (Acts 27:13). You know what happened next: "a wind of hurricane force … swept down from the island" (v. 14). The location of their peril has been called St. Paul's Bay by many for centuries. "Only a few years ago dozens of yachts, some of considerable size, were wrecked here under just such conditions as Luke describes."[1]

This particular peril in the apostle's life struck a chord in my heart for reasons I couldn't quite identify. I finally realized why—he and the others met great difficulty because of someone else's poor judgment.

I've gone through storms as a direct result of my own rebellion. I've also gone through storms as a result of spiritual warfare. Others were ordained directly by God for His glory, but sometimes the most difficult storms of all can be those which result from another person's poor judgment. A wrong decision by a business partner, a boss, a driver, a jury, a teacher, or a spouse can have devastating repercussions on other lives.

Of the four origins of personal storms we've identified, the one caused by someone else's poor judgment has its own unique difficulty. Why? We have someone else in flesh and blood to blame! We feel much greater potential for bitterness and unforgiveness.

$\mathcal{H}$ave you ever been in a storm due to another person's poor judgment? If so, without mentioning names, describe how you felt.

The sailors took steps to deal with the storm that enveloped their ship. In their actions I see practical behaviors we can also apply in our lives for surviving our personal *storms*. Although the points I am about to make might not apply to a literal ship on an angry sea, they will be helpful in the storms we encounter when someone close to us exercises poor judgment.

1. Don't pull up the anchor (see Acts 27:13). Jesus Christ is our anchor beyond the veil (see Heb. 6:19-20). When gentle breezes blow in our lives and all seems calm and peaceful, we often become less attentive to Him. We're not as aware of our need for the One who secures our lives and holds us steady until the storms begin to rage. Don't let a few calm breezes give you a false sense of security in yourself and your surroundings. Stay anchored in Christ in gentle times, too.

When gentle breezes blow, do you tend to pull up the anchor and ignore your relationship to Christ? ❑ Yes ❑ No If so, what would help your faith become more consistent and less regulated by circumstances?

_____

_____

2. Don't give way to the storm (see v. 15). Peril caused by another person's poor judgment can often cause feelings of immense helplessness. Don't give way to the storm. Give way to the Master of the seas.

*W*hat did the disciples say about Christ in Mark 4:41?

_____

3. Do throw some cargo overboard (see v. 18). Raging storms have ways of identifying some old cargo we're still hanging onto. When we're upset over someone's poor judgment, we have a tendency to drag up memories of other times we've been wronged as well. Storms complicate life enough. Ask God to simplify and clarify a few things in your life by helping you throw some old cargo overboard.

*C*an you think of the last time you dragged out some old cargo in the midst of a new storm? Explain briefly.

_____

_____

4. Do throw the tackle overboard (see v. 19). The *tackling* on a ship included all kinds of gear: ropes, pulleys, spars, masts, and planks. These objects were man-made provisions to master the storm. Storms are seldom pleasant, but they can serve an important purpose. They help us to see what man-made solutions we are substituting for depending on and getting to know God.

5. Never give up hope (see v. 20). Notice Luke uses the word *we* when identifying those who gave up hope. He wrote one of the Gospels! How could he lose hope? He witnessed miracles! Today's text reminds us anyone can lose hope when a storm rages. The original word for *gave up* in Acts 27:20 is the same one translated *cutting loose* in Acts 27:40. We might say Luke and the others *cut loose* their hope when the storm continued to rage day after day. The psalmist offers us a lifesaver in our raging storms in Psalm 62:5.

*W*rite the verse in the space below:

_____

_____

The original Hebrew word translated *hope* in Psalm 62:5 is *tiqvah* which literally means "a cord, as an attachment" (Strong's). The psalmist contrasted the disappointment

161

he often experienced in man with the security he found in his faithful God. His cord or rope was attached to God alone. We're all holding onto a rope of some kind for security; but if anyone besides God is on the other end, we're hanging on by a thread! Hang on to Christ for dear life when the waves break harshly against you. He will be your survival no matter what the storm may destroy. Only He can keep you from becoming bitter. Only He can rebuild what gale-force winds tear apart. Be very honest. Picture the rope you are hanging onto for security. Is God on the other end, or have you placed your hopes and expectations in someone who might not be able to deliver?

6. Listen for God to speak (see v. 24). Incline your ear to the Master of the seas when the storms rage. He will not be silent. He will probably not send an angel from heaven to speak audibly to you, but He may send a fellow believer, a neighbor, a pastor, or friend. You can also hear Him speak through His Word anytime you are willing to open the Bible and receive. Job suffered, for reasons outside his control, in ways we will never experience. He had plenty of places to lay blame. I believe one reason he survived such tragedy was because God proved not to be silent as Job had feared. The place in which He spoke to Job is very applicable to us today.

*H*ow does God want you to respond to what He showed you today?

_____

_____

_____

_____

_____

_____

*F*ill in the following blank based on Job 40:6.

"Then the Lord spoke to Job _____"**

God will speak to you, too —straight to your heart. Sometimes others can make decisions which are devastating to our lives. I cannot promise you everything will be OK. It may be. It may not be. But I promise you based on the faithfulness of God that you can be OK. Just don't pull up that anchor. And never let go of the rope.

D A Y   2

An Umbrella in the Storm

Today's Treasure
"'God has graciously given you the lives of all who sail with you'"
(Acts 27:24).

As today's study unfolds, we join Paul and the crew aboard their tossing ship in a terrible storm. In our previous lesson, we discussed a difficult scenario: when suffering results from the foolishness of another. Today's reading develops the opposite scenario: when blessings result from the faithfulness of another. Let's allow God to open our eyes to the importance of faithfulness and obedience through a lesson in contrasts today. Our reading will overlap with the reading on day 1, so we can recapture the scene and a sense of continuity.

*R*ead Acts 27:13-44. Try to picture the events and hear the waves breaking harshly against the boat. Complete the following based on verses 27-44. How many nights passed before the crew realized they were approaching land? Choose one.
    ❏ 3   ❏ 7   ❏ 14   ❏ 40

Why did the sailors pretend to lower anchors from the bow?

_____

162

Our children might call the apostle a *tattletale* in verse 31! This scenario offers a great rule of thumb for appropriate times to be a *tattletale*. What might be the rule of thumb?

_____

The crew of 276 was scared and hungry. How did God use Paul to specifically meet both their needs in verses 33-36?

_____

What did they do right after they ate? Choose one.
- ❏ They swam to shore.
- ❏ They gave thanks.
- ❏ They threw the grain overboard.
- ❏ Other _____

Reread verses 42-43. Why were all the prisoners spared?

_____

By what two methods did everyone reach land safely?
- ❏ swimming
- ❏ lifeboats
- ❏ assistance of islanders
- ❏ planks or pieces of the ship

What an exciting event! Paul's life lends constant proof that the most outlandish works of God are often seen in the most difficult circumstances. This shipwreck was unfortunately not Paul's first.

*H*ow many times was Paul shipwrecked? Read 2 Corinthians 11:25.

_____

This shipwreck is the only one described in detail, however. The reason may be the lesson in contrasts we should not miss. Paul's voyage to Rome teaches us that one life and one man's decision can dramatically affect many, whether positively or negatively.

Julius, the centurion, was a good man, but he made a foolish decision. In Acts 27:11, he took the advice of the pilot and owner of the ship who were motivated by profit rather than good judgment. The owner gambled everything he had to gain a little more but ended up losing everything. Although the entire crew suffered because of one man's selfish motive and another man's poor judgment, they ultimately kept their lives because of a third man's faithfulness. The angel of God spoke clearly to Paul in Acts 27:24, "'God has graciously given you the lives of all who sail with you.'" Clearly all life was spared because of Paul. From either viewpoint, we can see one moral to the story: The umbrella of protection or destruction in one man's hand can often cover many heads.

Let's think of the effects of one person's actions being like an umbrella over several other heads today. One holds the umbrella, but several others are under the influence. What kind of *cover* these figurative umbrellas provide is not only determined by belief in God versus unbelief but also in faithfulness versus unfaithfulness. In Acts 27 God gave Paul an *umbrella* of protection because of Paul's obedience in ministry. Whether or not they realized it, many were gathered under the *umbrella* and found safety.

Let's take a look at another kind of *umbrella* in the storm. Ask God to give you fresh insight into the familiar story of the prophet Jonah.

*R*ead Jonah 1:1-17. Consider the *similarities* between Jonah and Paul. In the space below write every similarity you discover.

_____

_____

Now consider the differences between Jonah and Paul. Write each one in the space below.

_____

_____

You may have discovered similarities I missed, but let's consider the following:
- Both men were Hebrews. Both had Jewish backgrounds and believed in the one true God.
- Both men were preachers. In Jonah 1:8, the crew asked, "What do you do?" The original Hebrew word for *do* is *melakah* meaning "deputyship, i.e. ministry" (Strong's). In essence the crew asked Jonah, "What is your ministry?" God clearly called Jonah to preach according to verse 2.
- Both men were called to preach unpopular messages in pagan cities. Nineveh and Rome were both powerful cities filled with wickedness.
- Both men boarded a ship.
- Both men experienced a terrible, life-threatening storm.
- Both men greatly impacted the rest of the crew.
- Both men knew the key to the crew's survival.

Paul and Jonah had many similarities, didn't they? We also share common ground with them. We are believers in the one true God. I think we each also realize we've been called to serve Him, but similarities can end dramatically at this point based on individual responses to God's directions. Let's consider a few contrasts between Paul and Jonah. They differed in at least the following ways:
- Paul was compelled by his calling to Rome. Jonah was repelled by his calling to Nineveh!

Use your imagination. Can you think of any reasons why the two men might have responded so differently to their commissions?

_____

_____

- Paul faced many obstacles on his way to Rome: imprisonment, many injustices, inclement weather, and other difficulties. Jonah's only obstacle was himself!
- Paul had to sit and wait for the Lord. Jonah stood and ran from the Lord!
- Paul felt a burden of responsibility for the crew, although the calamity was not his fault. Jonah slept while the others worked diligently to survive his calamity.
- Although both men were frightened and probably felt hopeless, Paul received courage from the Lord. Jonah revealed a rather amusing cowardice. In Jonah 1:12, the fugitive preacher told them, "'Pick me up and throw me into the sea....

164

I know that it is my fault.'" Notice he never offered to jump in! Sadly, heathen men showed more character than God's servant. Jonah 1:13 says, "Instead, the men did their best to row back to land." They did not want to throw him overboard and risk offending Jonah's God.

Paul and Jonah are great characters to compare and contrast because we can relate to both of them! Sometimes we respond with obedience like Paul. Other times we run from God with aerobic velocity like Jonah. Let's ask a fair question based on their examples. Does prompt obedience really make much difference? When all was said and done, didn't Paul suffer through a terrible storm although he had been entirely obedient? Didn't Jonah get another chance to obey, and an entire city was spared?

What difference does prompt obedience or faithfulness make anyway?

_____

_____

God loves us whether or not we are obedient, but the quality of our Christian lives is dramatically affected by our response. In addition to your thoughts above, allow me to add one very big difference between the obedient Christian and the disobedient Christian—between obedient times and disobedient times.

Read John 15:10-11. What is the result of obedience according to verse 11?

_____

_____

Although Jonah was ultimately obedient and surprisingly successful, you will search in vain for a single hint of joy in his life. Although Paul seemed to suffer at every turn, he had more to say about joy than any other mouthpiece in the Word of God.

I think we've learned a few important lessons today. An attitude of obedience makes a difference to the servant and to those close by. Servants of God can dramatically affect the lives of others positively or negatively. Under Jonah's umbrella in the storm many experienced calamity. Under Paul's umbrella many found safety. Is the sky rumbling? Are clouds darkening? Is a storm rising in the horizon? If you are a child of God, you will hold an umbrella in the storm. You will not be under the umbrella alone. Neither will I. Our children will be under there with us. Our coworkers may be, too. The flocks God has entrusted to us will be there. Even the lost are often drawn to people of faith when hurricane winds begin to blow. Child of God, you and I are centered on the bow of the ship when storms come and the waves crash. May the rest of the crew find an umbrella of blessing in our midst.

How does God want you to respond to what He showed you today?

_____

_____

_____

_____

_____

_____

D A Y   3

Island Wonders

After 14 days of stomach-turning terror, the ship ran aground on an unexpected island. Some swam to shore, but others paddled their way on planks and pieces of the ship. I would have been the one clinging to the biggest piece of the ship and hollering for Keith.

I've had my own terror in the tropics: a snorkeling expedition off the coast of Maui in 1995. I assure you Keith will never forget it either. Fifteen minutes after everyone else

Today's Treasure
"Once safely on shore, we found out that the island was called Malta. The islanders showed us unusual kindness. They built a fire and welcomed us all because it was raining and cold" (Acts 28:1-2).

jumped in the water with gear intact, I was still standing on the back of the boat. The captain found the tragic scene rather amusing.

The trouble really began once I got into the water. They told us to simply breathe normally and enjoy the scenery. I really tried. But I couldn't see a single fish for the fog in my mask. Keith swam over to me and said, "Elizabeth, every swimmer within 10 nautical miles can hear you breathing all the way under the water." He appeared to be losing patience with me. We were supposed to have snorkeling buddies so Keith had to swim close to me. Every time I turned my head, I accidentally smacked him in the face with the breathing tube sticking out in the back. After three or four rounds, I looked up and my buddy was nowhere to be found. We didn't meet up again until the captain pulled me back into the boat. Keith and I have shared some great laughs over parting waters in the deep and in case you're concerned, we're still buddies! Hopefully my story will not take the luster from Paul's.

> **Read Acts 28:1-10. What was unusual about the islanders according to verse 2? Choose one.**
> ❏ their language ❏ their dress ❏ their customs ❏ their kindness
>
> **Why did the islanders suspect Paul to be a murderer?**
>
> _____
>
> **When Paul suffered no ill effects, what opposite assumption did the islanders make?**
> ❏ He must be a saint. ❏ He must not be a murderer.
> ❏ He must be a king. ❏ He must be a god.
>
> **What special treatment did Paul and his associates receive in Malta?**
>
> _____
>
> **How did God reveal His power throughout the island?**
>
> _____

As Paul and his coworkers paddled their way from the sinking ship to shore, they must have wondered what they would find. On the island of Malta they made at least six discoveries. Let's consider them together.

1. They discovered "unusual kindness." Paul and the crew could have easily stumbled on unhappy natives. Instead, God prepared a safe haven for them among kind and civilized people. Luke tells us the people of Malta were not just kind; they were "unusually kind." This was not always the case. Ancient islanders often considered visitors to be unwelcome intruders. The original Greek word translated *islanders* in Acts 28:2 is *barbaros* which means "a barbarian."

Everyday I pray for a different country specified in a prayer guide. Not long ago, I was to pray for missionaries in the Pacific Islands that day. My first thought was, *what an easy life, serving on some beautiful tropical island.* Then the first two sentences grabbed my attention: "The Pacific was one of the first areas to be evangelized in the modern Protestant missionary era. Few areas of the world have claimed more missionary lives through disease, violent death and cannibalism."[2] Numerous believers exist on those islands today because many missionaries suffered to take them the message.

166

Can you think of a time when you were shipwrecked, in a manner of speaking, and encountered unusual kindness?

_____

At the time did you recognize God as the source of the unusual kindness for you? ❑ Yes ❑ No

Not long ago my assistant and I had a flat tire. We took the first possible exit, and right before our eyes was a car repair shop. A kind man dropped everything he was doing and fixed our tire. We were overwhelmed at his kindness.

2. They discovered warmth. The water was cold! Furthermore, rain was falling. I don't mind being cold for a few minutes if I can then put on a warm coat, but I don't like to be cold *and* wet! Just as Paul promised, not one hair was lost—but you can be sure each was standing on end! When you're wet and cold few things are more comforting than a warm fire. In fact, you can't truly appreciate warmth until you've experienced cold. Picture the crew huddled tightly around the camp fire warming their trembling hands. God met their most immediate need—warmth—first.

3. They discovered snakes! A viper indigenous to this region is a small but poisonous snake. Interestingly, it looks similar to a dead branch when immobile, so in all likelihood Paul picked up the snake as he was gathering brushwood. (Doesn't that give you the creeps?) When he put the branches in the fire, the viper took the first way out: Paul's hand. Can you imagine what Paul was thinking as the snake dangled from his hand? "Five times I received … forty lashes minus one. Three times I was beaten with rods, once I was stoned, three times I was shipwrecked" (2 Cor. 11:24-25) *and now this!* God used the creature, however, to reveal the beliefs of the islanders.

4. They discovered limited knowledge. The response of the islanders to Paul's snake bite was, "'This man must be a murderer; for though he escaped from the sea, Justice has not allowed him to live'" (Acts 28:4). Even though their assumption was incorrect, they revealed a limited knowledge of the one true God. If you have a *New International Version* of the Bible, you may have noticed the word *justice* was capitalized as a proper noun. I discovered the reason when I researched the original Greek word. The word *dikastes* actually means "a judge. One who executes justice. One who maintains law and equity." Although the island of Malta had presumably never been evangelized, they revealed an awareness of a divine judge who maintains justice.

Out of love for the world, God makes Himself known even in the most remote places on earth. Some call this self-disclosure *natural revelation*. He desires for people to seek the unknown through the known and discover a greater knowledge leading to salvation.

Read Romans 1:20. **What can be seen by all humanity, even those who have never heard of the God of the Bible?**

_____

_____

Through physical nature and perhaps human nature, the islanders of Malta perceived the existence of a divine Judge who ultimately enforced justice—even on those who thought they had escaped.

God is so merciful, isn't He? He doesn't just want people to be without excuse. He doesn't want people to be without a Savior. Justice was the natural light through which the people of Malta first perceived the one true God.

5. They discovered spiritual need. The people of Malta were walking in the natural light they had received. They believed in justice and equity but their knowledge was incomplete. When Paul shook off the snake and suffered no ill effects, they changed their minds and said he was a god. Although they believed in a divine Judge, they also believed in other gods. Many peoples of the world have received enough natural light to recognize the existence of deity, but they do not realize only One is truly God. They are dependent on missionaries, preachers, and teachers to come in their midst and be used of God to bring supernatural light. This supernatural light is described beautifully in 2 Corinthians 4:6.

*W*here does this supernatural light shine?_____

Where can the light of the knowledge of the glory of God be seen?

_____

Paul and his associates didn't just happen on the island of Malta. God sent them to bring the Word of God. The apostle surely preached to shine supernatural light on the face of Christ.

6. They discovered physical need. Something very unique happened on the island of Malta. All the sick were healed. Through this awesome, miraculous work, I believe God still prioritized their spiritual need. Three details suggest God worked in the physical realm for spiritual reasons.

*N*ote **Paul's action before he placed his hands on the chief official's father in Acts 28:8. "Paul went in to see him and, after _____, placed his hands on him and healed him."**

Paul did not want the people of Malta to think he was a god. He definitely would have wanted this healing to bring glory to and shine a spotlight on the face of Christ.

*A*ssume **Paul prayed aloud and write a brief petition he might have prayed.**

_____

_____

Prayer helped redirect their attentions to the source of all healing—Jesus Christ, the Great Physician. The second detail which suggests God used physical needs to shed light on spiritual realities was His means of healing. He used Paul to heal, yet Luke was a physician. Why? I believe God wanted the people of Malta to recognize God instead of some well-educated professional, as the source of their healing. No doubt God used Luke many times to tend the sick; but when He wanted to leave no room for doubt, He used someone with no knowledge of medicine.

The last detail that suggests God was up to something spiritual is wholesale healing. Sadly, an evangelist may not pack the house with good preaching and Spirit-filled worship, but he could draw the attention of every inhabitant in the land with rumors of healing. Yes, God cares about the sick. He cares deeply. And He often heals physical ill-nesses, but seldom in Scripture did He use a servant to bring physical healing to an entire land. I believe God used the physical needs of those in Malta to draw attention to the only One who could meet their spiritual needs. He trusted Paul not to take credit for a work only God can do. He knew the apostle would point the people of Malta to *Jehovah Rapha* —the One who said, "I am the Lord, who heals you" (Ex. 15:26).

We must also be careful to give God the glory when He uses us to accomplish things only He can do. Every time you lead someone to the Lord, the Holy Spirit is accom-plishing His work through you. Every time you exercise a spiritual gift, God is accom-plishing His work through you. If you are a servant of God and you have known Him long, He has used you to do something only He can do.

*N*ame a work He has accomplished through you. If you're uncomfortable with this request, you still may be taking too much credit. I'm asking you to boast in God, not in yourself. Go ahead. Name something!

_____

_____

If you sense the direction of the Holy Spirit now, write a brief prayer of availability for any work He might use you to accomplish. Then commit to give Him the glory.

_____

_____

*H*ow does God want you to respond to what He showed you today?

_____

_____

_____

_____

_____

_____

God used the apostle Paul to do something only God could do. He will use you and me too, but we must be trustworthy. Acts 28:11 tells us God allowed Paul and his coworkers to remain on the island for three months. You can be sure they heard more preaching in a few short months than most people hear in a lifetime! The angel told Paul in Acts 27:24: "'God has graciously given you the lives of all who sail with you.'" Then Paul revitalized the crew by saying, "'So keep up your courage, men, for I have faith in God that it will happen just as he told me. Nevertheless, we must run aground on some island'" (vv. 25-26). Little did Paul know he would run aground on an island called Malta where God had a glorious agenda planned.

D A Y   4
Brothers Among Strangers

Today's Treasure
"There we found some brothers who invited us to spend a week with them. And so we came to Rome" *(Acts 28:14).*

In the early spring of A.D. 61, God fulfilled His promise to Paul. The apostle arrived in Rome. Our text in Acts is very brief today and may leave some of us yearning for details. Although Luke wrote about the shipwreck in comparative detail, he left us very little with which to grasp Paul's reaction when he reached Rome. Surely, he was overwhelmed by the imposing sight; yet more so by his faithful God. Some things aren't easily expressed in words. The times I'm fullest of feelings, I seem most lacking of words.

During those times, I often say to God, "Please hear my heart." No doubt God heard volumes from Paul's heart. Please sift every word of your first reading through the sieve of God's faithfulness.

*R*ead **Acts 28:11-16 tracing Paul's final steps to Rome on your map; then complete the following.**

Another Alexandrian ship docked for the winter in Malta before the sea became so treacherous. Paul and his crew boarded this ship when winter passed. The figureheads on the ship were Castor and Pollux, "the guardian deities of sailors."[3]

*J*ulius, **the centurion from the Imperial Regiment, obviously trusted Paul. While docked in Puteoli, where was the apostle allowed to stay for a week? Choose one.**
- ❏ **with Christian brothers**
- ❏ **with relatives**
- ❏ **with friends**
- ❏ **with an evangelist**

Look at your map once again. A number of Christians from Rome traveled to meet Paul as far as the Forum of Appius and the Three Taverns, the former totaling 43 miles and the latter totaling 33 miles. They were not old acquaintances of Paul's. They had never met him.

*L*ist **as many reasons as you can why they traveled so far to greet the apostle and escort him into Rome.**

_____

_____

Why was Paul so thankful for and encouraged by the sight of these men?

_____

_____

Describe Paul's immediate living conditions in Rome.

_____

Paul had never seen anything like Rome. At the time of his arrival, Rome was inhabited by one million citizens and approximately the same number of slaves. By today's standards the city was gigantic. Rome shared a number of characteristics with many current overcrowded inner cities. Although magnificent buildings and luxurious villas begged to steal the onlooker's attention, he would have to tear his focus from seas of tenements on the verge of collapse. These four-to-five story *insulae,* with no running water or sanitary restrictions, housed most of the city's population. "Like many modern cities, Rome had an urban police force and firefighters, and prostitutes, who registered with the courts and paid their tax, wandered the streets in identifying clothing."[4] Even though Claudius formerly ordered all Jews to leave Rome, the edict either lapsed under Nero's rule or was rescinded. At the time Paul entered Rome, a large number of Jews once again populated the city.

As Paul approached the gargantuan municipality, I believe God knew he would be overwhelmed by a great sea of strangers and the certainty of enemies. Not coincidentally, God met him at each stepping stone to Rome with brothers; therefore, the concept of brotherhood in Christ will occupy our attentions as we study this season in the apostle's life. Keep in mind that brotherhood in Christ is not a term related to masculinity. It rather refers to the unique fellowship of brothers and sisters in Christ.

How important was brotherhood in Christ to the apostle Paul? Scripture refers to a natural sibling of Paul's only once, yet I counted 99 times in his Epistles when the apostle referred to other Christians as brothers. The original Greek word for *brothers* is *adelphos*. In reference to fellow believers in Christ the term "came to designate a fellowship of love equivalent to or bringing with it a community of life." As Paul approached Rome, God knew he needed "a fellowship of love" or "a community of life."

Paul's need was not unique. People are desperate for a sense of community today. We all want to feel like we belong somewhere. Some would even say anywhere! God recognizes man's need for community and desires to meet the need through His church. I'm not talking about a building or a denomination. I'm referring to the body of believers God organized to offer a community of life.

God is not the only principality who recognizes our need to belong. Satan, the enemy of our souls, also sees our need for community—and he constantly capitalizes on it. He entices people toward many forms of community which can lead to destruction.

*W*hy do you think many people choose other forms of community over the body of Christ expressed through the local church?

_____

_____

Have you personally discovered a strong sense of community in the body of Christ? ❑ Yes ❑ No Explain briefly why or why not.

_____

_____

Paul obviously sensed a very strong bond of brotherhood with other believers. Many Christians existed in Rome probably as a result of the outpouring of the Holy Spirit on the Day of Pentecost. According to Acts 2:10, Roman Jews were in Jerusalem for the festival and heard Peter preach. Obviously many believed in Christ, returned to Rome, and were used by God to bring a greater harvest. Paul presumably never met the Christians in Rome, yet he clearly considered them his siblings in the faith (see Rom. 1:13). Paul's strong bond of brotherhood with other believers was not accidental nor was it the natural outcome of his salvation.

Many people believe in Christ as Savior yet never sense a brotherhood or sisterhood with other Christians. I believe imitating his approach to other Christians would lend the same sense of community for any of us who dared. In preparing for his visit to Rome, Paul wrote the Romans a letter. From this we can identify three strands which formed the cord of brotherhood he felt toward believers in Rome.

*R*ead Romans 1:8-13 to see the three strands in the cord of brotherhood.

Prayer—In a previous lesson, we considered Paul's request for the Christians of Corinth to pray for him. Although he certainly wasn't bashful about asking for prayer, he returned the favor many times over.

What words or phrases in verses 8-9 characterize Paul's prayer efforts on behalf of the Christians in Rome?

_____

Paul believed in the power of prayer and in our spiritual poverty without it. His intercession on behalf of the Romans was not an exception. Over and over in his letters, Paul assured churches throughout the civilized world of his prayers. He didn't just ask God to bless them. Paul jealously sought God's best for them.

Using these references to some of Paul's intercessory prayers, list specific petitions he made for fellow believers.

Ephesians 1:17 _____

_____

Ephesians 1:18 _____

_____

Philippians 1:9-10 _____

_____

Colossians 1:9 _____

_____

Paul asked big things of God because he knew God had big things to give. Paul had experienced the riches of an intimate relationship with Christ. He wanted other believers to experience those same riches. Take another look at his specific requests for fellow Christians. Each one of those are available to you. Christ makes far more available to us than most people ever dream of receiving.

Be bold in your prayers! Ask for these riches and ask for them in behalf of others, too! What was the result of Paul's constant prayers for other believers? He had a strong bond of brotherhood with them. His unceasing intercession fueled a sense of camaraderie and unity in his heart. Likewise, our sincere intercession for others will also result in a sense of closeness, strengthening our family ties in Christ.

Have you ever experienced a strong tie to someone you hardly knew as a direct result of your intercessory prayer for that person? ❑ Yes ❑ No

Why were you interceding for that particular person?_____

Without a doubt, one primary reason why such a strong cord of brotherhood tied Paul to fellow believers was his faithful practice of intercession.

*M*any of us feel or have felt alienated from others in our church family. What impact do you think interceding for brothers and sisters in your congregation could make in your sense of belonging and bondedness?

_____

Obligation—Paul's strong sense of obligation was the second strand forming his strong ties to the body of Christ. He believed that part of his calling was to share his gifts and his faith with other Christians. He truly believed Christians have an obligation to one another as well as to the lost. In 1 Corinthians 12:12 he said, "The body is a unit, though it is made up of many parts; and though all its parts are many, they form one body. So it is with Christ." Without apology, he instructed believers, as "parts" of the "body" of Christ, to recognize their obligation to one another—and their need for one another. Generally speaking, my spiritual gifts were given for your edification. Your spiritual gifts were given for mine. Paul presented our mutual encouragement more as an obligation than an invitation. Paul's sense of obligation didn't result in resentment toward the body of Christ as some might imagine. Rather, his sense of obligation resulted in strong bonds of brotherhood.

*I*n addition to prayer, what could we do to strengthen ties to our fellow

believers? _____

According to Romans 1:11, why did Paul long to see the Christians in Rome?

_____

Equality—I see this as one more strand forming the cord of brotherhood Paul felt toward Christians in Rome and elsewhere.

*R*ead Romans 1:16 and fill in the blank. Paul knew the gospel was "the

power of God for the salvation of _____ who believes."

Paul desired to see all people come to Christ: Jews and Gentiles, wise and foolish. He preached to anyone who would listen, and he considered any convert a brother or sister. All are equally in need of salvation, and all are equally loved by God.

At first consideration, we may fully believe we share his attitude; but sometimes we struggle with the equality of all believers. We may desire to see all people saved regardless of race and position, but we don't necessarily want to receive all of them as brothers and sisters. The status struggle is still alive and active in the church. We tend to be selective about those we want to associate with as brothers and sisters.

*R*ank each of the following factors from 1 to 10 where 1 means you have major difficulty accepting a brother or sister in Christ and 10 means you can easily love and accept the person:
____ a person of another socio-economic status
____ a person with habits I find offensive
____ a person of another race
____ a person who dresses poorly and doesn't maintain good hygiene

173

How does God want you to respond to what He showed you today?

_____

_____

_____

_____

_____

_____

I believe God used Paul's memories of his murderous fanaticism and relentless persecution to keep him humble. He considered himself the worst of offenders, esteeming others better than himself. We tend to think a sense of community comes from others accepting us. Paul's sense of community came from his acceptance of others.

As Paul reached the Forum of Appius and the Three Taverns on his way to Rome, he was greatly encouraged by a group of strangers who met him there. Why? They were his brothers. In a sea of strangers, he had a family. Their faces were unfamiliar, but they had each been washed in the blood of Jesus Christ. God used prayer, a sense of mutual obligation, and a sense of equality to bind their hearts.

Paul's example teaches us that a sense of brotherhood and community is not derived from the actions and attitudes of others toward us, but our actions and attitudes toward them. As we imitate his approach to other believers, we will form cords of love not quickly broken.

DAY 5
Ears, Eyes, and Hearts

Today's Treasure
"For this people's heart has become calloused; they hardly hear with their ears, and they have closed their eyes. Otherwise they might see with their eyes, hear with their ears, understand with their hearts and turn, and I would heal them"
(Acts 28:27).

As we conclude week 8, we will also conclude our studies in the fascinating Book of Acts. I've relished every second of our journey. In a blinding light on the Damascus road, I saw God's mercy. In a midnight song from a dungeon, I heard authentic worship. In every miracle on the island of Malta, I felt hope. The Book of Acts has quickened my senses and involved me. I pray you've also gotten involved. Much more awaits us; but not from the pen of Luke, a faithful physician who took his sign off the door, hit the road, and gave his all. Our final two units take us to the letters Paul wrote during the last six years of his earthly life. Luke's final account of the apostle Paul provides a fitting conclusion to the Book of Acts.

Read Acts 28:17-31. Based on our numerous stops with Paul on his missionary journeys, how were his first ministry attempts in Rome typical of many of his other attempts? Name as many similarities as you can based on verses 17-24.

_____

_____

_____

Paul borrowed the expressions of the prophet Isaiah to make what specific charges against the Jews in Rome?

_____

_____

How long did Paul retain these specific living conditions? Choose one.
❏ 2 months   ❏ 6 months   ❏ 1 year   ❏ 2 years

Check the statement below which you believe to be *most* accurate.
❏ Paul made the best of his difficult circumstances.
❏ Though Paul was confined, in other ways, Paul was unleashed.
❏ Paul was devastated by the rejection of many Jews.
❏ Though Paul spent many hours alone, Christ ministered to him.

Cite evidence to support your choice. _____

_____

Recently a friend asked me what impressed me most from my research about the apostle. I didn't hesitate to answer. God used Paul's unparalleled passion for Christ to woo me into the study and his inconceivable perseverance to sustain me. When I was a child, someone gave my brother an inflatable clown with sand in the base. No matter how we socked that clown, he always came back up for more. The apostle was no clown; but, every time he got hit, he bounced back up for more. Of course, the reason for his perseverance was his deep passion for Christ.

As today's reading unfolded, Paul hardly had time to brush his teeth before he assembled the leaders of the Jews. Ordinarily when he arrived at a new city, he made a beeline for the synagogue, but his new living arrangements necessitated others coming to him. No matter how many times he had been rejected by the Jews, he bounced back up and tried again. He approached them with the same method and the same message. He tried to convince them about Jesus from the law of Moses and from the prophets. Based on Old Testament prophecy, Jesus was unmistakably the Messiah. Paul tried very hard to make the Jews see the obvious fulfillment, too.

When Paul realized that many were intentionally closing their eyes to the truth, he responded with an updated application of Isaiah's revelation (see Acts 28:26-27). Be careful not to miss one of the most tragic elements of the Jews' rejection: Paul was not trying to take anything away from them. He had something more to give them. He never asked them not to be Jews. He simply pleaded with them to receive their Messiah.

How terribly we cheat ourselves when we have as much as we want from God. Although many of us have received the gift of salvation, in other ways, we are not unlike some of the Jews Paul encountered. We sometimes hold up our hand to God and say, "That's enough. That's all I'm comfortable with." In our previous lesson, we discovered a host of extraordinary blessings available to us as we considered Paul's intercessory prayers. Each of us is probably aware that God offers more than we accept.

God's gift of salvation is complete. Although we can't accept more salvation, we can receive on a daily basis:
- a greater filling of the Holy Spirit
- a deeper wisdom
- a more obvious disclosure of God's activity (see John 14:21)
- more effectiveness in service
- character more conformed to Christ, and best of all
- a more intimate relationship with Christ

𝒲hy do you think we sometimes resist the increase God has for us?

_____

Whatever the reason for our resistance, we may suffer from our own rendition of Paul's diagnosis of many Jews. Is it possible we could resist what God is trying to tell us, give us, and work in us? We need to be aware of the possible outcome: our spiritual ears don't hear as well, our spiritual eyes don't see as well, and our hearts develop a toughness. Based on my own experience, I recognize the danger. At times I've resisted what God wanted to do in me or through me. I seemed to hear Him less, see His activity less, and, tragically, love Him less. Thankfully, when I finally relented and became receptive, my spiritual ability to hear, see, and love were restored to me.

Let's examine the expressions Paul used and consider the abilities at risk when God desires to give and we continue to resist. Those who continue to resist God will be:
- ever hearing but never understanding
- ever seeing but never perceiving
- developing calloused hearts

1. "Ever hearing but never understanding" (Acts 28:26). By the word *hearing*, Paul referred to the basic physical ability. By the phrase *never understanding*, he referred to a crippling inability. The original Greek word for *understanding* is *suniemi* meaning "the assembling of individual facts into an organized whole, as collecting the pieces of a puzzle and putting them together." *Suniemi* is exercised when "the mind grasps concepts and sees the proper relationship between them." Do you see the tragedy at stake?

When we continue to resist what God has for us, we may cripple our ability to understand how the pieces of our puzzle fit together. We will constantly single out our experiences rather than understand them as parts of a whole. The things we go through may never make any sense to us. Preachers and teachers may tell us God is at work in our lives; but, although we physically hear, we have little ability to understand. Although we will not understand everything until we see Christ face-to-face, God often blesses us by letting many things make sense during our lifetimes. Most things I've encountered eventually made sense as I developed a more cooperative spirit and a greater understanding of God's purposes. Many of those experiences still hurt, but I find comfort in seeing their eventual usefulness as parts of the whole. You might think of the process this way: God is faithfully putting a puzzle together in each life so the final picture will resemble Christ (see Rom. 8:28-29). If we continue to resist this further work, we will be less likely to see the pieces fit.

*N*ame something you've experienced which eventually seemed to fit in the puzzle of God's conforming work in you.

_____

God gave you the gift of *suniemi*. You eventually saw how the piece fit in the puzzle. Can you see how difficult life would be without some ability to understand? God's working an awesome puzzle in you and me. We don't want to miss the blessing of seeing pieces fit together.

2. "Ever seeing but never perceiving" (Acts 28:26). Again, Paul referred to a basic physical ability as he used the word *seeing*. *Perceiving* is translated from the Greek word *eido* which merges the ability to see with the ability to know. *Eido* is "not the mere act of seeing, but the actual perception of some object." If we continue to resist the further blessings and works of God in our lives, we may lose some ability to see past the obvious and the physical. Those who allow God to unleash His Holy Spirit in their lives are those who often perceive spiritual and eternal works in the physical and temporal realm. People who never see with spiritual eyes can't comprehend how others claim to see God at work.

176

I'll never forget the time Amanda's seat belt in our old station wagon would not fasten. Five years old at the time, she pushed and pushed on it to no avail; and I finally told her to crawl into the front seat. Seconds later, the window where she had been sitting unexplainably imploded and pieces of glass imbedded into the seat she had just evacuated. I exclaimed, "Thank you, Dear God!"

Later she said, "Do you really think that was God?"

I said, "No, Baby. I know that was God." Every now and then God blesses us with a good dose of *eidos*. We not only see, but we know.

*C*an you think of a time God gave you the ability to see past the obvious and perceive His activity? If so, explain briefly.

_____

_____

When Paul tried to point out Christ's fulfillment of Old Testament prophecy, many Jews chose to close their eyes and refuse to see.

*D*escribe a time God tried to show you something you didn't want to see.

_____

_____

God wants to give us supernatural sight. Let's not resist Him. Our lives are so much richer when we not only see, but we also perceive!

3. Developing calloused hearts (see Acts 28:27). I was surprised when I discovered the meaning of the word *calloused*. You may be, too! The original Greek word is *pachuno* meaning "to make fat ... calloused as if from fat." According to Acts 28:27, people who continue to resist God can develop fat around their hearts. Let's try to determine what Paul meant. Whether or not we consider physical fitness a personal priority, we are inundated with fitness information.

*B*ased on any knowledge you may have, what causes fat to develop?

_____

In the physical realm, one reason fat develops around the heart is a lack of exercise. In spiritual matters, many of the Jews had ceased exercising their hearts. Religion for them involved more of a state of mind and intellect than the heart.

*T*hink of several ways we exercise our hearts in spiritual terms.

_____

_____

At one time or another, we've all been hurt in love relationships. But if we cease to exercise our hearts by loving God and loving others, getting involved, and taking risks, our hearts will become diseased and hardened.

177

*R*ead Acts 28:27.

Through the prophet Isaiah and the apostle Paul, God revealed three dangers and three opposite blessings. By heeding Paul's warning, we can have ears willing to hear, eyes willing to see, and hearts willing to be exercised. Today we've discovered three gains which can accompany a receptive attitude toward God: understanding, perception, and an uncalloused heart.

Reflect on each original definition once more. How could God use each of these spiritual abilities to enhance your life?

Understanding: the ability to put puzzle pieces together—

_____

Perception: the ability to see past the obvious and "know" God is at work—

_____

*H*ow does God want you to respond to what He showed you today?

An uncalloused heart: the willingness to remain tender and open to God and others—

_____

_____

_____

_____

_____

_____

_____

God has so much to give us. Today we caught a glimpse of the risk man takes when he puts his hand up to God and says, "No more. I'm comfortable this way." We've also realized what we have to gain by remaining receptive to God. His greatest riches are those things which are conformable, not comfortable. As we conclude the Book of Acts, I pray we've each had our eyes unveiled to the extraordinary works God can do in ordinary lives. As we've sojourned from chapter to chapter in Luke's wonderful book, we've met Stephen, Paul, Barnabas, John Mark, Timothy, Silas, Aquilla, Priscilla, Philip the evangelist, his four daughters, and many more. They all shared one thing in common: they were simple flesh and blood infiltrated by the awesome power of the Holy Spirit. All because they didn't resist.

[1]Ernle Bradford, *Paul the Traveller* (New York: Barnes & Nobles, 1993), 226.
[2]Patrick Johnstone, *Operation World* (Grand Rapids, MI: Zondervan Publishing House, 1993), 81.
[3]Kenneth Barker et al., eds., *The NIV Study Bible* (Grand Rapids, MI: Zondervan Bible Publishers, 1985), 1700.
[4]*The Revell Bible Dictionary* (Old Tappan, NJ: Fleming H. Revell Company, 1990), 871.

The Pathway to Rome

Romans 6:1-23

Slaves to Righteousness

1. By reminding ourselves we are _____ to sin (v. 11).

   Count means "to occupy oneself with reckonings or calculations."

2. By deliberately _____ the _____ of sin (v. 12).

3. By deliberately _____ ourselves to God (v. 13; 12:1).

4. By knowing our _____ as those united with Christ (v. 14; Gal. 5:1).

5. By not misapplying the doctrine of _____ (v. 15).

6. By realizing no substitute exists for _____-_____ _____

   in our quest to be free from slavery to sin (v. 17).

7. By facing the _____ of our natural selves (v. 19).

8. By acknowledging the _____-_____ nature of wickedness (v. 19).

9. By never forgetting the _____ feeling of being out of control (v. 20).

10. By counting the _____ of slavery to sin (v. 21).

11. By recognizing the _____ of slavery to God (v. 22; Mic. 7:8, 18-19).

WEEK 9

Letters Bridging the Miles

Day 1
Don't Be Kidnapped!

Day 2
A Profound Mystery

Day 3
A Ready Warrior

Day 4
A More Excellent Way

Day 5
A Rare Gem

We will finally see Paul in his long-awaited destination. He had faith to believe God would send him to Rome, but surely he would never have guessed how! We can sometimes relate, can't we? As we approach our ninth week of study, I am reminded how many remaining riches we won't have time or space to discover. God appointed the great apostle to pen 13 books of the Bible. I have chosen to emphasize His life and passion for Christ rather than his writings; however, this week we will seize an opportunity to glance at 4 letters believed to have been written during Paul's house arrest in Rome. Each of them is like a plate overflowing with rich foods. We will only get to sample and taste, but I pray our appetites will be kindled to return to them after our study. We will discover the answers to the following questions.

Principal Questions
Day 1: How can we protect ourselves from being kidnapped by hollow and deceptive philosophy?
Day 2: What are a few things submission does not mean?
Day 3: Which exhortation spoke most clearly to you in your battle against an unseen enemy?
Day 4: How did Paul demonstrate wisdom as he sought reconciliation between Philemon and Onesimus?
Day 5: What are the thieves of contentment?

Allow this week's study to cause a little soul-searching—a little reevaluating. Strive not just to attain further knowledge, but seek the courage to adjust your life to His truth! Let God get very personal with you this week!

DAY 1

Don't Be Kidnapped!

Paul's incarceration took away his ministry of traveling and preaching, but it necessitated his second method—letter writing. We have four significant reasons to be thankful for Paul's first imprisonment in Rome: Colossians, Ephesians, Philemon, and Philippians. Each of these letters almost certainly was written at this time. God used the apostle's inability to travel to force him to sit and write. Ultimately, Paul was imprisoned a second time in Rome, but this week we will focus on his first imprisonment.

The openness of Paul's first imprisonment in Rome enabled him to receive ample information about the churches. One of the letters he wrote during this two-year period became the Book of Colossians. Though Paul never visited the Asian city of Colosse as far as we know, he obviously received word about the false teaching in Colosse and wrote his Epistle as both a warning and an encouragement. You would benefit most by reading all four chapters of Colossians. Understandably, you may not have time. The primary purpose for Paul's Epistle appears in Colossians 2.

*R*ead at least the second chapter of Colossians and complete the following. According to Paul, what is the "mystery of God"? (vv. 2-3)

_____

Paul made one primary purpose for the letter clear in verse 4: "So that no one may deceive you."

*H*ave you, or someone you know, ever been "taken captive" through some "deceptive philosophy"? If so, briefly describe the belief or idea.

_____

_____

Based on Paul's arguments in verses 9-23, what do you assume were several of the deceptive influences the Colossians encountered?

_____

_____

Try to capture Paul's frame of mind as he wrote the Christians in Colosse. He described himself as struggling (2:1). The original Greek word is *agon* from which we derive the English word *agony*. *Agon* means "strife, contention, contest for victory or mastery such as was used in the Greek games of running, boxing, wrestling, and so forth." By using the word *agon* Paul implied he was figuratively boxing or wrestling with Satan for the minds and hearts of the Colossians and Laodiceans. No sooner had the people of Colosse and Laodicea received the Word than Satan began infiltrating them with deceptive doctrines. Satan used at least four *isms*. Let's briefly consider each one.

1. Gnosticism: The word *gnosis* means *knowledge*. Followers of the gnostic belief system believed knowledge, rather than faith, led to salvation.

Today's Treasure
"See to it that no one takes you captive through hollow and deceptive philosophy, which depends on human tradition and the basic principles of this world rather than on Christ" (Col. 2:8).

*A*lthough we are not gnostics, can you think of a way we might be tempted to replace faith with knowledge? Write your ideas in the margin.

Focusing on knowledge instead of Christ is harmful. We should study the Bible to know and glorify Jesus rather than to impress others with knowledge.

The gnostics could not accept both the deity and the humanity of Christ, so they tried to reduce Him to the status of an angel. Paul responded to gnosticism clearly in verse 9: "For in Christ all the fullness of the Deity lives in bodily form."

2. Legalism: In verses 11-17, Paul addressed the fruitlessness of keeping endless laws that condemn rather than liberate the believer to pursue godliness.

*W*hich of the following are contemporary forms of legalism?
- ❑ seeking to be more "spiritual" by keeping man-made, extra-biblical rules
- ❑ believing that God requires harsh treatment of the body
- ❑ elevating one Christian above another based on keeping rules
- ❑ the refusal to accept those who have committed certain sins
- ❑ attempting to restrain sin by making lists of do's and don'ts.

3. Mysticism is the belief that we can obtain direct knowledge of God from our internal thoughts and feelings or from our experiences. It conflicts with biblical faith because Jesus Christ is the source of our knowledge about God. In verses 18-19, Paul addressed a mystical belief recently infiltrating our own society—the worship of angels. Angels have important positions in God's creation, but Paul helps us find the balance. Angels were created to praise God and act as messengers and ministering servants. We worship angels when we disconnect them from their original purpose and focus on them.

4. Asceticism: In verses 20-23, Paul addressed the practice of denying the body and treating it harshly in order to achieve holiness. Followers of asceticism do not stop at the wise denial of dangerous, perverse, or unhealthy practices. Ascetics deny the body unnecessarily. In Paul's day, as in ours, some people branded, burned, starved or cut the body in an attempt to force it into submission. Most of us have discovered that unnecessary denial arouses more desires.

*H*ave you ever practiced an unwise form of self-denial or treated your body badly in an attempt to bring it into submission? ❑ Yes ❑ No
If so, what were the results of your self-denial?

_____

_____

We still battle many of the same destructive philosophies faced by the early believers. Though the list of *isms* may change, Satan is still up to the same old tricks. He seeks always to infiltrate with false teaching. Paul instructed the believers in Colosse: "See to it that no one takes you captive through hollow and deceptive philosophy" (v. 8). The original Greek word for *captive* is *sulagogeo* meaning "to lead off as prey, carry off as booty, rob, or kidnap." Recently my community was devastated over the kidnapping of a 13-year-old girl. I cannot imagine anything worse than the agony of one of my children being kidnapped. Paul responded with agony (*agon*) when he felt a kidnapper (Satan) was after some of his children in the faith.

*A*ccording to the apostle, who was vulnerable to being kidnapped? To discover the answer, check the recipients of this letter in Colossians 1:2.

_____

Paul was addressing believers, faithful believers. Not even the faithful are completely immune to deceptive doctrine. Had Paul's recipients not been Christians, he would not have referred to the act as a kidnapping. Kidnapping takes place when someone steals a person who belongs to another.

No matter what a kidnapper does, he cannot make a child no longer belong to her family. The same is true spiritually. Once we accept Christ as Savior, we become joint heirs with Christ (see Rom. 8:17), and God becomes our Father (see John 20:17). Satan may try to kidnap us by enticing us away from the truth, but no matter what he does he cannot make us his. My security in God's family comforts me, but I don't ever want to be kidnapped, do you? The safeguards Paul taught the believers at Colosse will also help protect us. Based on Colossians 2:6-7, let's discover how we can protect ourselves from being kidnapped by "hollow and deceptive philosophy."

1. Remember how you received Christ. None of us entered God's family through our own effort. We received Christ as a gift of grace. Now Paul tells us "the way we got in is the way we go on." We must not believe any teaching or philosophy that replaces God's grace with our performance.

2. Continue to live in Christ. The best way for a child of God to avoid getting kidnapped is to stay close to home. Children in natural families cannot live their entire lives in their yards, but children in the spiritual family of God can! Continuing to live in Christ means remaining close to Him and retaining a focus on Him. Any other focus can lead to deceptive doctrine, even if the focus is a biblical concept. Satan's favorite trick is to twist the Word of God (see Gen. 3). Remember, any doctrine which loses connection with the Head has been twisted into deception.

Name subjects in the Bible that can become a focus or an obsession causing Christians to temporarily lose sight of the Head, Jesus Christ.

_____

Can you think of a time when Satan tempted you to misappropriate a biblical concept and prioritize it over Christ? ❏ Yes ❏ No If so, explain.

_____

_____

Many of us have probably let something under a religious umbrella temporarily become a greater focus than Christ Himself. We are less likely to be kidnapped when we stay close to home by staying focused on the Head, Jesus Christ.

3. Grow deep roots in Christ. The more we feel like family the less likely we'll be enticed. A very important part of feeling like family is knowing your family history and the belief systems handed down through the generations. Spiritually, we have difficulty growing up until we've grown down. We form deep roots by knowing the basics of our faith. We can receive Christ and be very enthusiastic and still fall into confusion the first time someone confronts us with strange doctrine. Our roots are our basics.

List a few truths you feel are foundations to our faith by completing this sentence. In my opinion, every new Christian needs to know:

_____

_____

You named roots that help us stand strong when winds of strange doctrines blow.

4. Grow up in Christ. In verse 7, the apostle exhorted believers to be "rooted and built up in him." After we've grown roots, we're ready to grow up.

Hebrews 6:1 strongly exhorts believers to a progression in Christ. **Fill in the blanks.**

"Therefore let us leave the _____ teachings about Christ

and go on to_____."

The Hebrew Christians knew the basics, and the writer knew they were ready for more. Paul suggested the same progression by a different analogy. In 1 Corinthians 3:2 he wrote: "I gave you milk, not solid food, for you were not yet ready for it." Paul was not implying infants in Christ should start with anything but milk. He was frustrated because people who should have been mature were still infants.

What will be the result if we "continue to live in him, rooted and built up in him"? We will be "strengthened in the faith" (Col. 2:6-7). Savor the definition of the original Greek word for *strengthened: bebaioo* means "to make firm or reliable so as to warrant security and inspire confidence." Satan is looking for victims. As we stay close to Christ, grow deep roots in the basics of our faith, and press on to maturity to become spirit-filled, power-packed believers, we won't be easy targets.

I understand that attackers target vulnerable-looking people. Being confident provides protection. The more you know about Christ, His Word, and His ways, the more confident you will feel. You will be the dread of those peddling strange doctrines.

A kidnapper is on the loose. If he tries to get his grasp on you or someone you love, Paul's exhortations can be easily summed up in the words of Christ in John 8:32.

Write them below and ask God to seal them in your heart forever.

_____

How does God want you to respond to what He showed you today?

_____

_____

_____

_____

_____

Today's Treasure "Wives, submit to your husbands as to the Lord.... Husbands, love your wives, just as Christ loved the church" (Eph. 5:22, 25).

D A Y   2
A Profound Mystery

For the next two days we will concentrate on the letter to the Ephesians. Most scholars believe Colossians and Ephesians were written early in Paul's two-year imprisonment, because he never hinted of a possible release as he did in Philemon (see v. 22) and Philippians (see 1:19-26).

The letter to the Ephesians differs from his letter to the Colossians. He never warned of deceptive philosophy; rather, Paul wrote about a greater knowledge and experience in Christ. We can easily deduce the reason for the omission of several basics. Remember, the Christians at Colosse had never met Paul while the people of Ephesus benefited from his teaching and an unparalleled demonstration of power for several years.

*W*hat did Paul say about his ministry in Ephesus in Acts 20:20? Choose any that apply.
   ❏ He preached house to house. ❏ He preached publicly.
   ❏ He convinced the Jews. ❏ He laid hands on them.
   ❏ He did not hesitate to preach anything helpful.

Obviously, Paul found receptive soil in Ephesus, even in the midst of terrible hardships. Publicly and house to house, he didn't hesitate to preach anything helpful. His lengthy and effective ministry in Ephesus not only resulted in deep bonds of love (see Acts 20:37-38), it also freed him to proceed to great depths in his letter. If you have a translation with chapter or paragraph headings, turn to Ephesians and look at the subjects Paul explored in his letter.

Space limits me to choose only two subjects from the Book of Ephesians. We will examine the subject of marriage today and spiritual warfare on day 3. (Perhaps you thought marriage and warfare were synonymous!)

Stop and pray for an open mind and freedom from the hindrances of negative preconceptions. After you have prayed, read Ephesians 5:21-33 and complete the following.

In one statement, write Paul's primary directive to wives.

_____

In one statement, write Paul's primary directive to husbands.

_____

What does Paul consider a profound mystery?

_____

_____

This portion of Scripture revolves around the biblical roles of three distinct figures intimately involved in marriage: wives, husbands, and Christ. We will approach each role individually today. Ladies, let's get the painful part over first!

Part 1: The Role of Christian Wives—First, notice verse 21. The attitude of all Christians is to be submissive to each other. No discussion of this topic can stay on track apart from that spirit.

How does the principle of mutual submission play itself out in marriage? The way I see it, Keith has to worry about things I don't. He sometimes has to come up with answers when I can't. He's responsible for things I'm not. Many times, I'm very happy to pass the proverbial buck. Keith would say the same about me. He really doesn't want to drive a car load of teenagers all over the city nor sit for hours on the end of our daughters' beds discussing matters of the heart. Usually we defer to each other on our "turf issues." When I'm not in agreement with Keith, I usually speak up, and we pray and work it out—at times less easily than others! This spirit of praying things through until we can come to consensus on important issues is the essence of mutual respect and the opposite of "lording it over one another."

You noted above that Paul's primary directive to women dealt with submission while his primary directive to men dealt with love. Could it be that he was targeting the area most likely to be our weaknesses? Before we learn what submission means for Christian wives, let's learn what it does not mean:

1. Submission does not mean women are under the authority of men in general. I love the *King James Version* rendition of Ephesians 5:22: "Wives, submit yourselves unto your own husbands." Guess what? Wives aren't asked to submit to anyone else's husband! Just their own! While I make this point somewhat tongue-in-cheek, many women assume the Bible teaches their general inferiority and subjection to men. Untrue. Paul is talking about marriage as a matter between each husband and wife.

2. Submission does not mean inequality. Paul, the same man who taught submission, made a statement in Galatians 3:28 pertinent to today's study.

*R*ead the Scripture; then fill in the blanks.
"There is neither Jew nor Greek, slave nor free, _____,

for you are all _____."

Spiros Zodhiates' definition of the original Greek word *hupotasso* explains that submission "is not due to her being inferior to her husband, for they are both equal before God."

3. Submission does not mean wives are to treat their husbands like God. The Bible Knowledge Commentary explains: "'As to the Lord' does not mean that a wife is to submit to her husband in the same way she submits to the Lord, but rather that her submission to her husband *is* her service rendered 'to the Lord.'"[1] I think most of our husbands are fairly relieved they are not called on to be God to their wives!

4. Submission does not mean slavery. Let's release a few old notions and fears! Paul uses an entirely different word in Ephesians 6:5 when he instructs slaves to obey their masters. This Greek word for *obey, hupakouo,* embraces more of the meaning people often mistakenly associate with marital submission. *Hupokouo* means "to obey, to yield to a superior command or force (without necessarily being willing)." The term draws a picture of a soldier saluting his officer, not a wife submitting to her husband!

*W*ere any of these four statements news to you? If any, which?

_____

_____

Now that we've learned a few things *submission* does not mean, just exactly what does it mean? *Submission* means "to place in order under." The Greek word for *submit* is *hupotasso. Hupo* means "under" and *tasso* means "to place in order." The compound word *hupotasso* means "to place under or in an orderly fashion." Paul didn't dislike women, he liked ORDER! He advocated order in the church, order in government, order in business, and, yes, order in the home. I'm convinced he even kept his cell in order! Galatians 3:28 and Ephesians 5:22 could spill from the same man's pen because Paul regarded husbands and wives as spiritual equals but with functional differences.

The concept of a submissive wife used to really go against my grain until I began to learn more about God. Two realizations have changed my entire attitude:

- God is good and loving. He would never give approval to meanness or abuse. Any misuse of submission by either the husband or wife is sin.
- God granted women a measure of freedom in submission we can learn to enjoy. It is a relief to know that as a wife and mother I am not totally responsible for my family. I have a husband to look to for counsel and direction. I can rely on his toughness when I am too soft and his logic when I am too emotional.

Certainly, I haven't just delivered the definitive dissertation on submission, but I believe I'm offering you sound doctrine. I hope it helps. Now, let's take a brief look at the role of husbands, according to Ephesians 5:25-31.

Part 2: The Role of Christian Husbands—Thus far Paul probably had the Ephesian Christians nodding their heads in agreement. Submission of the wife to the husband was codified Hebraic law. Nothing new here. Now Paul raises eyebrows in a hurry. He tells husbands to love their wives. The original Greek word for *love* is *agapao* meaning "to esteem, love, indicating a direction of the will and finding one's joy in something or someone." Notice the phrase indicating a direction of the will. A husband is called by God to exercise his will to love his wife. Love is not simply an emotion or a feeling. Love is a willingness to continue in devotion and goodness toward the spouse.

For a society where women were little more than property, passed from father to husband, the command to love their wives was a radical idea. Paul knew few role models existed for the men to follow. He gives them the best role model possible: Jesus Christ.

1. Husbands should love their wives sacrificially "as Christ loved the church and gave himself up for her" (v. 25). Just as a husband must be careful not to abuse his wife's exhortation to submission, a wife must not abuse her husband's exhortation to sacrifice. Some men work several jobs sacrificing time at home in an effort to continually raise the standard of living for their families.

2. Husbands should love their wives in ways that encourage purity. Christ encourages purity in His bride, the church, desiring for her to be holy and without stain. God calls upon husbands to treat their wives as pure vessels even in physical intimacy.

3. Husbands should "love their wives as their own bodies" (v. 28). I have to snicker when I think about verses 28 and 29. I wonder if Paul might have been thinking, "If you love yourself at all, Mister, then love your wife—because life will be far more pleasant under the same roof with a well-loved woman!" I also have to wonder if Paul's reference to a man treating his wife as he does his own body, feeding and caring for it, implies that husbands are supposed to cook for their wives. Don't take me too seriously, but I would submit to my husband's cooking any day!

I would like to suggest one last responsibility for both husbands and wives based on the final phrase in Ephesians 5:31: "and the two will become one flesh." The original Greek word for *flesh* in this passage is *sarx* which means "flesh of a living creature in distinction from that of a dead one." May I interject that our marriages were meant to be alive not dead! Is your marriage more like romance or roadkill?

In all seriousness, where would you place your marriage on this scale?

Lifeless and dull   Alive

No matter where you have charted your marriage on the scale, list several reasons why you think you are there.

_____

_____

Too

We were much too young
Much too selfish
Much too blind
To make it

Much too wounded
Much too frightened
Much too hurt
To take it

Too much we said
When love seemed dead
To go on
And forget

Too little learned
From anger burned
Too much
We both regret

Yet God's been

Much too good
Much too faithful
Much too kind
To walk away

Much too patient
Much too present
Much too able
Not to stay

Too much harm
To children's charms
To tear our home apart

Too much time
For nursery rhymes
To give away our hearts

Too much we've shared
With no one else
To go on and forget

Too many years
Of drying tears
To do what we'd regret

Too many laughs when
thinking back
Remind me what is true
I find that I still love you
And I think you love me,
Too.

187

Think of marriage as a three-legged stool. The legs are a submissive wife, a loving husband, and Christ. All three legs must be in place for marriage to work as God intended. A wife submitting to an unloving husband is as lopsided as a loving husband sacrificing for a domineering wife. When Christ is not the head of the marriage relationship, the stool falls indeed. Paul pictures for us God's ideal marriage relationship. Sadly, many Christian women are trying to keep their stools balanced with only one leg in place–their submission.

Over the course of the last 20 years, my marriage has been at both extremes and everywhere in between, but Keith and I have never been the types who could tolerate dull for very long. God has always been faithful to restore the life, passion, and active care to our marriage, and we have worked very hard to cooperate. You may need help from a real marriage expert like we have at times. I'd like to recommend the one who saved our marriage. His Name is Wonderful Counselor, and His office is open 24 hours a day. He also uses human Christian counselors to help with His caseload!

Part 3: The Role of Christ in Marriage—Not only has Christ set the standard for a good marriage and the example of a loving husband, He offers sound counsel. Then He supplies every ounce of power necessary to make a marriage work.

How does God want you to respond to what He showed you today?

*R*ead Colossians 1:16-17. Fill in the following blanks based on the first phrase of verse 16 and the last phrase of verse 17.

"For by him all things were _____:

"… and in him all things _____."

Beloved, God created marriage (Gen. 2:21-24). Figuratively speaking, before Adam and Eve said "I do," God did. No one helped Him. Only God created marriage, and only He can hold it together. Many people live in the same home and share a joint checking account under the same name, but they don't have a clue about the true covenant of marriage. Marriage as the institution and wonderful mystery God created cannot exist nor hold together without Him.

I want to conclude today with a poem I wrote for Keith a number of years ago after a difficult season of our marriage. I pray God will use it to speak to you or encourage you. It appears in the margin on page 187.

D A Y 3
A Ready Warrior

Today's Treasure
"Put on the full armor of God so that you can take your stand against the devil's schemes" (Eph. 6:11).

You may recall we dedicated day 2 to "Helps for War in the Home" and, as promised, we'll dedicate today to "Helps for War in the Heavenlies." Paul had specific reasons for teaching on spiritual warfare to the Christians in Ephesus. Please review the paragraph with the heading, *God made His power over the occult obvious,* on page 112.

*R*ead Ephesians 6:10-20. What is God's general responsibility in warfare?

What is the believer's general responsibility in warfare? _____

_____

Let's approach today's lesson as a battalion of soldiers in the middle of a heavenly war. Lives are at risk. Casualties may be high. Our Commander-in-Chief issues orders. The victory is sure, but the fight will be difficult. Hear the voice of your Commander in Ephesians 6:10-20 as He exhorts you to do the following:

1. Realize your natural limitations (see v. 10). We cannot enjoy spiritual victory without actively calling on the power of God. We are only strong when we are "in the Lord and in His mighty power."

2. Remember the "full armor" (v. 11). Paul exhorted us to use every weapon available. Picture your Commander-in-Chief standing behind a table displaying 6 tools or weapons. He says, "I've tailormade each of these for you. You may take only some of them if you choose, but they were designed to work together. Your safety and effectiveness are only guaranteed if you use them all."

Don't underestimate the enemy's ability. He is an expert archer. He's had at least six thousand years of practice on human targets. He won't waste arrows on well-armed places. He will aim for the spots you and I leave uncovered. Trust me, I know.

3. Recognize your real enemies (see v. 12). The struggles of warfare you and I experience do not originate in spouses, in-laws, neighbors, coworkers, or even our earthly foes. Spiritual forces of evil exist. The original word for *struggle* in verse 12 is *pale* which was "used of the wrestling of athletes and of the hand-to-hand combat of soldiers."

Not every problem we have is warfare. Yes, Satan is ultimately at the origin of every temptation, but we're not perpetually going hand-to-hand with principalities of darkness. Some of my problems have resulted from personal rebellion. Sometimes I sense Satan is very actively opposing my life. Other times, I sense he is more passive; because he sees me doing a fine job of getting myself into difficulty! We are wise to pray for discernment to know the nature of our problems. Sometimes the prescription is repentance. Other times it is fortification against the evil one.

*H*ave **you considered that a Christian friend may be used of Satan in your life? Or have you been used unknowingly by Satan to be an enemy to someone, maybe even a sister in Christ?** ❑ Yes ❑ No

4. Realize our enemies' limitations (see v. 13). Satan and his powers and principalities cannot do anything they want with us. They have certain limitations. One is absolutely crucial for believers to understand: Demons cannot possess Christians. They can oppress, but they cannot possess. In his letter the apostle assured the Ephesians of their security in Christ before he ever warned them about warfare.

*R*ead **Ephesians 1:13 and 4:30. What principle did Paul repeat in each verse?**

_____

The original Greek word for *seal* is *sphragizo* meaning "to seal, close up and make fast with a seal signet such as letters or books so that they may not be read; generally to seal ... for the sake of security." When you and I received Christ, God dropped His Holy Spirit into us, slammed on the lid, and tightened the cap. We've been closed and sealed every moment since. Nothing can get in. Furthermore, Satan cannot read our minds.

Check the definition once more. The kind of seal to which Paul referred closed a document so it could not be read. You may be thinking, "Satan sure seems to read my mind at times." My children used to think I could read their minds, too. In reality, I simply knew them so well that I sometimes guessed what they were thinking. In the same way, because of our past behavior, Satan can often guess what we are thinking.

5. *Retain an active stance (see v. 13)*. Notice two appearances of the word *stand* in verse 13. Actually, each one has a different Greek word. The first appearance of the word *stand* is in the phrase "to stand your ground." A more accurate translation of the word is *withstand*. The second appearance of the word is rendered accurately as *stand*.

*D*escribe the difference between "withstanding" something and simply "standing". In the margin write your thoughts or you may check a dictionary.

The word *withstand* draws an image of a soldier occupying his own piece of land and an enemy threatening to take it from him. Ephesians 4:27 warns us not to "give the devil a foothold." The original term for *stand,* paints the picture of the evil one trying to grab a believer's foot to pull him off the ground he is occupying.

In the years we have known Christ, hopefully we have gained some ground. We're beginning to occupy some of the victorious space God desires for us. Satan wants to force us off our property and make us feel like we've gone nowhere. Believer, you are getting somewhere! Your dedication to study God's Word is proof! You and I must actively guard the gains we've made in Christ. Paul exhorts us to stand our ground!

*C*an you identify an area in your life where Satan tried to seize ground you had gained? ❏ Yes ❏ No If so, were you able to stand against him and refuse him an inch? ❏ Yes ❏ No If not, pray and ask God to give you the strength to do so now!

6. *Reject personal hypocrisy (see v. 14)*. The "belt of truth," represents not living a lie in any part of our lives, living free of secret areas of hypocrisy. King David learned the hard way how quickly a man can fall when living a lie. Satan loves to blackmail believers who have a secret they want to keep hidden.

*R*ead David's words in Psalm 51:6. In your opinion, how do these words relate to "the belt of truth"?

_____

7. *Resist snares of unrighteousness (see v. 14)*. "The breastplate of righteousness" is the protection we receive when we choose the right even when we feel like choosing the wrong thing. Not only will we find protection from disaster, God will honor our obedience by changing our hearts if we'll let Him.

*C*an you think of a time when you wore "the breastplate of righteousness" in a difficult situation and found protection?

_____

We will find great protection in learning to pray Psalm 141:4. "Let not my heart be drawn to what is evil."

8. Remain balanced! (see v. 15). Good soldiers have their "feet fitted with the readiness that comes from the gospel of peace." The word for *readiness* is *hetoimasia* meaning "firm footing." Roman soldier's boots had cleats on the soles to give them firm footing. Our feet give our bodies balance. We can remain balanced because, although we are at war with Satan, we are at peace with God. Sink your feet into "the gospel of peace!"

9. Refuse unbelief (see v. 16). "The shield of faith" is our protection when Satan tempts us to disbelieve God. A big difference exists between doubting what God may do and doubting God. Even when you have no idea what God is doing, your protection is in never doubting God *is* God. We're not called to have faith in our faith. We are called to have faith in God and never doubt Him.

10. Reinforce your mind (see v. 17). "The helmet of salvation" protects our minds. The best way to protect our minds is to fill it with the Word of God and things pertaining to godliness. We need to deliberately avoid destructive influences.

*R*ead 2 Corinthians 10:3-5. In what way is Paul, in essence, describing a helmet over the minds of believers?

_____

_____

11. Raise your sword (see v. 17). You've probably noticed the defensive nature of all five previous weapons. "The sword of the Spirit" is our only offensive weapon against the evil one. Christ taught us to be expert swordsmen. In His wilderness temptation Jesus attacked Satan with "the Word of God" until the enemy gave up. Know and use "the Word of God" persistently!

12. Retain an active prayer life (see v. 18). Prayerless lives are powerless lives. Active prayer lives equip us with the power and motivation to put on the full armor of God. Because Paul mentioned praying for others next, I believe this first exhortation was primarily about praying for ourselves.

13. Remember one another in warfare prayer (see v. 18). Power results from collective prayer. God delights in our petitions for each other's strength in battle and victory in warfare. Soldiers depend on one another to watch their backs! Not long ago, I realized I was having an internal problem with anger. I was caught off guard because ordinarily I do not struggle with anger. I prayed many times; finally I shared my struggles with a friend. She began to join me in prayer and the anger ceased immediately. I cannot explain why. I only know Satan's secret was out, prayer doubled, and God acted.

*H*ave you ever had a similar experience with the power of collective prayer in warfare? If so, what happened?

_____

_____

14. Remember spiritual leaders in warfare prayer (see v. 19). Notice Paul ended by asking for prayer. Again, I believe he was talking about warfare prayer, because he asked specifically for intercession regarding fearlessness. According to 2 Timothy 1:7, God does not give us a spirit of fear (KJV). Satan is the one who fuels fear in an attempt to keep people from serving God effectively. If the great apostle needed prayer to fulfill his calling fearlessly, we all need prayer! Our missionaries, pastors, leaders, and teachers need our prayers. The enemy wants to destroy ministries. Our prayers help build a hedge of protection around them.

The following list includes each of Paul's 14 exhortations about warfare. Evaluate yourself on each of the actions with either a 3 for consistent behaviors, a 2 for need improvement, or 1 for much improvement needed. Although I encourage you to discuss the test in general you will not need to share your score or specifics in your small group.

_____ I realize my natural limitations.
_____ I remember (keep in mind) the importance of the full armor.
_____ I recognize my real enemies.
_____ I realize my enemies' limitations.
_____ I retain an active stance.
_____ I reject personal hypocrisy.
_____ I resist snares of unrighteousness.
_____ I remain balanced.
_____ I refuse disbelief.
_____ I reinforce my mind.
_____ I raise my sword.
_____ I retain an active prayer life.
_____ I remember others in warfare prayer.
_____ I specifically remember spiritual leaders in warfare prayer.

_____ TOTAL SCORE

If your score is 34-42, shout Hallelujah! You are presently a well-equipped soldier and an asset to your battalion. Two suggestions: 1) Note exhortations you marked 2 or 1 and ask God to help you become fortified in those areas for your own protection or the protection of your fellow soldiers. 2) Keep up the good work and don't let down your guard! First Corinthians 10:12 applies here!

If your score is 24-33, you have some definite strengths, but you are at risk in several areas. Suggestion: Prioritize becoming more fortified and more effective as a soldier at war. Today's exercise helps you identify strengths and weaknesses so you know where to begin.

If your score is 14-23, shout Help! You are at great risk just like the rest of us have been at one time or another. You are most likely living in painful defeat. Suggestion: Begin praying immediately for God's help and let this be your last day of defeat. "The one who is in you is greater than the one who is in the world!" (1 John 4:4).

DAY 4
A More Excellent Way

By this time, Paul had written the following Epistles, probably in this order: Galatians, 1 and 2 Thessalonians and 1 and 2 Corinthians, Romans, Colossians and Ephesians. In the last years of the apostle's life, four out of five of his letters were written to individuals rather than a body of believers. Philemon was the first of Paul's personal letters divinely chosen to be part of Scripture. Philemon was a believer from Colosse whom Paul probably met while ministering in a nearby city.

How does God want you to respond to what He showed you today?

_____
_____
_____
_____
_____
_____

Today's Treasure
"I appeal to you on the basis of love"
(Philem. 1:9).

$\mathcal{R}$ead Philemon and complete the following. According to verse one, who was obviously at Paul's side while he was under house arrest?

_____

Based on every reference to Philemon and your own conclusions, describe the recipient of Paul's letter as thoroughly as you can.

_____

_____

_____

In one sentence, state Paul's basic purpose in writing to Philemon.

_____

On what basis did Paul appeal to Philemon according to verse nine?
❑ friendship ❑ partnership ❑ love ❑ fairness

What did Paul tell Philemon to do if Onesimus owed him anything?
❑ Cancel his debt. ❑ Charge it to me.
❑ Forgive him. ❑ Charge him interest.

Why is the inclusion of Mark, formerly called John Mark, among Paul's fellow workers especially significant? Acts 15:37-38 will refresh your memory.

_____

_____

Why do you think God deemed this personal letter to be in Scripture?

_____

I am a hopeless romantic. I hate conflict, and I love happy endings. Of all 50 lessons God gave me for this series, week 4, day 1 was one of the most difficult. I had grown to love the partnership between Paul and Barnabas so much. My heart ached over their disagreement about John Mark, which caused dear friends to separate. The last we saw John Mark, he was with Barnabas headed for Cyprus. Twelve years passed. Paul was placed under house arrest in Rome. Now we see Mark with him once again. Time heals and, if we're the least bit cooperative, matures. Praise God, sometimes we live and learn.

You may be wondering why I am focusing on Paul and Mark when the letter is obviously about Paul and Onesimus. I think Mark may have been Paul's inspiration for seeking restoration between Philemon and Onesimus. A dozen years earlier, Paul had been hard and unyielding. Perhaps he had since learned a more excellent way.

Let's compile a few facts and assumptions necessitating Paul's personal letter. Based on his statement in verse 19, Paul apparently led Philemon to Christ. They developed a friendship, and Paul saw Philemon become an active worker for the gospel. Philemon must have been a wealthy man to be a slave owner and own a home large enough to serve as a meeting place for the church. At some point Onesimus, one of his slaves, ran away. Verse 18 indicates he also may have stolen something from Philemon: "If he has done you any wrong or owes you anything, charge it to me."

We have no way of knowing for certain, but while he was on the run Onesimus may have stolen again and been incarcerated with Paul. Imagine how strange their meeting must have been once they realized they both knew Philemon. You can be sure their meeting wasn't a coincidence. No doubt, God ordained the fugitive slave to have a heart-to-heart collision with the most well-known slave of grace in Christendom.

Paul could have dealt with the situation in one of several different ways, but the wise apostle chose the most excellent way taught in both the Old and New Testaments. In terms of Old Testament teaching, Paul portrayed a beautiful example of Micah 6:8.

*P*lease read Micah 6:6-8; then complete verse 8 below: "He has showed you, O man, what is good. And what does the Lord require of you? To...

_____

_____

The original Hebrew word for *good* in Micah 6:8 is *tob*. A few of the English definitions are "beautiful, lovely, delightful, and excellent."[2] In Micah 6:8, God tells us justice, mercy, and humility are more beautiful than burnt offerings.

Far more than our greatest sacrifices or offerings, God desires three things from us: to act justly, love mercy, and walk humbly with Him. The solution Paul sought in the conflict between Philemon and his fugitive slave, Onesimus, met all three requirements.

1. Paul acted justly. One easy way Paul might have handled the situation was to consider Onesimus absolved from all responsibility after he repented and accepted Christ. However, Onesimus wronged Philemon in several ways. He ran away from his legal owner, and he possibly stole from him. In Paul's estimation, the restoration of two Christian men was priority. The issue could not be resolved fully unless Onesimus returned to Philemon and recompense was made for all he owed.

*W*ho did Paul assign to pay the debt? _____

For justice to prevail, someone had to take responsibility for Onesimus' actions, and someone had to pay his debt. Paul responded with great wisdom. Paul insisted that Onesimus take responsibility for wrong doing, yet he took on the debt. Likewise we must take responsibility for our sins; but, thankfully, Christ has paid the debt!

2. Paul loved mercy. Paul did more than preach to people. He lived the concepts he taught. When he met Onesimus, he saw a man in desperate need of a Savior; Paul didn't just preach to him about the mercy of God, he showed it to him. He took Onesimus' debt not only out of justice, because the debt needed to be paid; but out of mercy because a sinner needed grace. Paul wanted Philemon to show mercy as well. According to the original language, Onesimus was a slave bound to permanent servitude to Philemon. His return to Philemon would mean the return to slavery.

*I*n the margin, write Paul's view of slavery based on Galatians 3:28.

You see, although Paul had to deal with slavery realistically as a part of his society, he believed in absolute equality. He believed that slaves must be obedient to their masters just like citizens must obey the law, but he was definitely not an advocate of slavery. He told Philemon he was returning Onesimus to him but "no longer as a slave, but better than a slave, as a dear brother" (Philem. 1:16).

God has very strong feelings about mercy. See His demand for mercy specifically applied to slaves in Deuteronomy 23:15-16.

*W*hat did God require of those with whom slaves took refuge?

_____

In the Old Testament God demanded mercy on slaves. God required His people to remember they had also been slaves and to have mercy on others.

As Christ's ambassador, Paul did not violate the Old Testament principle. He had the full cooperation of Onesimus, who was willing to return so restoration would ensue. Paul also asked Philemon to be an ambassador of Christ by abolishing Onesimus' slavery and receiving him as a brother. Paul's proposal was to let mercy reign.

3. Paul walked humbly with God. Anyone who truly walks with God, walks humbly. The closer we draw near to Him and behold His majesty, the more we relate to the psalmist who said "What is man that you are mindful of him, the son of man that you care for him?" (Ps. 8:4). Like the psalmist, Paul recognized the pit from which God had pulled him. Both men enjoyed an intimate relationship with God, yet neither of them viewed Him as a chum or a running buddy. They each knew grace had bridged the wide gulf fixed between them. To walk with God is to walk humbly. We cannot help but confront His holiness. Paul's proposal for restoration between Philemon and Onesimus required both men to walk humbly with God.

In what way did Paul's proposal require Onesimus to humble himself?

_____

_____

In what way did Paul's proposal require Philemon to humble himself?

_____

_____

Paul also had to humble himself by resisting the temptation to be bold and order Philemon to do what he ought to do (v. 8-9). Instead, he appealed to him on another basis which brings us to our final point.

When God sent His Son to be an atoning sacrifice for our sins, He showed mankind a more excellent way: He fulfilled the law with love (see Rom. 5:8). Paul could have demanded certain actions from Philemon, but he appealed to him on the basis of love. I'm going to ask you to read this most excellent way with a freshness of spirit and an openness of heart.

*P*lease read 1 Corinthians 12:31; then 13:1-13, aloud if possible. In one sentence, write a summation of Paul's teaching.

_____

How does God want you to respond to what He showed you today?

_____

_____

_____

_____

_____

Paul learned the hard way how meaningless gifts, talents, and sacrifices were without love. Paul's repetition of the pronoun *I* in 1 Corinthians 13 reveals that he learned the lesson personally before God could use him to teach it to anyone else. In his earlier years Paul attempted to exercise his gifts and make extreme sacrifices without love.

The hollowness of works without love becomes evident to all who seek to serve God. We cannot serve God wholeheartedly without the whole heart. Even though many years earlier Paul and Barnabas had probably made the right decision to divide and multiply, I'm not sure Paul responded to the conflict with John Mark in love. I think a hollowness accompanied Paul everywhere he went until the gulf was bridged with grace. Somewhere along the way, Paul learned the most "excellent way." And he showed it by personal example to others like Philemon and us.

The rich Book of Philemon ends with Paul's request for Philemon to prepare a guest room for him in hopes he would be there soon. I grin as I imagine Philemon receiving his runaway slave as a brother just as Paul asked. After all, Paul might be on his way.

D A Y   5
A Rare Gem

Today's Treasure
"I know what it is to be in need, and I know what it is to have plenty. I have learned the secret of being content in any and every situation, whether well fed or hungry, whether living in plenty or in want" (Phil. 4:12).

Today we conclude the letters we believe Paul wrote during his house arrest in Rome. Our thoughts will center on the glorious Book of Philippians. You may recall that most scholars assume Colossians and Ephesians were written earlier in the two-year period. Both Philemon and Philippians refer to the possibility of Paul's release, leading us to believe they were written in the latter part of his house arrest.

Relish every word of Philippians 4:1-23 and complete the following. Imagine you are writing a Bible study. List key words from the chapter.

_____

_____

Which of the words would interest you most as a topic for study?

_____

Can you see ways in which your other key words may relate to the topic you've chosen? Explain.

_____

_____

If I don't choose your topic, God may be leading you to do a little research of your own! I asked you to choose the key words in the chapter because God has taught me many things through this method. After the steps above, I then use my topic and other key words as a springboard for word studies and cross references. I check commentaries to make sure I'm not departing from sound doctrine. All the while, I pray Psalm 119:18.

"Open my eyes that I may see wonderful things in your law." Whether or not you teach, perhaps you might be blessed by trying the same method occasionally in your own personal quest. We don't have to be scholars, just willing, teachable students.

I consider the entire Book of Philippians as a discourse on the higher life in Christ. Every precept he taught the Christians in Philippi can be a reality for any believer; however, open hearts and cooperative wills are necessities for those who can truly proclaim, "For to me, to live is Christ and to die is gain" (Phil. 1:21). As you read Philippians 4, no doubt you gathered many treasures. Sift through the treasures until you find one of the rarest of all gems: contentment.

How many truly contented people do you know? They are rare gems, aren't they? The enemy loves to see our discontentment. Why? Contented Christians live a powerful and effective testimony. Their lives are walking witnesses proving Christ can deliver what the gods of this world can't. You can be sure of this: Wherever a rare gem exists, a jewel thief is closely lurking. Today, let's reveal five thieves of contentment based on Philippians 4.

*R*eread verses 2-3. How did Paul know Euodia and Syntyche?

_____

What general problem were they having? _____

1. The first thief of contentment is *pettiness*: To everyone who thought the apostle Paul did not believe in women in ministry—allow me to introduce Euodia and Syntyche. They worked right beside him. They were *fellow workers*! They had just one little problem: they couldn't get along. Let's admit it: People can be petty!

A good reason exists for our tendency toward pettiness. Satan tries his best to counterfeit the works of God. God intentionally made women sensitive. I believe the counterfeit of sensitivity is pettiness. We tend to get our feelings hurt easily and take things personally. We can pick out imperfections with mind-blowing velocity. God gave us a special tenderness and sensitivity to lend a sweetness to our service. Pettiness sours a servant's heart and steals contentment. Let's learn to take the mask off pettiness and identify it as a thief breaking in to steal the rare gem of contentment.

*H*ave you ever been in a situation like Euodia and Syntyche? If so, how did pettiness steal your contentment in the situation?

_____

_____

2. Does anything rob us of contentment more than *anxiety*? I personally can't think of a more successful jewel thief.

*H*as anxiety robbed you of inner contentment recently? If so, why have you been anxious?

_____

No anxiety—what a thought! How do we turn off the valve pumping anxiety into our souls? Paul proposes an answer—prayer. You might say, "A better solution to fighting

The Five Thieves of Contentment

1. Pettiness

The Five Thieves of Contentment

1. Pettiness
2. Anxiety

anxiety must exist. I've prayed—and still been anxious." I want to suggest gently that you haven't necessarily been practicing the kind of prayer Paul was describing as a prescription for anxiety.

*H*ow did the apostle describe anxiety-relieving prayer in verse 6 (KJV)?

_____

The verse describes a very intimate and active prayer life. Notice Paul's words for prayer and supplication. The word *prayer* refers to a very general kind of prayer. The word *supplication* is translated from the Greek word *deesis* describing a very personal kind of prayer. *Deesis* is "the petition for specific individual needs and wants." Paul exhorted believers to come to God with general requests and needs as well as the details that cause us anxiety. Then don't give up! Persist until peace comes.

*W*rite your most specific need. _____
Hopefully you are aware of things God has done for you during the weeks of this study. Thank Him for several specific things He's done for you recently.

Keep praying not only about this specific need but also about everything! An open line of communication with God reminds you He is real and active in your life. Peace overflowing from an active prayer life lends contentment.

3. Another thief of contentment is ***destructive thoughts.*** Proverbs 23:7 describes man with the words, "For as he thinketh in his heart, so *is* he" (KJV). We might apply the proverb this way: A person feels like he or she thinks. Our human natures tend toward negative and destructive thinking. If 10 people complimented you today and 1 person criticized, which would you go to bed thinking about tonight? Probably the criticism!

Destructive, negative thinking is a habit which can be broken, but this thief takes diligence to overcome. God knows the tendency of the mind to meditate on things. Meditation is simply the thinking and rethinking of certain subject matter. Paul gave us a wonderful checklist for determining whether or not our thoughts are worth thinking!

*R*eread Philippians 4:8. What did Paul identify as worthy thoughts?

_____

_____

I struggle with destructive thinking just like you. In my journey, God has used Scripture memory and Bible study to set me free. I continue to make a priority of His Word daily, but He also blesses refreshment I gain from school events, an occasional decent movie, a wholesome magazine, a good documentary, or a funny book. Worthy thought patterns are a key to contentment.

4. A ***resistance to learn*** is a successful thief of inner contentment. This thief is sneakier than his counterparts, because he's less obvious. We lose so much when we refuse to learn from our experiences with God.

*R*ead verses 11 and 12 carefully; then fill in the following phrase underscored by the apostle Paul:

"I have _____ the secret of being content in any and every situation."

The Five Thieves of Contentment

1. Pettiness
2. Anxiety
3. Destructive thoughts

The Five Thieves of Contentment

1. Pettiness
2. Anxiety
3. Destructive thoughts
4. Resistance to learn

We do not suddenly get contentment. We *learn* it. No one was born with contentment. Paul said he had learned to be content "whether well fed or hungry, whether living in plenty or in want." He learned from experience that God was faithful no matter what circumstance he met. Had he never been in want, He never would have learned! Often we're in no mood to learn when we're in difficult circumstances, but God desires to show us that we can't meet a circumstance He can't handle. If we do not respond with teachable hearts as we meet each new circumstance, we've stifled the purpose—and all our discomfort is in vain! As circumstances inevitably change, we handcuff a sly thief of contentment when we ask God to give us hearts willing to learn.

Have you ever learned to be content in a situation that formerly brought dissatisfaction? ❑ Yes ❑ No If so, how did you finally learn to be content?

_____

_____

5. *Independence:* We now unmask the fifth thief that steals the rare gem of contentment. Refusing to rely on God robs us of some of God's most priceless riches.

*R*ead verse 12 again. I purposely waited until now to pinpoint a wonderful word in this verse. Paul tells the secret of being content in verses 13 and 19. Write both verses below. No doubt you will see a common thread.

Philippians 4:13 _____

_____

Philippians 4:19 _____

_____

Through countless ups and downs, Paul learned he could do everything God called him to do, but only "through him [Christ] who gives me strength" (Phil. 4:13). Through the multitude of needs Paul encountered, he learned that "God will meet all your needs … in Christ Jesus" (Phil. 4:19).

I believe Paul considered reliance on God a secret because everyone has to discover it for themselves. I can tell you God will meet your every need. I can say that you can do all things through Christ; but until you find out for yourself, it's still a secret. I can tell you, but He can show you. Let Him. He is so faithful.

Contentment is a rare gem. Because Paul ceased letting thieves steal his contentment, his testimony was powerful. Even many who belonged to Caesar's household were compelled to know Christ! (see Phil. 4:22). My guess is, Paul had a secret they wanted to know.

The Five Thieves of Contentment

1. *Pettiness*
2. *Anxiety*
3. *Destructive thoughts*
4. *Resistance to learn*
5. *Independence*

*H*ow does God want you to respond to what He showed you today?

_____

_____

_____

_____

_____

_____

¹John F. Walvoord et al., eds., *The Bible Knowledge Commentary New Testament* (Wheaton, IL: Victor Books, 1983), 640.
²Spiros Zodhiates, ed., *The Hebrew-Greek Key Study Bible* (Chattanooga, TN: AMG Publishers, 1996), 1519.

Letters Bridging the Miles

Philippians 3:3-14

Ten Goals from Paul's Heart

1. To count on _____ when we've _____ for the sake of Christ (v. 8).

   Knowing means "present and fragmentary knowledge."

2. To identify the primary gain as _____ _____ (v. 8).

3. To be _____ in Christ (v. 9).

   The word *doulos*. He was the bondslave of Jesus Christ.

4. To possess the _____ that comes from God (v. 9).

5. To _____ Christ (v. 10).

   To know implies "something we know by trial/examination/seeking to find out."

6. To be unhindered by personal _____ (v. 12).

7. To _____ on (v. 12).

8. To _____ _____ of Christ's purposes for me (v. 12).

   Take hold means "to be seized with eagerness or suddenness!"

9. To _____ former trophies (vv. 13-14, v. 5).

10. To _____ for the prize (v. 14).

Going Home

Day 1
A Sharp Memory

Day 2
Spiritual Fitness in Ministry

Day 3
Woman to Woman

Day 4
Come Before Winter

Day 5
Finishing the Race

In the introduction to our Bible study, I told you I had been a fan of the apostle Paul for years. As we prepare for the final week of our study, I must confess; my "fan-dom" has grown. I am a greater fan not only in spite of his frailties and weaknesses, but in some ways because of them. He gives me hope. He reminds me none of us are beyond grace, beyond use. Only God can make the common sacred. We've learned so much about this man who once persecuted the people of Christ with such vengeance; yet, to me, the best of him is yet to come. Finishing the race is not all that matters. HOW we finish the race is sometimes our most powerful testimony. Join me on our last excursions together, and let's attempt to answer the following questions.

Principal Questions
Day 1: How was the apostle Paul able to retain his spiritual passion through so many years and experiences?
Day 2: What are several imperatives for strong ministry?
Day 3: What are several characteristics of an effective mentor?
Day 4: How did Paul's second imprisonment in Rome differ from his first?
Day 5: How did Nero's experience in an Olympic race contrast so vividly with Paul's experience in life's most important race?

Withhold nothing from God during this last week of study. Stop and pray right now for Him to have full access to do anything still lacking among His goals for you in this journey. Let God's Word break every chain and loosen you to be a mighty servant of God. He is life—and life more abundant.

DAY 1
A Sharp Memory

Today's Treasure
"I was once a blasphemer and a persecutor"
(1 Tim. 1:13).

I can hardly believe we are beginning our final unit. The apostle Paul has occupied my thoughts for more than a year. His experiences have permeated every circumstance I met. Each sermon I hear sparks thoughts of one of Paul's. Virtually every prayer I raise is now marked with phrases and concepts I learned from his petitions. Each time I approach the end of a study, I have the same overwhelming feeling: "Lord, keep the truths I've learned in this journey as fresh on my heart as they are at this moment. Never let me forget!" Today I realize why refusing to forget the glorious works of God is so important. As we will soon see, Paul's refusal to forget brought immeasurable benefit.

Before we begin our reading, let's recapture our context. Our previous unit carried us through the two-year period Paul spent under house arrest in Rome in A.D. 61-62. We believe during this time he wrote the books of Colossians, Ephesians, Philemon, and Philippians. In this final unit, our focus is the last five years of his life.

Our tenth week unfolds with Paul's release from house arrest and his presumed freedom for about four years. Scholars debate his exact whereabouts during his last season of freedom, and whether or not he finally made it to Spain. We do know that Paul wrote three personal letters to a couple of young preachers during his last five years. He wrote 1 Timothy and Titus during his season of freedom, and he penned 2 Timothy during his final imprisonment. We will focus on 1 Timothy today and tomorrow.

*R*ead 1 Timothy 1:1-2. How did he refer to Timothy? _____

Although many fellow workers endeared themselves to Paul, I'm not sure anyone ever shared Timothy's place in his heart. He referred to several people as sons in the faith but no one seemed to compare to Timothy. I'm sure one reason Timothy was so dear to Paul was his young age when Paul met him. All Jewish men longed to be fathers and deeply desired to have sons. Perhaps Timothy filled a gap in Paul's life at a crucial time. He deeply loved this young man and felt an obvious freedom to both praise and correct him.

Paul and Timothy spent years together, yet oddly the apostle hardly greeted the young preacher before he repeated his testimony. Remember, God inspired this letter to be written, and He had purpose in Paul repeating his testimony.

*R*ead 1 Timothy 1:1-17 giving special attention to verses 12-17. If you had to give a profile of Paul's state of mind at this point in his life, how would you describe him?

_____

_____

Twenty-six years had passed since a blinding light opened the eyes of a persecutor named Saul. Why was he still repeating his testimony to those who certainly knew it? Because he never forgot. He remembered like it was yesterday.

I don't know how you feel about Paul or the journey we've shared, but I know I want his unquenchable passion! Fortunately it's contagious. We catch it by imitating what he did to get it. The apostle retained his spiritual passion through a roller-coaster existence for at least six reasons based on 1 Timothy 1:12-17.

1. He never forgot the privilege of ministry (v. 12). Decades later, Paul was still amazed to have been appointed to Christ's service. When Jesus first appointed him, He said to Ananias, "This man is my chosen instrument.... I will show him how much he must suffer for my name'" (Acts 9:15-16). Paul's life obviously fulfilled Christ's testimony. Unlike most of us, Paul's conversion and subsequent ministry took him from a life of relative ease to almost constant pressure and turmoil. He was beaten, stoned, whipped, jailed, and starved in the course of his ministry; yet he considered his calling to serve God to be the greatest privilege anyone could receive.

Why do you think Paul felt this way after all he had been through?

_____

How did the writer of Psalm 84:10 reveal a similar heart toward ministry?

_____

A host of reasons probably existed for Paul's continued gratitude. One possibility stands out most in my mind. His chief desire was "to know Christ" (Phil. 3:10). I believe the more he knew Christ, the more he saw His greatness. The more Paul saw His greatness, the more amazed he was to have the privilege to serve Him. We will also become more amazed over our privilege to serve as we seek to know Christ better.

2. He never forgot who he had been (v. 13). God used Paul to perform more wonders and birth more churches than any other human in the New Testament. In a quarter of a century, Paul had plenty of time to forget who he had been and take pride in his powerful ministry. One reason God leaves our memories of past repented sin intact, but disengages His own, is because the memory is of no use to Him. On the other hand, a twinge of memory is indeed profitable to us because pride is the arch enemy of ministry.

I think one reason why Paul continued to remember who he had been was because his love for Christ continued to grow. The more he loved Christ, the more he wondered how he could have sinned against Him so horrendously in his past. I've personally experienced this. Even though I know I am fully forgiven; the deeper my love for Christ has grown, the more I regret past sins.

Who are we according to 2 Timothy 2:19? _____
Does God ever forget who we are? ❑ Yes ❑ No

We are wise never to forget who we *were*. God never forgets who we *are*. Never forgetting who we were lends a far greater appreciation for who we now are!

3. He never forgot the abundance of God (v. 14). Paul discovered God's intent was not just for us to get by. He is not the God of barely enough. Paul encountered a God who super-gave! The word *abundantly* in verse 14 means to "superabound" (Strong's).

What three contents did God pour on Paul from Heaven?
❑ knowledge ❑ wisdom ❑ grace ❑ favor
❑ faith ❑ love ❑ blessing

Did you know God has poured out more than enough grace to keep you covered? Did you know God has poured out more than enough faith for you to trust Him? Did you know God has poured out more than enough love to never let you go?

*C*an you think of a time when you were aware God had poured grace, love, or faith on you in superabundance? ❑ Yes ❑ No If so, in the margin briefly describe the experience.

Paul never forgot the abundance of God. Greater still, God never forgets the abundance of our need.

*H*ow strong is God's devotion to His children according to Isaiah 49:15?

_____

He sees our needs like a mother sees her helpless infant's needs. Like a loving mother He will never forget one of His children.

4. He never forgot the basics (v . 15). Can you imagine the wealth of knowledge Paul gained in his quest for God? Still he never lost sight of the most important truth he ever learned: "Christ Jesus came into the world to save sinners." May we also never forget! We don't have to lose touch with our most basic belief to press on to maturity.

How long has it been since tears stung your eyes when someone received Christ? Or how long has it been since you felt deep gratitude for the simplicity of your salvation?

*P*lease use this space to thank Christ in your own words for coming into the world specifically to save you.

_____

_____

_____

Read the familiar words of 2 Peter 3:9. Each day He prolongs His return,

why does He tarry? _____

Salvation is God's primary agenda. Never lose sight of this marvelous basic of life.

5. He never forgot his primary role (v. 16). According to the apostle Paul, God saved "the worst of sinners," to "display His unlimited patience as an example." The Greek word for *example* means "to draw a sketch or first draft as painters when they begin a picture." Paul saw himself drawn in that picture. You are painted in the portrait. I am painted in. The worst of sinners—the spiritually blind, lame, and lost—find unlimited patience in our God! If we look on the era of Paul's life and his contemporaries to be the last great movement of God, then we have tragically misunderstood. If our conclusion is "Wow! Those were the days," we missed the point. God is still painting the portrait of His church. Paul was only an example of what God can do with one repentant life.

*P*aul wrote one of my favorite Scriptures in Philippians 1:6. Paraphrase this verse in your own words.

_____

_____

God hasn't finished the picture—but one day He will.

*P*ray for someone you know who has not received Christ. Picture his or her face in the portrait and ask God not to rest until the person is on His canvas. Ask that you might be an example from which this person can see God's unlimited patience.

6. He never forgot the wonder of God (v. 17). Twenty-six years after he fell to his knees, he still felt so overwhelmed by the awesome work of God that he exclaimed, "Now to the King eternal, immortal, invisible, the only God, be honor and glory for ever and ever." I wish I could have seen Timothy's face reading Paul's words. Perhaps he thought, *How has he kept his wonder?* The answer? He never forgot who he had been. He relished the abundance of God. He never lost sight of the basics.

When my oldest daughter was little and I offered her a treat which had lost its luster to her, she responded politely, "No thank you, Mommy. I'm used to that." The apostle Paul had known Christ for 25 years. Still he looked back on his salvation and the privilege to serve and never got "used to that." May God grant us a memory like Paul's.

*H*ow does God want you to respond to what He showed you today?

_____
_____
_____
_____
_____

D A Y   2

Spiritual Fitness in Ministry

Glance through the Book of 1 Timothy. You will notice a continuing exhortation for order in the churches. Paul wrote about deacons, overseers, widows, elders, and slaves. In stressing order in the church, he made some statements about women that raise controversy. Although these statements are not our focus today, I do not want to be charged with cowardice by omitting any mention of them. We are wise to view Paul's exhortations in context. He used far more ink to address deacons and overseers.

*R*ead 1 Timothy 2:11-12. Do these verses trouble you? ❑ Yes ❑ No If so, in the margin describe why.

When Paul said, "A woman should learn in quietness" and "be silent," he did not use a Greek word which meant "complete silence or no talking. [He used a word] used elsewhere to mean settled down, undisturbed, not unruly."[1] Remember, Paul's primary ministry was geared toward Gentiles who had never been trained to have respect and reverence in worship. Paul encouraged women to observe traditional customs lest the young churches suffer a bad reputation.

Consider a traditional Jewish worship service. Men sat on the lower floor of the synagogue while women sat in the balcony or at the back of the room. Women were not allowed to utter a word; they merely listened. Contrast this picture with a Christian worship service in the New Testament world. The men and women were together in a private home. The worship centered around praising God, singing, fellowshiping, eating together, sharing testimonies, and receiving instruction in their new faith. Women were included as never before. Talk about a radical idea!

The Christian movement was new and fragile. Any taint of adverse publicity could greatly hinder the mission of the church and mean persecution for believers. Women had to restrain their new freedom in Christ (Gal. 3:28) so as not to impede the progress

*T*oday's *T*reasure
"*Train yourself to be godly. For physical training is of some value, but godliness has value for all things, holding promise for both the present life and the life to come*" (1 Tim. 4:7-8).

of the gospel. Paul's "weaker brother" principle (1 Cor. 8:9) applies. He said, "Be careful, however, that the exercise of your freedom does not become a stumbling block to the weak." Thus, women were to learn quietly, without calling attention to themselves.

In regard to instructing women not to teach men, you must understand that women in Paul's day were illiterate. They were not taught in synagogue schools nor trained by a rabbi. Paul goes on to say in verse 12 that women should not usurp authority over men. The Greek word *authenteo*, "one who claims authority," is used only this one time in the Greek translation of the Bible. This word refers to an autocrat or dictator. Paul says women were not to come in and take over!

We cannot regard verses 11-12 as a prohibition against women opening their mouths in church or men learning anything biblical from women. Paul gave instructions for how women are to pray and prophesy (1 Cor. 11:5). He was fully aware of Priscilla's role in teaching Apollos in Ephesus (Acts 18:26). Paul issued differing instructions for churches based on their cultural settings and his desire for order in the church.

Our focus today is on Paul's personal exhortations to Timothy, his son in the faith. Midway through my preparation for this series, I began to realize one of God's priority goals for this study is to raise up and encourage passionate, persevering servants completely abandoned to His will. Paul's exhortations to Timothy stand as timeless words of advice to every servant of the living God, regardless of generation or gender.

*R*ead 1 Timothy 4:1-16; 5:22; and 6:11-21. Look for the following six imperatives for strong ministry.

1. *"Train yourself to be godly"* (4:7). Instant godliness does not accompany salvation. Remember, salvation is a gift. Godliness is a pursuit. The word meaning "to train" is *gumnazo* from which we derive the word *gymnasium*. The apostle drew a parallel between an athlete preparing for the Greek games and a believer pursuing godliness. An athlete preparing for intense competition makes frequent visits to the gym.

*E*xpound on Paul's parallel by thinking creatively. List as many parallels as you can between an athlete training for intense competition and believers training for godliness.

Athletic Training	Spiritual Training
_____	_____
_____	_____
_____	_____

On the lists you just created, underline ways you are presently training yourself to be godly as one frequenting a gym. Circle any ways you are not now training that you need to begin to practice.

2. *"Set an example"* (4:12). Although Timothy was young, Paul exhorted him not to let others who were older intimidate him. Rather, he should "set an example ... in speech, in life, in love, in faith and in purity."

God wants us to set good examples for others to follow. People are desperately looking for lives and philosophies that work. God is practical. His Word works. He wants us to be living proof by our example.

*W*hat did Paul tell others to do in Philippians 3:17?

_____

_____

The key to understanding how Paul had enough nerve to invite people to follow him is in 1 Corinthians 11:1. What was his obvious philosophy on Christian leadership?

_____

This verse defines the single most important characteristic for all church leaders. If we're leading but we're not closely following Christ, we are misleading.

3. "Do not neglect your gift" (4:14). Spiritual gifts must be cared for, cultivated, and developed. Paul felt so strongly about this exhortation to Timothy, he gave it even greater emphasis in his second letter. In 2 Timothy 1:6 Paul told Timothy "to fan into flame the gift of God."

When we receive Christ, God gives us spiritual gifts, but they must be developed. For example, I received Christ as a young child, but I did not use the gift of teaching until I became an adult. Then God opened a door for me to teach Sunday School. Although He gave me the spiritual gift and opened the door for me to use it, God expected me to accept the opportunity and fan the gift into a flame. Every week I had to study. I also spent numerous hours listening to other teachers. I asked one to disciple me personally. I had to develop a consistent prayer life. I also had to learn from my blunders and lessons that flopped! Still I kept asking God to teach me His Word so I could be obedient. These are a few ways God directed me to "fan into flame" one gift He gave me.

Name one of your spiritual gifts and describe the ways you are fanning it into flame.

_____

_____

God honors a beautiful blend of gift and grit! He gives the gift, and He expects us to have the grit to practice and learn how to use it effectively.

4. "Watch your life and doctrine closely" (4:16). The Greek word for *watch* is *epecho* meaning "to hold upon" (Strong's). Paul exhorted Timothy to keep tight reins on how he lived and what he taught. Remember, Timothy was a young preacher. We could never overemphasize the importance of preachers and teachers keeping tight reins on what they teach. Teaching is a tremendous responsibility, because we risk compromising the truth. God intends for teachers and preachers to instruct soberly with an ongoing sense of reverence for God and responsibility toward man.

*R*ead James 3:1. What does this Scripture say about teachers?

_____

_____

James warns us that teaching and preaching call for a stricter judgment due to the great responsibility involved. In James 3:2, we read, "We all stumble in many ways." Everyone has been at fault in what he has said at some point. None of us are immune; therefore, all of us are warned to be cautious.

5. "Keep yourself pure" (5:22). Paul exhorted Timothy to watch his life closely. He then became more specific by directing Timothy to keep himself pure. Nothing marks the erosion of character or has the potential to destroy ministries and testimonies like impurity. Paul told Timothy to keep himself pure. The original word for *keep* comes from the word *teros* meaning "a warden or guard." Paul told Timothy to stand as a guard over purity in his own life. I must take responsibility for purity in my life. You must take responsibility for purity in your life.

*D*o you want to be used mightily by God? You must answer two questions.
1. Have you renounced all forms of impurity in your life? ❏ Yes ❏ No
2. Are you guarding against future impurity? ❏ Yes ❏ No
Name several specific strategies you use to guard against impurity.

_____

_____

_____

If you are trying to keep yourself pure but you continue to fall, please seek godly counsel. A mature and discerning believer can help you identify reasons why you continue to be drawn to impurity. It is not too late to consecrate your life to God and find victory.

6. "Turn away from godless chatter" (6:20). Paul literally drew a line to help Timothy pursue godliness. The original word for *godless* is *bebelos* which speaks of "a threshold, particularly of a temple." This "threshold" separates the profane from the holy. If we are believers in Christ, we are sacred temples of His Holy Spirit. We have a choice what crosses the threshold and finds a place in our temples. Paul exhorts believers to discern a line in conversation which should not be crossed.

Picture yourself as a temple. We often have a choice of what we allow in and what we turn away. When we are filled with the Holy Spirit, we have an acute awareness when the threshold is crossed or when conversation we're hearing is inappropriate.

*R*ead 2 Timothy 2:16. Why should we avoid godless chatter?

_____

Sometimes we have to think of ways to turn away without deeply offending another person or disrespecting someone in authority. Consider the following scenarios and suggest ways we can turn away from "profane" (KJV) or "godless chatter."

*Y*ou have friends over for lunch and the conversation turns to gossip.

_____

Your boss uses profanity when he or she talks to you.

_____

You go to a movie with several friends from church. The sexual innuendos are inappropriate but no one else says anything.

_____

Pursuing godliness isn't always pleasant. Sometimes we are forced to make difficult decisions. He will direct us how to turn away appropriately. If we turn away proudly and self-righteously, we, ourselves, have crossed a very important threshold. Humility is the earmark of God's genuine servant. Even when we turn away, we should be humble.

The apostle Paul spoke to Timothy from experience about safe and strong ministry. He knew the pitfalls. He knew how quickly lives could be shipwrecked. Paul knew that integrity is more easily maintained than regained. I believe Paul would offer us the same advice today: "Train yourself to be godly" (1 Tim. 4:7). Set an example! Don't neglect your gift! Watch what you teach! Keep yourself pure! Turn away from profanity!

I pray that Paul's life has compelled you to be an active part of God's agenda. I hope you will never again be satisfied to sit on the sidelines. I pray you want your life to leave footprints someone else could follow straight to Christ. None of these things will happen accidentally or coincidentally. Godliness and effective ministry take attention, but nothing you could pour your energies into will ever have a greater pay off.

How does God want you to respond to what He showed you today?

_____

_____

_____

_____

_____

D A Y 3

Woman to Woman

The second epistle Paul wrote during his final five years was to another young preacher he nurtured in ministry. This youthful Gentile was named Titus. When Paul wrote the letter we are studying today, Titus was a busy preacher on the island of Crete. Paul's associates were family to him. No doubt he hated to part with them, but his passion for Christ and the holy calling greatly exceeded his possessiveness.

Though **our study will settle on one central theme today, please read all three chapters of the Book of Titus. The reading is brief and helpful.**

Note any new concepts Paul taught Titus or anything unfamiliar to you personally.

_____

_____

Paul introduced a wonderful concept to Titus that we don't want to miss. It's tucked into chapter two: women mentoring women. Let's check out Paul's instruction to men; then we'll focus on the biblical relationship between older and younger women. I believe he prioritized some of the instructions each needed most. We tend to think Paul picked on women, but please notice his priorities for older men.

In **the margin list what Paul instructed Titus to teach older men according to Titus 2:2.**

Today's Treasure
"Then they can train the younger women to love their husbands and children" (Titus 2:4).

Notice Paul's words, "sound in faith, in love and in endurance." The word *sound* means healthy. Paul told Titus to prioritize teaching men how to exercise healthy faith, love, and endurance.

*C*an you think of a way in which someone could exercise unhealthy faith?

_____

Think about men specifically. Why might men need to learn how to exercise healthy kinds of endurance?

_____

_____

Now take a look at the word *love*. He used the same original root word for *love* that is used in Ephesians 5:28 when he commanded husbands "to love their wives." You may recall the sacrificial, nurturing nature of this love. Paul did not assume all men knew how to love their wives in healthy ways. Tragically, not all men have seen good examples of healthy love. Through his letter to Titus, Paul charged preachers with teaching men healthy ways to live, exercise authority and faith, and love others. All of us need to be taught not only what is God's will, but how to do it!

*N*ow consider Paul's instruction to Titus for teaching young men in verse 6. He only gave one instruction. Why do you think he might have prioritized this specific teaching for young men?

_____

Immediately, Paul charged Titus with the responsibility for setting an example for young men. In essence, he said, "Don't just command it. Show it!" Titus was also a young man. Nothing would be a more effective teaching tool than his own example. Most teenage boys are so inundated by excess and opportunity, they don't view self-control as a possibility. Even many Christian young men feel self-control is momentarily out of their reach and something they have to grow up to grasp.

Few lives have greater impact than one self-controlled teenage boy. Whether or not they admit it, others take notice. Seeing a living, breathing example of a self-controlled teenage boy is sometimes confrontational. Such an example proves it can be done. Paul called Titus to be living proof.

*D*o you know a young man who is seeking to live a self-controlled life against the odds? If so, write his name in the margin; then spend a moment praying earnestly for God to surround him with strength and protection. After you intercede for him, circle his name as a symbol of what you've asked God to do for him.

Now let's turn our thoughts to the wonderful concept of women mentoring women. I wish I had the space to share about the older women who have mentored me as a Christian woman, wife, mother, and servant of God. Instead, I will ask you to also remember those who have mentored you.

In the margin write your mentors' names and a phrase describing the way each helped you most.

You know, none of those women were in your life accidentally. God brought you into their sphere of influence purposely to fulfill one of His roles for women. Let's look at Paul's charge to older women. Notice he began by pointing out certain qualifications for a mentor to younger women in verse 3.

1. Reverent in the way she lives. Having researched the original language, allow me to paraphrase: Her actions are becoming to a woman who respects God. Each of the women who have mentored me were quite different in personality, but they all shared one common denominator: their lives were replete with a reverence for God. Those I respect most are those who respect God.

When you think of an older woman who deeply reverences God, how would you describe her? In other words, how does reverence look?

_____

_____

2. Not slanderous. I believe older women may have more opportunities to remain active today than in Paul's day. One of my 83-year-old friends told me the other day she was too busy to die! Still, for some who have grown idle, slanderous talk can become a means to keep life interesting. Younger women struggle with temptation to slander, too. The word *divide* is associated with the original definition of slanderous. Slanderous people thrive on conflict and division. The godly mentor sets an example by edifying others through her speech—rejoicing over their victories and hurting with them in defeat.

3. Not addicted to much wine. The original word for *addicted* is *douloo* meaning "to enslave" (Strong's). In Paul's generation, wine was the primary substance to which a woman might become addicted. Today we could fill a grocery shelf with potentially enslaving substances.

Think about the average woman in an average home. What potential addictions could she have?

_____

_____

I have two very dear friends whose mothers were alcoholics. They still struggle with the painful results. So many women in our society are enslaved to different substances. Alcohol, prescription and non-prescription drugs, diet pills, sleeping pills, and illegal drugs are readily available to anyone the least bit desperate or vulnerable.

Why do you think Paul was adamant about mentors having no addictions?

_____

The general purpose for older women mentoring younger women is stated at the end of Titus 2:3: "to teach what is good." The original Greek word for *good* is *kalos* which "expresses beauty as a harmonious completeness, balance, proportion." Older women are to teach younger women about genuine beauty: God's idea of a beautiful woman.

*R*eread Titus 2:4-5. List the areas in which older women can be very helpful to younger women.

_____

_____

_____

Because our space is limited, please allow me to emphasize three areas in which older women are to help younger women. We've had previous opportunities in our study to discuss self-control, purity, kindness, and submission. Let's look at the remaining three subjects older Christian women should prioritize with younger Christian women.

1. Love their husbands. Interestingly, the original word used for *love* is not *agape* this time. It's *philandros* which speaks of "loving [someone] as a friend." Romantic love is so important in a marriage but, in addition, Titus 2:4 expresses our need to learn to be a friend to our husbands. Women often have several good friends, but men tend to have fewer close friendships. A man often needs his wife to be a friend as well as a lover. Not long ago, Keith said to me so sweetly, "Elizabeth, you're my best friend." Keith is my husband and my love for him is totally unique, but I have so many close girlfriends that I didn't think of him as my best friend. I nearly cried and prayed silently, *Oh, God, help me be a good best friend to my husband—and make him mine.*

Even if you are not married, can you think of several ways a wife can also be a friend to her husband?

_____

_____

_____

Phileo love, which is central to *philandros*, grows from "common interests." By our feminine natures, women don't often share the same interests as men. But we can learn to share their interests! I'm intimidated by deep water, so I rarely fish with my husband. But we've spent many nights by the fire at the deer lease, and we love to watch basketball together. One common bond which Keith and I share is humor. Rarely a day goes by that we don't share a painful belly laugh. A good laugh has healed many hurts in our home! We make an effort to spend lots of time together and share each other's worlds. I want to be a better friend to my husband. If you're married, let's make this commitment together and start working on it right away.

2. Love their children. You may be thinking, *Who needs to be taught how to love her children?* Lots of wounded people, that's who. As recently as three days ago a woman at a conference whispered in my ear, "I don't know how to love my children." I've heard those words a staggering number of times over the course of my ministry.

*C*an you think of several reasons why some women may not have strong maternal feelings? ❏ Yes ❏ No List your ideas in the margin.

I had the great blessing of a family where children are virtually royalty. Each of my parents' nine grandchildren have gotten the chance to be the star of the entire extended family. My mother has mentored me to love children. Many women haven't had a mentor like my mom. I would make four heartfelt suggestions to those who have difficulty loving their children: 1) Seek a mentor who can help train you to be a loving mother. 2) Seek sound godly counsel to discover why your heart is hindered and how you can find freedom in Christ. 3) Do the right things until you feel the right things. In other words, hug your children and tell them you love them whether or not these actions are easy for you. Please. They so much need hugs and reassurance. 4) Take up their interests. Attend their school functions, go to their games, have their friends over for pizza! Whether or not parenting comes naturally to you, it's hard work! Nothing has ever drained me nor thrilled me more on this earth than motherhood. Hang in there and seek some good support!

3. Be busy at home. The original word for *busy* means "one who looks after domestic affairs with prudence and care." I believe Paul wanted older women to teach younger women that homes and families do not take care of themselves. Someone has to watch over the priorities. Children don't raise themselves. Someone has to watch over them and be involved. A marriage doesn't improve itself. Someone has to watch over it and encourage growth and intimacy. Even if we work, wise women still remain very involved in their homes and families. The wife and mother has something to give her home and family no one else can supply as effectively: tenderness, nurturing, a personal touch.

How does God want you to respond to what He showed you today?

_____

_____

_____

_____

_____

D A Y   4
Come Before Winter

The year was A.D. 67, the place was Rome, and the conditions inhumane. A crazed emperor named Nero ruled the Roman Empire. The horrors began when a fire broke out in the Circus Maximus in Rome on July 18, A.D. 64, burning for nine days and consuming two-thirds of the city. Rumor began to circulate that Nero had ordered the fire so he could rebuild Rome in his own honor. With his last shreds of sound mind, Nero realized he must offer a scapegoat. He chose a despised group of people commonly called *Chrestiani,* or Christians. Numbers only Christ Himself could count were put to death. Nero applied every ounce of his creativity to appoint means of death. Many were nailed to crosses. Others were covered with animal skins, tied down, and devoured by dogs. Still others were doused with flammable fluids and set on fire as torches in the night.[2] Nero exercised such unimaginable cruelty toward Christians that many believed he must be the antichrist.[3]

Peter lost his life in this terrible wave of persecution.[4] We have no idea whether officials captured and brought him to Rome or whether he came to help. We can, however, be reasonably sure Paul was Nero's prime trophy. Nero could not tolerate the zealous apostle, but the Emperor would have to be careful how this Christian would meet his death. After all, Paul was a Roman citizen.

Today we approach the final letter from the pen of the apostle Paul. He wrote his second letter to Timothy during his last imprisonment in Rome, shortly before his death. Our goal today is to capture the state of mind and physical conditions of the great apostle in the final season of his life.

Today's Treasure
"Do your best to come to me quickly"
(2 Tim. 4:9).

213

*Y*ou would benefit immensely from reading 2 Timothy in its entirety. If your time is too limited, read at least each of the following Scriptures. Record any conclusions you draw about Paul's conditions or state of mind.

2 Timothy 2:9 _____

2 Timothy 1:17 (What does this verse imply about Paul's accessibility?)

_____

2 Timothy 4:13, 21 (Look for inferences to a certain need in both verses.)

_____

2 Timothy 4:10, 16 _____

2 Timothy 4:11 _____

2 Timothy 4:9 _____

2 Timothy 4:17 _____

2 Timothy 4:18 _____

Let's reiterate several descriptions of Paul's condition and state of mind during his final imprisonment:

1. He was in physical discomfort. Some criminals were simply incarcerated behind locked doors with no chains. Paul was held under conditions like those of a convicted killer. He was bound by heavy chains—the type that bruise and lacerate the skin. He was almost 60 years old and had taken enough beatings to make him quite arthritic. The lack of mobility greatly intensified any ailments or illnesses. He most likely was reduced to skin and bones. The cells where the worst prisoners were chained were usually filthy, wet, and rodent-infested dungeons. Paul was cold. He wanted his cloak and begged Timothy to do everything he could to come before winter.

*D*escribe briefly the last time you were physically miserable.

_____

You probably had great difficulty concentrating didn't you? Severe physical conditions such as extreme temperatures, chronic pain, or hunger are quite consuming. The beauty and articulation of Paul's final letter cannot be fully appreciated without realizing how physically uncomfortable he must have been when he wrote it.

2. He was probably humiliated. In ancient prisons, captors often thought of ways to shame their captives. Perhaps the least of their inhumanities was disallowing prisoners to wash and dress themselves adequately. Their confines doubled as bedroom and bathroom. In 2 Timothy 1:12, Paul said, "That is why I am suffering as I am. Yet I am not ashamed." Paul's words may hint at the attempts of his captors to shame him. He told Timothy several times not to be ashamed of him (see v. 8). As much as Paul had suffered, he was unaccustomed to the treatment he received in the final season of his life.

3. He felt deserted and lonely. Some deserted him. Others, like Onesiphorus, had trouble finding him. Paul told Timothy in 2 Timothy 4:16 that everyone deserted him at his first defense. Since he was a Roman citizen, he had a hearing. People could come forward in his defense. No one came forward at Paul's first hearing. Can you imagine the loneliness he must have experienced as the bailiff called for defense witnesses, and silence fell over the courtroom? I don't believe they deserted him because they didn't love him. Many probably grieved because they did not come to his defense, but they were frightened for their lives. As far as most of them were probably concerned, Paul was on death row anyway. They couldn't save him. After all, he was certainly guilty of denying the deity of Nero.

*A*t this point what can you tell about Paul's attitude from his words, "May it not be held against them" (v. 4:16)?

_____

I keep staring at the words "Only Luke is with me" (2 Tim. 4:11). Sometimes I think nothing is dearer than an enduring friendship between two men. Maybe because it's rarer than those among women. Now do you see why God appointed Luke to tell Paul's story in the Book of Acts? Who on earth loved him more? Who was more devoted?

Picturing these two men in a rancid cell moves me. One was bound to the floor with chains, the other chained to his friend with heartstrings. You can be fairly certain whatever wrap Luke had, he draped around the frail shoulders of his friend. I wonder if the Paul of the old days was hardly recognizable. Paul had been so fiery, so temperamental. Luke had watched the great apostle speak with indescribable authority. He saw him perform wonders and woo people to Christ. In that prison cell in 67 A.D., he saw a frail man, cold and lonely. I think perhaps Luke would rather have seen his friend dead than chained like an animal and humiliated.

God was gracious to sustain Dr. Luke's life so he could care for Paul in his last days. Luke was an old man by this time with few tools to take care of his beloved patient. But perhaps most important of all, as the weakening apostle struggled in the blackness of a dungeon night, his old friend could say, "I'm here, Paul. Right here."

4. He longed for normalcy. Although Paul's life was seldom normal in our terms, in his last season I believe he longed for the things that were normal to him. Notice how he wanted his oldest friends. He asked for Mark (see 2 Tim. 4:11). He spoke of Luke at his side. He sent greetings to Priscilla and Aquilla. He begged Timothy to come quickly. His request for his scrolls, especially the parchments also tenders my heart. His scrolls were probably copies of Old Testament Scriptures. Very likely he had also recorded on parchments facts about the earthly life of Christ, based on the stories of Peter and Luke. I can't begin to put myself in Paul's position, but if I were away from loved ones and facing certain death, I would want several things.

If you were in similar conditions and you could only ask for three things (not people), what would they be?

1. _____

2. _____

3. _____

Now, try to explain why you would want those particular items.

_____

_____

Paul probably had reasons very similar to yours. I have stacks of journals recording prayers too private to allow anyone to read, yet I cannot bring myself to throw them away. During uncertain times when I am called to walk by faith, I can turn back to personal records of God's faithfulness and find strength again. My Bible and my journals are my most treasured tangible belongings. During difficult days, even holding my Bible close to my chest brings me comfort. No doubt, Paul longed for these things.

A person confined and facing death inevitably turns the mental pages of the past. Surely, Paul was no different. He must have thought about Tarsus. His mother's face. His father's voice. His childhood in a Jewish community. His first impressions of Jerusalem. The classroom debates he enjoyed. The way people whispered about his genius behind his back. His bright future. His return to Tarsus and the respect he commanded. His drive to persecute the people of the Way. The blinding light that sent him to his knees. He traded a life of respect and honor for one of rejection and tribulation. If his childhood friends could have seen him in that horrendous dungeon, they might have surmised he traded everything for nothing.

So, what do you have when you have nothing left? You have what you know. Faced with humiliation, Paul proclaimed, "Yet I am not ashamed, because I know whom I have believed, and am convinced that he is able to guard what I have entrusted to him for that day" (2 Tim. 1:12). Paul's sanity was protected by his certainty. He knew the One in whom he believed. Years earlier he stepped out in faith, but faith gave way to sight as Paul witnessed the power of God. God's invisible hands left far too many visible prints for Paul to doubt. He knew Him—with the kind of knowledge that was worth any loss (see Phil. 3:8). If we're going to survive the faith walks of our lives, we must know whom we've believed. No matter what you lose, no one can take what you know. No one can take Who you know.

Paul had entrusted everything to Christ. Every effort. Every tear. Every drop of sweat. Every mistake. Every victory. Every ability. Every sermon. Paul placed everything he had in one set of hands. No matter how difficult circumstances grew, he never tried to take it back. As the chains gripped his hands and feet and the stench of death assailed him, he recalled everything he had entrusted to his Savior and said, "[I] am convinced he is able to guard what I have entrusted to him" (2 Tim. 1:12).

Paul used a terminology that painted a graphic image. The original term used for *guard* is *phulasso*. The noun form of the word is *phulakterion*. Do you know what this word meant? *Phylacteries*! Paul's father wore *phylacteries*. As a young rabbi, Paul wore *phylacteries*. Years later, his thoughts obviously returned to the many experiences leading him to this place where he was bound in chains and he said, *Christ is safely keeping everything I've entrusted to Him. Every time I've chosen Him over the world. Every time I've chosen to believe rather than doubt. Every time I've been willing to be a fool for Him. Every record is kept like words on a scroll—every trust tucked safely in His care. He will not forget.* With chained hands, Paul could still touch the face of God.

*M*y friend, what have you entrusted to Christ? What have you chosen to entrust to an invisible Savior while a visible world begs to differ? What kind of risk have you taken on Him?

_H_ow does God want you to respond to what He showed you today?

_____

_____

_____

_____

_____

_____

He is able to guard every single thing you have entrusted to Him. Never will you choose to believe or trust, then be forsaken. He is keeping every record, every scroll, every trust. You may walk in faith and never see with your human eyes how trustworthy He really is until that day when you come face-to-face. But you can know the One in whom you believe and be convinced He is able. You have not been foolish to trust an invisible God. One day you'll see.

D A Y   5

Finishing the Race

We have journeyed with the apostle for many weeks. We've met many interesting characters. We've been thrown out of cities, boarded boats, and battled waves. We've been in and out of prison. We've been to the heights and to the depths. We've walked next to one of the most influential men in Christendom. He was far from perfect. Indeed, we've seen ourselves in him. But more than anything, we've seen Christ in him.

I've prayed so for you on this trip. I've asked God over and over to reveal Himself to you at every stop. As we conclude today, I am reminded of my earliest prayer when I began this study. I asked God to meet each of us on our roads to Damascus and cause the scales to fall from our eyes. I've prayed that we would live the rest of our lives with new vision. Not because of my feeble prayers but because of the faithfulness of God, I wonder if scales have fallen from your eyes in any way through this journey.

Do you see anything differently now? If so, explain briefly.

_____

We can be sure God will take His Word from the page to the pavement and challenge us to live the truths we've learned. I do not want this journey to end. I don't want to unpack and go back to life as I knew it before this trip. I don't want to pull out a few snapshots and toss them in a drawer. I want where I've been to impact where I'm going. Too many times we've said farewell with the words, "God be with you." He's already promised He would. My farewell today is, "Go with God," suitcase packed and ready to go. In the spirit of the apostle Paul, go wherever Christ may lead.

Before we continue our own journeys, let's join a certain sinner saved by grace on his final flight. Even if you read the entire Book of 2 Timothy in our previous lesson, please complete each of today's reading assignments.

*R*ead 2 Timothy 3:10—4:6 and complete the following.
I'm sure you sensed the fatherly tone of Paul's instructions to Timothy. An urgency is evident in Paul's words to his dear son in the faith. Cite three points you sense Paul was prioritizing in this section of his letter.

1. _____

2. _____

3. _____

Today's Treasure
"I have fought the good fight, I have finished the race, I have kept the faith" (2 Tim. 4:7).

We are also wise to heed Paul's advice to Timothy in verse 5: "But you, keep your head in all situations." What did Paul mean by this expression?

_____

_____

How do you think Paul's life was like a drink offering?

_____

_____

The apostle knew without a doubt he was about to die. If any man ever had enough faith to "name and claim" an earthly deliverance, Paul did. He knew how to pray believing yet also to pray accepting. Paul probably prayed for God to release him once again to minister in the midst of chaotic Rome. Paul may have believed his death at that exact time was totally illogical, yet he also had surrendered his life to God's perfect will. God's glory was the issue in every situation he encountered (see 2 Cor. 4). Whether or not he felt the timing of his death was logical, clearly he realized it was inevitable. He knew the Romans could not lay a hand on him without God's permission. Paul was no masochist. We don't find him striking a martyr's pose nor singing "Nobody Knows The Troubles I've Seen." He wasn't begging for the guillotine. He simply looked at life through the window of Philippians 1:21.

*P*lease write Paul's one-sentence philosophy below.

_____

_____

Our entire journey has been an effort to study the heart of a man who could sincerely make such a statement. After all you've learned about the apostle Paul, what do you think he meant by this statement?

_____

_____

_____

Christ had profoundly transformed Paul's attitude toward life and death. Having spent his entire adult life in pursuit of Christ, Paul saw death as:

1. A departure. He did not say, "the time has come for my death." He said, "the time has come for my departure." His entire life was a series of departures. He followed the leading of the Holy Spirit through Judea, Syria, Cilicia, Galatia, Pamphylia, Asia, Macedonia, Achaia, and Italy. He never knew what awaited him as he entered a city, but one possibility was inevitable—as surely as he arrived, he would depart. God never let him hang his hat for long. "Our citizenship is in heaven," Paul said in Philippians 3:20. To him, settling in would be pointless until then. Paul had faithfully done his time in Rome and, predictably, another departure awaited him. This time, he was going home.

*H*ave you ever known anyone personally who faced death like Paul? If so, what explanation would you offer for their attitude?

_____

_____

2. A rescue. Read 2 Timothy 4:18. Paul didn't see death as a defeat. He did not believe the enemy finally had his way. He saw death as a rescue! We tend to define the word *rescue* an entirely different way. If we are pursued and we cry out to be rescued, you and I usually are not referring to death! We're referring to earthly deliverance. God certainly rescued Paul many times on this earth, just as He has rescued us; yet Paul knew the greatest rescue of all awaited him. Death was not God's refusal to act. Death was God's ultimate rescue. Oh, if we could only understand this difficult truth, how different our perspectives would be. Paul not only saw death as the ultimate rescue from evil; he saw death as a rescue from frail, limited bodies.

> *R*ead 2 Corinthians 5:1-10. What did Paul call our bodies?

_____

Remember, he was a tentmaker by trade. The parallel was irresistible to him. I can say to you confidently based on 2 Corinthians 5:8 that not one moment will lapse between our earthly departures and our heavenly arrivals. Before these tents have dropped to the ground, we'll be clothed with immortality.

3. A safe passage. Reread 2 Timothy 4:18. God will not only rescue us but He will bring us safely to His heavenly kingdom. In week 5 we learned the original Greek meaning for the word *rescue. Rhuomai* means "to draw or snatch from danger, rescue, deliver. This is more with the meaning of drawing to oneself than merely rescuing for someone or something." God is not simply trying to snatch us from danger. He desires to draw us to Himself spiritually, then one day physically. When our ultimate rescue comes, God's purpose is to deliver us to Himself—safely.

In our most vulnerable moments, all of us fear death. When the time comes, God will deliver us safely. You may say, "But what if we die a violent death?" Paul was about to die a violent death—yet God would deliver him safely. To the heartbreak of all of us in the Houston area the young kidnapped girl I told you about in week 9 was found dead several days after I wrote those words. She died a violent death, but she was a believer. I stand on what Scripture teaches: God delivered her "safely to His heavenly kingdom."

> *W*hat scriptural basis do I have besides 2 Timothy 4:18? Read Hebrews 2:14-15. What is God able to do for us according to Hebrews 2:15?

_____

One of the most innate desires of any decent parent's heart is to soothe his child's fears. God is not just a decent parent. He is the perfect parent. I believe He is far more concerned with calming His beloved child than with calming a raging storm.

Each nightfall in that dark dungeon in Rome, Paul knew he was one day closer to certain execution. The only reason he was spared so long was the problem of his Roman citizenship. Many Christians were fed to lions in an amphitheater packed with spectators. Nero could not legally sentence Paul to such a death; hence, Paul's literal expression in 2 Timothy 4:17: "I was delivered from the lion's mouth"—not by Nero but by God. I believe the crazy emperor incited more anger and revulsion than fear in Paul. Paul had grown and changed in so many ways during his lifetime with Christ. He grew less harsh and more understanding. Yet some things never changed—like Paul's propensity to have the last word. Let me show you something absolutely vintage Paul as we draw our series to a close.

*R*eread the awesome words of 2 Timothy 4:7-8; then write verse 8 below:

_____

_____

_____

_____

Paul wasn't just pulling a word picture out of a hat. Anyone in the Roman Empire would know exactly what he was talking about. I wouldn't be the least surprised if these words spread and ultimately hastened his death. In the year A.D. 67, the year of Paul's death, Nero had the audacity to enter himself in the Olympic games. Mind you, Olympic athletes trained all their lives for the games. The thirty-year-old, soft-bellied emperor used medications to induce vomiting rather than exercise to control his weight.[5] He was in pitiful shape and ill-prepared, but who would dare tell him he could not compete? He cast himself on a chariot at Olympia and drove a ten-horse team. "He fell from the chariot and had to be helped in again; but, though he failed to stay the course and retired before the finish, the judges nevertheless awarded him the prize."[6]

Nero did not finish the race. Nevertheless, a wreath was placed on his head, and he was hailed the victor. He showed his gratitude for their cooperation in the ridiculous scam by exempting Greece from taxation. For his processional entry into Rome he chose the chariot Augustus had used in his triumph in a former age, and he wore a Greek mantle spangled with gold stars over a purple robe. The Olympic wreath was on his head. "Victims were sacrificed in his honour all along the route."[7] You can be fairly certain they were *Chrestiani.*

Needless to say, word of the humiliating victory spread faster than the fire of A.D. 64. Soon after Nero returned to Rome, the apostle wrote his stirring final testimony: "I have fought the good fight, **I have finished the race,** I have kept the faith. Now there is in store for me the **crown** of righteousness, which the Lord, the righteous Judge, will **award** to me" (2 Tim. 4:7-8). The edict was signed for his execution. The apostle Paul desired one thing of his death. The same thing he desired in his life.

*W*hat was his eager expectation according to Philippians 1:20?

_____

God did not allow the death of His beloved apostles to overshadow their lives. Their departures were intimate encounters between themselves and the One for whom they laid down their lives. Traditional teaching handed down through the ages tells us two soldiers by the name of Ferega and Parthemius brought Paul word of his death. They approached him and asked for his prayers that they might also believe in his Christ. Having received life from his instruction, they then led Paul out of the city to his death.[8] Traditional teaching claims he prayed just before his execution. At this point in our study, I would have trouble believing anything different. Wouldn't you?

*Y*ou've come to know the apostle. What do you suppose he said in his last prayer, considering all you know about him? In the margin write several sentences just as you believe he may have said them.

220

After saying words probably much like the ones you've written, the apostle Paul gave his neck to the sword. Before his earthly tent had time to collapse to the ground, his feet stood on holy ground. His eyes, possibly scarred and blurred from a glorious light on a Damascus road, saw their first crystal-clear vision in 30 years. Paul, himself, had written, "Now we see but a poor reflection as in a mirror; then we shall see face to face" (1 Cor. 13:12). Faith became sight and the raptured saint saw His face. He beheld the ultimate surpassing glory.

*W*hat had the apostle Paul written in Romans 8:18? _____

_____

_____

No thought of beatings. No questions of timing. No pleas for vengeance. No list of requests. Just the sight of unabashed, unhindered, unveiled glory. And he had not yet looked past His face. "The glory of God in the face of Christ" (2 Cor. 4:6). He was seeing the face he had waited 30 years to see.

The Righteous Judge raised a wreath of righteousness and placed it on the head of His faithful servant. He had finished the race. More impressively, he had kept the faith. Never doubt the difference.

Paul once wrote, "Now I know in part; then I shall know fully, even as I am fully known" (1 Cor. 13:12). The partial knowledge of Christ Paul had acquired in his lifetime was the same knowledge he claimed to be worth every loss (see Phil. 3:8-10). Oh, my friend, if partial knowledge of the Lord Jesus is worth every loss, what will full knowledge be like? "Oh, the depth of the riches of the wisdom and knowledge of God!" (Rom. 11:33). One day the prayer of the apostle will be answered for all of us. We will indeed "grasp how wide and long and high and deep is the love of Christ, ... and know this love that surpasses knowledge" (Eph. 3:18-19).

Until then, may God find us faithful, unstoppable servants of the One who saved us, and waiting to hang our hats on heaven's door. "For I am convinced that neither death nor life, neither angels nor demons, neither the present nor the future, nor any powers, neither height nor depth, nor anything else in all creation, will be able to separate us from the love of God that is in Christ Jesus our Lord" (Rom. 8:38).

> *Most Worthy Lord,*
> *make me a drink offering*
> *and take me not home*
> *until the cup is overturned*
> *the glass broken*
> *and every drop loosed*
> *for Your glory.*

---

[1] John F. Walvoord et al., eds., *The Bible Knowledge Commentary New Testament* (Wheaton, IL: Victor Books, 1983), 735.
[2] Will Durant, *Ceasar and Christ* (New York: Simon & Schuster, 1944), 280-281.
[3] John Foxe, *Foxe's Book of Martyrs* (New Kensington, PA: Whitaker House, 1981), 12. Used by permission of the publisher–Whitaker House, 30 Hunt Valley Circle, New Kensington, PA 15068.
[4] *The Revell Bible Dictionary* (Old Tappan, NJ: Fleming H. Revell Company, 1990), 775.
[5] Robert Graves, *The Twelve Caesars* (New York: Penguin Books, 1957), 222.
[6] Ibid., 226.
[7] Ibid., 226.
[8] John Foxe, *Foxe's Book of Martyrs* (New Kensington, PA: Whitaker House, 1981), 12. Used by permission of the publisher–Whitaker House, 30 Hunt Valley Circle, New Kensington, PA 15068.

Going Home

Ephesians 2:8-10

Workmanship in the original Greek is _____.

Poiema (workmanship) means "poem (or masterpiece)."

1. The poet writes from strong _____ (Eph. 3:17b-19).

2. The poet pens some of the most beautiful lines from _____ (2 Cor. 12:7-10).

3. Faith lives _____ _____ _____ (2 Cor. 5:7; Titus 1:2).

4. Our poems are not _____ (Phil. 1:6; 1 Cor. 13:12).

   _____ _____ means "clear and exact knowledge."

5. One day all the lines will _____ (Rom. 8:28).

Preparing Christians to Serve

In the **Christian Growth Study Plan (formerly Church Study Course)**, this book *To Live Is Christ: The Life and Ministry of Paul* is a resource for course credit in the subject area BIBLE STUDY of the Christian Growth category of diploma plans. To receive credit, read the book, complete the learning activities, show your work to your pastor, a staff member or church leader, then complete the following information. This page may be duplicated. Send the completed page to:

Christian Growth Study Plan
127 Ninth Avenue, North, MSN 117
Nashville, TN 37234-0117
FAX: (615)251-5067

For information about the Christian Growth Study Plan, refer to the current Christian Growth Study Plan Catalog. Your church office may have a copy. If not, request a free copy from the Christian Growth Study Plan office (615/251-2525).

To Live Is Christ
COURSE NUMBER: CG-0420

PARTICIPANT INFORMATION

Social Security Number (USA ONLY)	Personal CGSP Number*	Date of Birth (MONTH, DAY, YEAR)
– –	– –	– –

Name (First, Middle, Last)		Home Phone
☐ Mr. ☐ Miss		
☐ Mrs. ☐		– –

Address (Street, Route, or P.O. Box)	City, State, or Province	Zip/Postal Code

CHURCH INFORMATION

Church Name

Address (Street, Route, or P.O. Box)	City, State, or Province	Zip/Postal Code

CHANGE REQUEST ONLY

☐ Former Name		
☐ Former Address	City, State, or Province	Zip/Postal Code
☐ Former Church	City, State, or Province	Zip/Postal Code

Signature of Pastor, Conference Leader, or Other Church Leader	Date

*New participants are requested but not required to give SS# and date of birth. Existing participants, please give CGSP# when using SS# for the first time. Thereafter, only one ID# is required. **Mail to:** Christian Growth Study Plan, 127 Ninth Ave., North, Nashville, TN 37234-0117. Fax: (615)251-5067

Nurture Your Spiritual Growth

Congratulations, you've completed the fascinating journey of discovering new insights about Paul, the Apostle to the Gentiles. Now catch your breath and get ready for Beth Moore's previous Bible studies: *A Heart Like His: Seeking the Heart of God Through a Study of David* and *A Woman's Heart: God's Dwelling Place.*

Similar in design and format, these in-depth Bible studies will encourage and challenge you and your friends to apply practical Bible truths with life-changing results.

Each study features a 224-page personal study workbook; a leader kit that includes the member book, leader helps, and six videotapes with administrative help plus Beth Moore's presentations; and audiotapes that feature the audio portions of the videotapes and a listening guide.

Living Beyond Yourself: Exploring the Fruit of the Spirit is a study of the Fruit of the Spirit. Like the other Beth Moore studies, *Living Beyond* will take you on an in-depth Bible-study experience, but with one difference. This 10-week study does not include video and may be completed with a 1-hour weekly meeting. *Whispers of Hope* is a unique prayer and devotional journal designed to help women develop a consistent, daily habit of prayer. Both *Living Beyond* and *Whispers of Hope* contain the group study guide in the back so your church has nothing more to purchase than the member workbooks.

Ask your church to schedule these studies soon—they're ideal in reaching and ministering to women of all ages.

To order these resources, write, call, or fax Customer Service Center, MSN 113; 127 Ninth Avenue North; Nashville, TN 37234; **1-800-458-2772.** Fax # (615) 251-5933. email to customerservice@lifeway.com.

Also available at your LifeWay Christian Store.

A Heart Like His: Seeking the Heart of God Through a Study of David member book
ISBN 0767325966

A Heart Like His Leader Kit
ISBN 0-7673-2653-9

A Heart Like His audiotapes
ISBN 0-7673-2652-0

A Woman's Heart: God's Dwelling Place member book
ISBN 0-8054-9836-2

A Woman's Heart Leader Kit
ISBN 0-8054-9826-5

A Woman's Heart Leader Guide
Included in kit.
ISBN 0-7673-3401-9

A Woman's Heart audiotapes
ISBN 0-8054-9797-8

Living Beyond Yourself: Exploring the Fruit of the Spirit
ISBN 0-7673-9275-2

Additional women's enrichment resources include:

Women Reaching Women: Beginning and Building a Growing Women's Enrichment Ministry
Compiled by Chris Adams, foreword by Anne Graham Lotz—A comprehensive leadership resource with the latest information on beginning and expanding women's ministry in your church.
ISBN 0-7673-2593-1

Journey: A Woman's Guide to Intimacy with God
This monthly devotional magazine helps women grow closer to God by addressing needs and issues unique to women. Available in multiple copies.

Whispers of Hope
Prayer and devotional journal by Beth Moore with study guide for a 10-week prayer group.
ISBN 0-7673-9278-7

For women's enrichment training, contact Chris Adams, (615) 251-2810, Fax# (615) 251-5058 or email to cadams@lifeway.com.

For women's events, contact Faith Whatley, (615) 251-2793, fax# (615) 251-5058 or email to fwhatle@lifeway.com.